TRADERS IN THE ANCIENT MEDITERRANEAN

PUBLICATIONS OF THE
ASSOCIATION OF ANCIENT HISTORIANS 11

EDITED BY TIMOTHY HOWE

ASSOCIATION OF ANCIENT HISTORIANS
MMXV

Publications of the
Association of Ancient Historians

The purpose of the monograph series is to survey the state of the current scholarship in various areas of ancient history.

Other publications by the Association

Makedonika: Essays by Eugene N. Borza
Edited by Carol G. Thomas

The Coming of The Greeks
James T. Hooker

Directory of Ancient Historians in the United States, 2nd ed.
Compiled by Konrad Kinzl

Continued publication of the series is made possible through the efforts of the AAH publications committee, Eugene Borza of the Pennsylvania State University; Lee L. Brice of Western Illinois University, president; Serena Connolly of Rutgers, The State University of New Jersey, chair; Denise Demetriou of Michigan State University; Steven Garfinkle of Western Washington University; Danielle Kellogg of Brooklyn College – City University of New York; Hans-Friedrich Mueller of Union College; Isabelle Pafford of Willamette University; and Jennifer T. Roberts of City College – City University of New York. Readers with questions about the series or topic suggestions for future volumes or manuscript questions should contact the current president of the Association of Ancient Historians.

FOR MY STUDENTS

PREFACE

In 2010, at the Annual Meeting of the Association of Ancient Historians in Salt Lake, Utah, the Publication Committee was discussing the need for some new PAAH projects that pushed the boundaries of both the evidence and existing theory. As the new member on the Committee, I kept pretty silent throughout, at least until Carol Thomas singled me out and said, "Tim, you've been uncharacteristically quiet, care to share your thoughts?" Put on the spot like that, I said the first thing I could think of: "As an agricultural historian and student of the ancient economy, I'd like to do a book on the movement of goods from the traders' perspective?" And so this project was born.

This monograph owes a great deal to a great many. Lindsay Adams, Eugene N. Borza, Carol Thomas, Jennifer Roberts, Lee L. Brice, Serena Connolly, Steve Garfinkle, Nicholle Hirshfeld and Eric Cline helped turn a proposal into a workable project by suggesting authors and reviewing chapter proposals. Claire Yancey and Elizabeth Bews did much of the copyediting and bibliography cross-referencing. The students from the 2014 Archaeological Field School at Antiochia ad Cragum, in Southern Turkey served as a general "focus group" and classroom test case. And the chapter authors—Christopher Monroe, David Tandy, Michael Kozuh, Joseph Manning, and David Hollander—turned my original proposal into the deeply-thoughtful and well-evidenced study that follows.

From the very first prospectus, I made a conscious decision that this study not duplicate other work on the ancient economy; thus, *Traders in the Ancient Mediterranean* takes a diachronic view of the Mediterranean trader from the Late Bronze Age through the Roman Imperial period, in an attempt to identify individual behavior and economic choice. The five scholars whose work is presented here, cunningly map ancient trading behavior and in so doing offer a framework on which to hang ancient Mediterranean buying, selling, and transporting of goods. In keeping with the mission of the PAAH monograph series to make new scholarship accessible to teachers, students and scholars of Ancient Mediterranean History, it is our hope that the patterns and behaviors analyzed here offer many points of departure for future conversation, in the classroom and beyond.

CONTENTS

INTRODUCTION:
SAILING THE ROUGH SEAS OF ANCIENT TRADE
Timothy Howe
St. Olaf College

The trader's dilemma, no matter the location, seems to have involved navigating the rough seas between tradition and commodification. By traders, I mean those who would consider their livelihood making goods available to consumers in exchange for other goods, precious metals, or more abstract services or favors (i.e. trade)—traders were professional "exchangers" of goods and must be distinguished from others who engaged in regional cabotage or tramping (Horden and Purcell 2000; Morley 2007, 77). But while picking out those who would identify themselves as traders narrows the field somewhat, it only serves as a beginning: in the ancient Mediterranean world there was often a fine line between what we might call a trader and a pirate (de Souza 1998; 2012), between a highwayman and a caravan driver (Monroe 2009), or between a farmer and a merchant (Tandy 1997). Context, that is human social and political relationships, assigns the decisive onomastic, often in pejorative ways.[1] To be sure, in regions of less governmental control individuals ventured out on the sea-lanes and highways to move goods much more freely than in areas of greater governmental control—though even in highly regulated environments traders sought to act more freely, often expending valuable resources to out-maneuver regulations and authorities.

As a rule, then, the ancient Mediterranean trader had to balance, in rational and (mostly) socially acceptable ways, a number of competing variables—such as investors, colleagues, agents, consumers, and producers—with competing priorities—such as local and regional traditions, individual and family needs, and internal and external social conventions. As Peter Bang puts it, unlike actors in modern or early modern capitalist economies, the ancient trader's "main concern was not the uninhibited operation of markets, but whether supplies were made available to consumers, mostly urban, while the rights of local aristocracies to

---

[1] As Philip de Souza (2012a) notes in his nuanced study of piracy, the term was often used to vilify and marginalize internal and external enemies; consequently one man's trader was another man's pirate. A similar dynamic seems at work among the literary sources, which prioritize farming as noble and trading as much less so (Howe 2008, 27-47).

control the agricultural surplus still had to be maintained" (Bang 2006, 76). With this balancing act between supplying urban consumers and not threatening the power of the traditional agricultural elites in mind, we might define Ancient Mediterranean traders as those individuals who moved goods from the periphery of an internally recognized socio-political entity (city-state, polis, empire, and so forth) to urban consumers, usually at the core of said entity, for the purpose of distribution in return for status, wealth, and/or influence, all without disrupting any local or regional power balances or socio-political structures.

Ancient Mediterranean traders exchanged goods for wealth and influence in ways that might seem idiosyncratic and even destructive to a modern audience. This confusion is not simply because of the complex balancing acts ancient traders performed as they navigated the rough seas of tradition and reward, but also because the surviving literary sources—our only "native informants" for the ancient Mediterranean world—are biased. The literary sources that mention trade and exchange of non-agricultural products are dismissive or scornful towards those who make their livelihood through moving and exchanging goods. As a result, ancient historians face a source tradition that seems at first glance suspicious of, if not outright hostile to, trade and traders (Bang 2009, 101).

Thus, the ancient historian interested in studying Mediterranean traders must sail carefully through the ancient literature. First, he or she must put aside modern concepts of supply and demand and embrace a traditional value economy that often sought reward not in profit but rather in influence. Second he or she must also confront the biases inherent in the sparse, anecdotal, and hostile literary evidence and tease out meaning. As we will argue in this volume, the best way to wrest meaning from the biased documentary record is by tempering and leavening it with archaeological data and economic theory. For example, even though most literary sources, from the Bronze Age to the Late Roman Period, assert that trading was uncouth, rather specialized and of negligible importance to individuals,[2] evidence from shipwrecks from all of these periods suggests that trade happed all the time, in a myriad of ways, for a myriad of reasons, and was of vital importance (Wilson 2011a). Indeed, the material record seems directly to contradict much of the literary

---

[2] The literary evidence seems equally to obscure and personalize traders and their activities. In addition, few of the thousands of administrative documents drafted by officials assessing productive capacities directly concern traders. See the chapters that follow for examples of this pattern in each historical period studied.

testimonia about grasping merchants unworthily making large profits from large shipments: the shipwreck data demonstrate that cargoes were small, ubiquitous, mixed, transported on small ships, and often split up among several shipments (Monroe 2009; Wilson 2011a; 2011b).

And so we come to a pivotal observation: Ancient societies were not commodified in the modern sense to expect large profit from distribution of goods. Wealth, per se, was not the end goal — status and influence were. Unlike much modern economic behavior, which we today see as disembedded and depersonalized, ancient transactions were wholly embedded, i.e. masked in terms of individual relationships, such as gift exchanges and obligations, and consequently much more personal and status oriented (e.g. Tandy 1997; Monroe 2009). And while there have been some excellent theoretical treatments to aid in tackling the literary and archaeological sources related to trade (e.g. Hopkins 1983), theory for interpreting ancient Mediterranean trade has been slow to come, as it has been generally for the ancient economy, and must be used cautiously in tandem with literary and archaeological evidence, not as a substitute for them (Bang 2008). New Institutional Economics (NIE), in particular, has recently shown great promise in this regard — the sheer number of studies conducted in the last 5 years has been both impressive and intimidating (e.g. Bresson 2007, 2008; Bang 2008; Gabrielsen 2011; Scheidel 2012, cf. Monroe 2009). And as these studies have shown, NIE's focus on institutions and structures seems to offer much more to ancient historians studying personal, embedded relationships, and webs of interaction than Neo-Classical Economics' focus on markets, supply, and demand. Nonetheless, the principal problems with the application of NIE to the ancient Mediterranean have come because the datasets are small. For ancient Mediterranean traders the datasets are smaller still.

So, why write a book about ancient Mediterranean traders and not ancient Mediterranean trade or the ancient Mediterranean economy? The answer is fairly mundane: there are a number of excellent studies analyzing the ancient Mediterranean economy and systems of trade (e.g. Scheidel 2007, 2012), but there are surprisingly few monographs on traders — Rauh (2003) and Monroe's (2009) studies really stand out here — and there are no studies on traders that offer a diachronic view that encompasses the entire Mediterranean, from the Bronze Age to Imperial Rome. This is partly because of the nature of the evidence — the small dataset problem again. The ancients did not share much information about those who made their livelihoods moving goods from the periphery to the center, perhaps because such activity was itself mundane and obvious, or perhaps because trading was not as worthy of comment as "proper" wealth-getting strategies, such as farming and animal husbandry (Howe 2008, 27-47; 2014a). That said, despite the small datasets and biased data, we can still discern much about traders and the economic patterns their activities generated.

Whether the literary sources choose to acknowledge it or not, traders played important roles in every ancient Mediterranean community, simply because they acted in geographically and socially liminal spaces. In fact, the information networks woven by ancient Mediterranean traders regularly spanned political and geographical boundaries. The ancient Mediterranean trader built links opportunistically between sources of information, labor, and wealth that benefitted the self, the family, the community, the state, or any combination thereof. Indeed, the chapters in this book attempt to show that ancient Mediterranean trade is primarily characterized by a general disregard for the "laws" of supply and demand, by quixotic consumer tastes and trends, and by intense official interference (and even competition) by revenue-hungry political entities. Consequently, for the ancient trader and the consumers he (or occasionally she) serviced, the prices of movable goods were always volatile, high risk was always a factor, and the integration of markets into an ordered economy superficial and tentative.

And yet, it seems that ancient traders were able to negotiate all of this complexity without any formalized economic theory. At times, ancient traders and governments even seem consciously to have rejected the integrated economies familiar to the modern world in favor of market chaos and the high levels of risk that resulted (so argues Bang 2008). By contrast, modern (and early modern) traders have had largely cooperative political entities and well-developed traditions of economic theory. Modern traders can therefore interpret consumer demand with a degree of confidence, diversify risk, and thereby create a predictable and transparent trading environment. For these reasons, modern perspectives about market supply, consumer demand, and state involvement can be distracting and misdirecting if one wants to make sense of ancient Mediterranean traders and the socio-political entities in which they operated. Consequently, without the familiar modern economic framework and terminologies, ancient trade can seem chaotic, idiosyncratic, and "bizarre." It was, but not hopelessly so, and certainly not as primitive or simple as M. I. Finley (1973) once argued.

4

As we look across time, patterns of ancient trade do move in and out of focus between two main types, what we might recognize as inter-regional and regional. It seems apparent that the political and social developments of the Late Bronze Age and the Hellenistic and Roman periods, characterized by the rise of what Manning (forthcoming) calls Leviathan States, facilitated a growth of cities, rise in population, and a wider use of precious metals as standards of exchange, all of which in turn facilitated increased volume and demand for long-distance, extra-mural trade. State formation, political and economic integration, and the resulting political stability and reduction of war, lowering of predation and costs of transactions, all facilitated inter-state trade and inter-nationally-connected traders. Alternatively, the political and social developments of the Early Iron Age (what in the Greek world is usually called the Archaic and Classical periods), while also facilitating a growth of cities, rise in population, and a wider use of precious metals as standards of exchange, tended to encourage international tension, fragmented trans-ethnic networks, predation, and increased the costs of transactions. The result was more regional, focused exchange onto smaller, local networks to such as degree that larger structures, and longer distance trade were slow to form and thrive.

When economic and political conditions are conducive, such as during the Roman Empire, or during the Late Bronze Age, much of the Mediterranean world could become an accessible, often integrated market, as Christopher Monroe (in Chapter 1), Joseph Manning (in Chapter 4) and David Hollander (in Chapter 5) will show. At other times, such as during the 5th century BCE Athenian Empire, or the Assyrian, Babylonian and Persian Empires, semi-porous, regional markets seem to dominate, as David Tandy (in Chapter 2) and Michael Kozuh (in Chapter 3) discuss. In a sense, these periods of Mediterranean-wide trade that we see in the Late Bronze Age and Hellenistic-Imperial Roman periods serve to bookend the (somewhat overlapping) periods of Greek and Near Eastern regionalism. Thus, with these five chapters we hope to offer a framework on which to hang ancient Mediterranean buying, selling, and transporting of goods. By also focusing on local traditions, the embedded historical context and the socio-political goals of traders as individual actors, we offer here contextualized analysis of the impact of trade on ancient Mediterranean life beyond the traditional boundaries of the "economy." As the readers will see, definite conclusions can be hard to come by, and this book will, perhaps, raise more questions than solid answers. But while this might disappoint some, we hope that readers will persevere and discern the larger patterns about the world of trade and traders that emerge from some quirky and often idiosyncratic actions and sources.

I

TANGLED UP IN BLUE: MATERIAL AND OTHER RELATIONS OF EXCHANGE IN THE LATE BRONZE AGE WORLD
Christopher M. Monroe
Cornell University

Although readers might think a chapter on Late Bronze Age trade is a fair beginning, historically we are already at an end.[1] The trading networks of the 14th and 13th century BCE Eastern Mediterranean were produced by centuries of individual and corporate entrepreneurship, diplomacy, and imperialism that culminated in the linkage of the Mycenaeans, Hittites, Cypriots, Egyptians, Assyrians, Babylonians and smaller polities amongst them. This International Age, as it is frequently called, collapsed ca. 1180 BCE in the midst of increasing aridity, grain shortages, violent migrations, and regional political-economic instability (Kaniewski et al. 2010; Kaniewski et al. 2013; Drake 2012).[2] But climate change is only part of the story of the Late Bronze Age (henceforth, LBA) collapse. How people adapted is more at issue in a human history, and trade is one of the most visible means humans have employed to improve their conditions. It is questionable and curious then, why traders themselves are still conventionally placed on the historical sidelines.[3]

While many scholars make trade a prime mover in the emergence of Bronze Age complexity across the Near East, eastern Mediterranean, and Europe,[4] a full appreciation of expanding trade must also recognize that increasing production, exchange, and consumption were sowing seeds of destabilization. In the LBA, as I will argue here, long-distance interdependencies developed out of the profit-seeking, risk-taking behaviors of traders and out-paced any royal, political or

---

[1] I wish to thank Nicolle Hirschfeld and Tim Howe for involving me in this volume.

[2] The most noted symptom of this environmental downturn was the "Sea Peoples" (Oren 2000) and other marine marauders that contemporary scribes in Egypt and Ugarit blamed for widespread destruction. In an Akkadian letter found at Ugarit the king of Alashiya warns his counterpart at Ugarit: "ships of the enemy have come. They have been setting fire to my cities and have done harm to the land ... (*Ug.* 5 24).

[3] In Van de Mieroop's history (2007, 188), e.g., trade of historical significance is state/royal trade, while traders themselves, whether Egyptian, Hittite, or Syrian, are all of supposedly low status.

[4] For a particularly expansive argument wherein trade drives complexity, see Kristiansen and Larsson (2005).

communal oversight of an immature international economic system. While not at all the focus of this chapter, collapse does serve to highlight how a productive system of international relations was ultimately beyond the control of those in power. Traders often acted in geographically and socially liminal spaces, and the information networks woven by their social relations of exchange became increasingly impactful in the 14th through early 12th centuries BCE. In short, traders—especially maritime traders—were deeply involved in both the rise and demise of that luminous period. On face such a conclusion sounds formalistic, but the ancient realities were far more complex than most of our well-worn rubrics. The evidence shows how trader behavior was shaped and constrained by cultural norms of the place and time; i.e. it was also quite substantive, or culturally embedded, in the terms inherited from Polanyi (1957) and Mauss (1990 [1925]). And, as will be shown, the evidence is often laconic and vague, and thus the theoretical framework should be one of ambiguity and balance, neither of which was captured well in the models of authority, control, and dependence (i.e. feudal, patrimonial, Asiatic, two-sector, theocratic, world-system, etc.) that dominated twentieth century discourse on ancient trade.[5]

How one sees traders naturally depends on the selection of evidence. Scholars tend to split into text or artifact specialists, both of whom rely heavily on theoretical models to fill out large lacunae. Archaeologists have many sites where material was produced for the market or consumed, but to witness goods actually in transit is much rarer. Few if any sites compare to the Uluburun shipwreck in numbers of artifacts or questions raised. The textual picture is not so different. Though the period is relatively well documented, compared especially with the succeeding Iron Age I (ca. 1200-1000), few of the thousands of cuneiform sources directly concern traders, as they were drafted mostly by administrators counting material indicators of productive capacities. Nevertheless there are currently around four hundred texts, mostly in Akkadian, that indirectly or directly involve traders (indexed in Monroe 2009).[6] Added to these are numerous texts in Ugaritic (a Northwest

---

[5] Summaries of the so-called substantivist-formalist debate can be found in, *inter alia*, Aubet (2013, 7-116), Monroe (2009, 4-9), Warburton (2009); Manning and Morris (2005), Van de Mieroop (2004), Snell (1997, 145–58), and Sherratt and Sherratt (1991).
[6] Most of those were written in the Middle Babylonian dialect of Akkadian, which became the scribal lingua franca of the LBA. The hundreds of relevant Akkadian texts

Semitic language written in cuneiform alphabetic script at Ugarit), Middle Assyrian tablets from several sites in Syria and Iraq,[7] some Egyptian papyri, and very limited material from Linear B tablets found at Pylos, Knossos and other Aegean sites. This varied assemblage includes administrative lists, scholastic lessons, legal documents, law codes, literature, and letters. As to historiographical sources for traders, the coastal city-kingdom of Ugarit (Ras Shamra, Syria) stands apart in the relatively high number of tablets authored in excavated residences where exchange was a professional matter, such as the houses of Rapanu, Rashapabu, Yabninu, and Urtenu (Van Soldt 2010; Yon 2006; Singer 1999). Van Soldt (1995) demonstrated the concentration of scribal "schools" at Ugarit, where boys were taught to write Akkadian and other languages in the private homes of merchants and other notables. As noted by Van de Mieroop (2007), scribes and writing, the remnants of a great information network, are what bound this world together; otherwise it was quite diffuse in terms of spoken languages and economic systems. Elsewhere I have examined this corpus of textual evidence for LBA traders in the Eastern Mediterranean, supported by a selection of archaeological assemblages (Monroe 2009). Here I attempt to summarize those findings in an effort to understand the experience of the LBA from the perspective of traders—those who were professionally involved in buying and selling or transporting goods.

I organize textual and supporting archaeological evidence for trade into types of socioeconomic relationships.[8] Technological relationships involve techniques and tools; these relations are material and relate to things such as balance weights, seals, ships, and donkeys. Recent inquiries into materiality and entanglement highlight the impact of such relationships, in effect how "sticky" they are in the dependencies created between human and thing (Hodder 2012; Maran and Stockhammer 2012). Financial relations deal with prices, negotiating, and how traders corresponded about money and valuable information. Political relations include those dealings between traders and rulers or their officers. Ethnic

---

from Emar and Ugarit in Syria, Boghazkoy in Hatti, and Amarna in Egypt are all Middle Babylonian.

[7] Provenance for much of the Akkadian material is summarized in Pedersén (1998).

[8] This is not a strict typology but a heuristic method for organizing evidence in a way that reflects its complexity. People and materials represented in the texts resist categories and dichotomies such as royal-private, dependent-independent, official-entrepreneur; even the lines between luxury and commodity frequently blur. Thus a single theoretical perspective would be difficult to maintain.

relations can be approached in the texts, though ultimately there is insufficient evidence to assess the importance of ethnic grouping among LBA traders. The conditions of the ethnic trader that anthropology has documented, however, are valuable for reconstructing in a theoretically informed, contextual manner how traders were perceived socially. Family, whether biological or socially constructed, proves unsurprisingly to be of first importance in relations of exchange, where trust is always paramount. I intentionally consider class (conventionally understood as relations to means of production) after other relations to avoid prioritizing presumed class distinctions; past studies have been compromised by deriving classes from poorly understood terms in lexical lists or on *a priori* dictates of a structural-functional model. Class is approached instead through evidence for modes of accumulation, which theoretically link to means of production *and exchange*. In considering the evidence that some LBA traders were engaged in a rational, continual pursuit of profit—what Weber (1996, 17) considered to be the essence of capitalism, it becomes impossible to avoid concluding that an incipient form of capitalism was being practiced. Finally, to augment these material relationships, I conclude with immaterial relations that concern anxieties, divinities and other phenomena that emerge from seeing traders as inhabiting a liminal condition. Together these social relations of exchange convey an impression of how a loosely-defined entrepreneurial class, divisible into terrestrial and maritime experts, played a vital role in LBA history by inserting itself into, and extending, networks of power and wealth that entangled much of the Eastern Mediterranean world.

THE MATERIAL WORLD: TECHNOLOGICAL RELATIONSHIPS

At Ugarit and Emar (Ras Shamra and Tell Meskene, Syria) at least three major weight systems were simultaneously used: the Hittite, Mesopotamian, and Levantine. Though the regional systems shared a talent of ca. 28.2 kg, the shekels carried by traveling merchants would cluster around 7.8 g (Mesopotamian), 9.4 g (Levantine) or 11.75 g (Hittite). Thus regional standards were differentiated and related by a simple 4:5:6 ratio, materialized by the size and weight of the balance-pan stones carried and the markings on them. Conversion was simple and formed in effect a "weighing koiné" (Alberti and Parise 2005, 387). Knowing these standards, merchants could quantify equivalences and calculate profit while tacitly referencing an impartial standard that would help maintain trust between transactors. Just such a procedure was recorded in the Ugaritic text KTU 4.709 where 7 talents of wool in the standard of Ashdod (Palestine) are equated to 5 talents and 1800 shekels in the Ugarit standard (Monroe 2009, 55). Prices of raw and finished goods, animals, even people were stated by weight in silver, less often in gold. Late Bronze Age weighing achieved all the functions of money or currency by facilitating shared price information, calculation, storage of value, and accumulation of wealth. Knowing the standards, how they were divided into larger and smaller units and converted, and what were acceptable prices constituted a technical jargon that could be called a "language of value" (Monroe 2005). The greatest concentration of weights, over 500, was found in various deposits at Ugarit (Courtois 1990), the next numerous at Uluburun, where 139 were recovered, including seven sets mostly from the Levantine standard (Pulak 2000).

Literary sources reveal that LBA societies associated weighing equipment not just with technical mercantile practices and ideals but traditional, substantive concepts of truth, fairness, and justice. This shared tradition stretches from ancient Egypt and Mesopotamia right through to the modern West without much interruption, with the scale-keeping role played similarly by the gods: Enlil, Zeus, Shamash, Anubis (with Thoth), Yahweh, Michael and Lady Justice (Monroe 2009, 40-47). One literary example, part of an "instruction" from Ramesside Egypt, might suffice to observe the commercial ideal of profit as socially embedded in traditional ideals:

> Do not move the scales nor alter the weights [...]
> Where is a god as great as Thoth,
> Who invented these things and made them?
> Do not make for yourself deficient weights
> They are rich in grief through the might of god (Lichtheim 2006, 156–7).

Seals, which in the LBA took the form of cylinder, stamp or ring, were used by many Bronze Age merchants. Seals found in trading contexts (such as on shipwrecks or in trader's houses) were rarely if ever inscribed, a fact running contrary to the demonstrable importance of literacy (below). The design of the seal had to suffice as one's impressed authorization when sealing clay labels or tablets. Sealing and seal-cutting appear to be less rigidly administered in the LBA than earlier periods, though sealing retained its signature function of marking authority (Collon 1987, 61-2). While it would seem easier from a modern hyper-textual perspective to use inscribed rather than just iconic seals, the latter apparently sufficed as historically they often have in complex societies and trading networks. None of the cylinder or stamp seals from the Ulu-burun or Cape Gelidonya shipwrecks is inscribed, and few are elsewhere. The evidence available suggests that traders drew from common seal iconography; one could not recognize impressions or a given seal as belonging to a trader. If traders wanted to demonstrate their membership in a group or class, they found other means of expressing that distinction (Monroe 2009, 56-65).

Sealing was instrumental in securely storing goods either before or during transit. Well-placed Assyrian officials like Babu-aha-iddina and Urad-Sherua had storehouse keepers to mind their locked and guarded "treasure houses" (or "bronze house" in one instance; Postgate 1988; Monroe 2009, 64-67), while merchants at Ugarit probably used their homes for storage, a practice known in the well documented Old Assyrian overland trade (Michel 1996). The corpus of labels or tags from Ugarit (Van Soldt 1989) shows how traders and officials annotated im-ported and exported goods. When a merchant from Emar named Dagan-belu wrote to Ugarit requesting shipments from two different merchants, he was careful to ask that the second merchant seal the goods with his seal so that the nearly identical cargoes would not be confused upon receipt (RS 34.134 = *RSO* 7 31, l. 36-42; Monroe 2009, 62):

> Seal (the goods) with your seal, and give (the goods) to
> the son of Urtenu and to the messenger of Shipti-Baal
> (so) they may take it on my account.

This is just one indication of the complex and rational manner in which traders pursued profit in the Late Bronze Age.

Gross transport costs will naturally increase with the volume of business, but rational traders use economies of scale to reduce net trans-port costs overall as business expands. Here the limits of technology (as Weber understood them) come into play. Using donkeys as trans-portation, one could increase the size of sacks and jars only so much until it became a matter of multiplying donkeys, each one incurring a main-tenance cost, to carry the load. There is little documentation of the pack-animals that bore the bulk of goods traded overland, but of course we know that donkeys carry at least a third of their weight, i.e. 50 kg, or close to two ancient talents. Thus any experienced caravan trader had at least a notion of the "tyranny of distance" problem created by the feed and care of these rather inefficient means of long-distance transportation—there was always a point of diminishing returns when profit would be outweighed by grain, water, lodging and other transport costs (Bairoch 1988, 11, 82). Nevertheless, donkeys were the means available, and one might surmise that they were abundant and cheap. Actual prices for donkeys in Ugarit texts and the Hittite Laws range between ten and forty shekels of silver (Heltzer 1999, 446; Hoffner 1997, §180), or more than a year's wages for an average worker making a few shekels of silver a month.[9] A single letter from Ugarit (RS 20.015) appears to be settling a matter regarding price for donkeys to be purchased from Rapanu, whose archives and preserved mansion at Ugarit testify to his successful business career (Monroe 2009, 72).

The Amarna Letters involving diplomatic marriages give us the only detailed recordings of caravan shipments in the LBA, though the so-called Great Kings were clearly above any concern with logistics. It is easy to be hypnotized by the glimmer of treasures listed in letters accompanying diplomatic marriages, such as EA 13, 22, or 25 (Moran 1992). But these wondrous accounts tell us mostly nothing about the people conveying the goods. Nevertheless, one of the Canaanite rulers, eager to impress pharaoh in EA 316, affords a glimpse of the caravan network:

> Who am I that I would not send on a caravan of the king,
> my lord, seeing that Lab'ayu, my father, used to serve
> the king, his lord, and he himself used to send on all the

---

[9] Wage data is lacking at Ugarit despite a wealth of evidence on prices (Heltzer 1978; Heltzer 1999; Vargyas 1986). However, silver was a common means of payment, equivalency, and labor compensation from as early as the third millennium in the region (Warburton 2009, 74-75), and monthly wages appear to vary from 1 to 4 shekels a month from Ur III (22nd cent. BCE) to Neo-Assyrian (7th cent.) times, depending on a variety of factors including status and skill level of the worker. Some of this is enshrined in well-known "law codes": Eshnunna §11 stipulates 1 shekel per month for a hired man; Hammurabi §273 implies a monthly wage of 1 shekel; closer in time and space, Hittite Law §158a implies about 1¼ shekels, using the barley to silver equivalency from §183, for unskilled agrarian labor (for law codes, Roth 1997). Supporting the evidence from law codes, Farber (1978) noted wages hovering around 1 shekel in Old Babylonian sources, and Radner (2007) found 7th cent. Assyrian contracts wherein wages range from 1 to just under 4 shekels silver per month. Thus 1 shekel per month can be used heuristically as a base minimum wage in several ancient Near Eastern periods.

caravans that the king would send to Hanagalbat [N. Syria]. Let the king, my lord, send a caravan even to Karaduniyaš [Babylonia]. I will personally conduct it under very heavy guard (Moran 1992, lines 12–25).

Legal texts from Ugarit convey more on the risks and techniques of the caravan trade. Close accounts were kept of the goods, including the differentiation between cargo and personal belongings. In a lawsuit one might call "Mashanda of Ura v. the prefect of Ugarit" (RS 17.346 = *PRU* 4:176–77) a foreign merchant (Mashanda) prevails in a large claim against him for 4000 shekels of silver only because he can swear by the contents of "the account of the caravan," a clay tablet listing contents of his merchant caravans. Mashanda claimed his caravans were being continually robbed by none other than the king of Ugarit, who was apparently subject to the commercial law of the land (Monroe 2009, 169-70). Such accounts also came into legal play when merchants were murdered, as in RS 17.146 (*PRU* 4:154 ff.), where the community in which the murder occurred had to pay colleagues of the deceased 3 mina of silver for each dead man, plus the value of all the cargo and personal belongings of the merchants. If the killers were not caught, with goods unrecovered, the payment was called "blood-money" and was limited to 3 mina of silver—still a prohibitive amount. To safely convey such treasures as listed in the Amarna Letters was surely an anxious undertaking, perhaps as risky as maritime ventures.

Maritime trading practices were documented no better than in other periods of antiquity, i.e. poorly. Brief anecdotal mentions of merchants underscore the activity we are missing in places like Hatti and Egypt that generally lack any administrative records concerning traders:

The traders fare downstream and upstream as they do business with copper, carrying goods <from> one town to another as they supply him who has not, although the tax-people carry gold, the most precious of all minerals (Pap. Lansing 4,8–5,2; Castle 1992, 256–57)

This is a rare glimpse from a New Kingdom satirical text that contrasts the hardworking pedlar of baser metals with the literate bureaucrat who controlled the gold. As a satire, its historiographical merit can be questioned, so one might correct the impression of the exploited, impoverished trader with an inscription of Ramesses II at Abydos:

> I gave thee a ship laden with cargo upon the sea, and great [marvels] of God's Land are brought in to thee; and the merchants ply their trade under orders, their labor being gold, silver and copper (Redford 1992, 227).

As in caravans, sailors could be liable for lost cargo. The best-known text documenting this is a legal case adjudicated by Queen Puduhepa of Hatti in which a ship captain named Shukku (probably from the Hittite controlled port of Ura) was held responsible for intentionally crashing a loaded ship into the quay at one of Ugarit's harbors: "may Shukku reimburse his ship (and) his goods which were set in his ship's hold" (RS 17.133 = *PRU* 4:118–19, lines 18-22). A few administrative lists and letters from Ugarit document both mixed and specialized cargoes being requested or sent, including materials such as building stone, cloth from Byblos, copper from Cyprus, and grain (Monroe 2009, 76-79). Unfortunately we lack any maritime "bill of lading" comparable to the caravan shipments in the Amarna Letters that were precisely described and weighed.

Maritime archaeology adds a great deal to the landed view received from ancient texts. The complete excavation of the Uluburun shipwreck has generated numerous publications of the material (see Pulak 2008 for the fullest synthesis). Elsewhere I have drawn on this material to address two questions: first, what was the scale of maritime shipping in the Late Bronze Age, or simply, how big were the ships? (Monroe 2007). And secondly, how valuable was the shipment at Uluburun? (Monroe 2010). Combining all the known textual data regarding ship size with the remains of the approximately 15 x 5 x 2 meter ship and its cargoes, one may postulate that this was both a large ship *for the times*, and furthermore that Bronze Age sailing ships probably never exceeded 20 meters in length, or about 15,000 liters in capacity, and probably little more than the 20 metric tons carried in the Uluburun ship. This corrects the widespread and misleading notion (Casson 1995, 36, e.g.) that ships many times this size, more befitting Hellenistic times, sailed during the Bronze Age, facilitating royal trade monopolies. The design advancements in shipbuilding that led to freighters exceeding 15-

20 meters in length and carrying hundreds of tons were still a long way off. It was not until the 6th or 5th century BCE that shipwrights altered the cross-section of the hull from a simple arch shape to a recurved or "wine-glass" shape that was inherently stiffer and stronger.[10]

Textual evidence for ship equipment is highly ambiguous, due in part to the infrequency of nautical terms used in Akkadian texts and to the un-vocalized Ugaritic script. Typical in this regard is the Ugaritic text RS 20.008: "Account of ship damage: 9 newly installed oars; and a latticed look-out (crow's nest?); and a mast and rigging; and a mast-cap/truck." Practically every word after "oars" is subject to interpretation (Monroe 2009, 91-93). Egyptian iconography and models, and archaeological evidence from elsewhere, is limited but arguably more informative in filling out aspects of ships that are not preserved on the seabed (which is most everything above the waterline); this material is fully presented by Wachsmann (1998).

Private ownership of ships is attested in texts from Egypt, Syria and Assyria, and there are numerous references to royally owned ships and fleets; the latter situation is actually the more ambiguous and may often mean ship(s) *in service* to a particular ruler (Monroe 2009, 94-97). Regardless of who technically owned a ship or its cargo, a single shipment in the Late Bronze Age could make or break a community. This conclusion is reached by matching textual evidence about prices and equivalences for copper, tin, resin, timber, silver, and gold to some of the materials found at the Uluburun shipwreck (Monroe 2010). A hypothetical minimum value for the wrecked ship and its cargo amounts to at least 12,000 shekels of silver on the Ugarit standard, a sum that could be contextualized in several ways: a thousand years of salary for a skilled worker; the annual payment to a thousand workers; enough capital to buy hundreds of cattle, donkeys, or horses; food for Ugarit's citizens for a year, or over three times what Ugarit had to pay Ramesses II in annual tribute. Even such a rough estimate of value emphasizes the impact maritime trade had whether in royal or entrepreneurial hands. There is still no

---

[10] Two momentous seafaring advancements of the LBA were the keel and the loose-footed, brailed sail. The former stiffened the hull substantially and gave better support to the mast. The latter constituted a lighter, safer means of controlling the sail that allowed the ship to close-haul as near as 50 degrees to the wind. But the LBA ship was still a heavy, overbuilt vessel that by design limitations, and perhaps design, drifted badly to leeward. One should avoid maximizing its sailing or storage capabilities (Monroe 2007).

way to know with certainty which or both was represented by the Ulu-burun shipwreck.

The above were not the only technological means available to traders, but they might suffice to illustrate how material relations (or means) operated alongside social relations in maintaining networks of exchange. Looking just at weights and ships, one has systems of things that are closely interrelated and mutually dependent. The balance pan metaphorically expresses how these relations intertwine around people and things in complex ways: a mass of silver is tied to one or multiple value systems; the silver is tied to an object bought or sold and possibly transferred into a new social context (much as foreign goods become recontextualized, as discussed in Maran and Stockhammer 2012); the merchant is tied to his customer and to the god of justice, etc. The ship is a carefully designed system that balances dependencies, redundancies, and opportunity costs to create not just a vessel for transporting goods but a floating cosmos, wherein humans contended against chaos in a constant, dynamic struggle that some innocently call "sailing."

PRACTICE: RELATIONS PERTAINING TO FINANCE, CONDUCT, AND LITERACY

Most societies are governed by traditions that limit or forbid the commodification of one's own people. This ideal is balanced by the need to exchange goods and services, and once the value of goods and labor can be stored and exchanged, commodification of people, or dehumanization, becomes inevitable. The trader's dilemma in any complex society involves navigating between tradition and commodification. Traders must discuss opportunity and commodification with investors, colleagues and agents, consumers, and producers in a rational way. But the form of this discourse is shaped by competing priorities: moral, communal traditions limited commodification and how traders could deal with other members of society (Evers 1994). By the LBA, the trader's dilemma was already a balancing act between tradition and an incipient capitalism, which can be defined as a rational pursuit of profit (Monroe 2009, 283; Weber 1996, 17).

Late Bronze Age sources document symbiotic relations between kings and merchants. Royal endowments could include real estate, office, capital, protection, tax exemption, and influence, thus providing merchants with means of production and exchange (especially for building information networks and reducing transport costs). Maritime financing methods are poorly documented but appear to include cooperatives among private citizens, as shown in the Akkadian text from Ugarit, RS 19.046 (*PRU* 6 138) where three men contribute silver to outfit a ship or ships with a number of crew members (Monroe 2009, 109-10). Another much-discussed Ugaritic text, KTU 4.338 (Pardee 2002; Hoftijzer and Van Soldt 1998, 337-38) probably accounts for a large amount of silver given by the king of Ugarit to the king of Byblos for buying and out-fitting a ship:

> 540 is the full amount of ship-silver that went into the ship for the king of Byblos, and 50 was the silver taken by the king of Byblos to "clothe" his ship. 40 silver is the market price here (Monroe 2009, 110-15).

This is unfortunately a unique text whose ambiguities are hard to clarify without suitable comparanda. My translation reflects a consensus that the tablet recorded a sale rather than a bottomry loan. In light of Ramesside and Akkadian price data used to estimate the value of the Uluburun hull (Monroe 2010, 25), the figure appears reasonable for the cost of a single ship, making the cost of a ship at Ugarit nearly 50 years of wages for a typical laborer paid a shekel a month, or maybe a decade of wages for a more skilled bureaucrat. In any case, these impressionistic figures agree with the historical truth that ships have always been expensive to build, maintain, and lose.

Given such costs it is not surprising to see maritime business protected by laws. Legal protection fostered trust among trade partners and induced financiers or modest contributors to invest in long-distance ventures. Kinship, marriage and adoption were all mobilized to accumulate capital by Ugarit's entrepreneurs. Rashapabu, for example, married into money and used it buy an olive grove and staff (RS 17.149 = *Ug.* 5 N 6).[11] The maritime merchant Sinaranu inherited his wealth before being granted the Cretan franchise by the king (RS 15.138+ = *PRU* 3:101–02). An Ugaritic text from the palace, RS 18.132 (*KTU* 4.394), records a reimbursement of silver (30 shekels) for a modest

---

[11] I consider the issue of whether money existed in the Bronze Age Near East to be long settled, in agreement with Powell (1996), Snell (1995), Castle (1992), Menu and Gasse (2001), and others who have demonstrated how weighed metal established standard prices, means of payment, means of storing wealth, portability, and easy convertibility.

amount of copper (perhaps 8 talents or about 225 kilograms) lost at sea that was worth 120 shekels of silver; one may surmise the reimbursements were made to those who contributed the copper to the lost venture, and that the tablet was intended to serve as legal proof that payment was made (Monroe 2009, 78-9).

Family members and property were sometimes used as security for loans, as is well documented in Assyrian texts. A 14th cent. text from the archive of Family A at Assur (*KAJ* 39; Monroe 2009, 117-19) uniquely specifies a monetary loan for a venture involving a caravan into northern lands. The sealed tablet specifies that 3 and 2/3 mina of silver is loaned to two caravaneers by two men who stand to collect fields and houses of the debtors should they fail to repay, which they are supposed to do when the caravan returns to Assur. Furthermore the loan is "bound upon their good credit and responsibility." In a loan contract from Tell Rimah, TR 3021 (Wiseman 1968), a man borrows over one talent of tin, sealed with the city-office seal, to be repaid with interest after two years. As his pledge to repay, the debtor's wife and children are sent to live and work in the house of the creditor's daughter (Monroe 2009, 120-21). The credit industry, including debt-slavery, seems to have thrived from Assyria to Ugarit. Metal loans are especially pervasive in the Assyrian sources, with large tin loans pointing to Assur's key role in moving tin from east to west. The documentation of a credit industry, and its rational organization, is much stronger in Assyria than in Syria, as in the archive of Urad-Sherua of Assur (Postgate 1988). However, an Akkadian letter-edict sent by Hattushili III to king Niqmepa of Ugarit addresses complaints of usurious activities of the merchants of Ura in Ugarit (RS 17.130+ = *PRU* 4: 103-04):

> His Majesty, Great King, has thus made a regulation concerning the men of Ura in their relations with the men of Ugarit. The men of Ura shall carry on their mercantile activities in the land of Ugarit during the summer, but they will be forced to leave the land of Ugarit for their own land in the winter. The men of Ura shall not live in the land of Ugarit during the winter. They shall not acquire houses or fields (in Ugarit) with their silver. Even if a merchant, a man of Ura, should lose his capital in the land of Ugarit, the king of the land of Ugarit shall not permit him to live in his land. If men

of Ugarit owe silver to men of Ura and are not able to pay it off, the king of the land of Ugarit must turn over that man, together with his wife and his sons, to the men of Ura, the merchants. But the men of Ura, the merchants, shall not claim houses or fields of the king of the land of Ugarit. Now His Majesty, Great King, has thus made a regulation between the men of Ura, the merchants, and the men of the land of Ugarit (Beckman 1996, 162–63).

Much space could be devoted to the implications of this edict, but here I would point mainly to the balancing of a capitalistic mode of accumulation on the one hand and the royal interest to maintain territory on the other. Contrary to some theories regarding the political economy and social organization of ancient Near Eastern states, kings did not simply own everything in the realm. Some land was alienable, and here doubly alienable to foreign merchants with enough capital, if left unchecked, to threaten the integrity of a kingdom.

Finally, concerning modes of finance, merchant associations are vaguely documented in one text referring to "organized, joined, or associated" merchants at Assur and in the problematic "decumates" (Monroe 2009, 123-25) at Ugarit. At present one may conclude only that decumates, some of which had ten members and some not (*DULAT*, 189–90), could include merchants but cannot be definitively identified as merchant associations.

Most of the evidence for practices or protocol of traders comes from Ugarit, though analogies from history and economic anthropology are key. In formalistic terms the main purpose of proper conduct was to maximize trust and flow of information while minimizing risk. Risks included losing bargaining strength by revealing privileged information, and suffering untimely delays, detainment, and mortal dangers.[12] If one or both parties in a documented partnership were royal, or if they had never done business before, the language of negotiation tended to follow the model of reciprocal gift exchange, as documented in Old and Middle Babylonian royal correspondence (Zaccagnini 1983; Liverani 1990). But the rules of commercial engagement above all seem to have been fluid

---

[12] Trust underlay all commercial relations, as has been documented anthropologically by Landa (1994). As Braudel (1982, 167) already knew, trade might thrive through ethnic networks because the trust was built in.

enough to adjust to given levels of trust.[13] Thus one notes the balancing of brotherly and other notions in an Akkadian letter from Burna-Buriash of Babylon to Akhenaten:

> Between kings there is brotherhood, friendship, peace and good terms, (if) there is plenty of (precious) stones, plenty of silver, plenty of gold (EA 11, rev. 22–23; Liverani 1990, 213).

Non-royal entrepreneurs might write in brotherly terms as if they were kings exchanging gifts, but if they have a prior business relationship, then one sees them freely engaged in discussions of profit. Such is the correspondence between Urha'e and Yabninu, who exchange pleasantries in RS 22.393, but in RS 19.050 (*PRU* 6 14) get down to business:

> Because Hatti loads up the caravan, to me Hatti is worthwhile. And when you go to the land of Egypt [...] I will take part in your venture because it (too) is propitious. And do give Kunaziti the news about when you are going to Egypt. I will participate greatly in your venture so in future days you will not say, "how profitable was my venture, (but) he did not participate!" (Monroe 2009, 134-35).

A letter from father to son (RS 34.133 = *RSO* 7 36) contains perhaps the most explicit expression of concern for proper correspondence procedures:

> A request is something *I* ask of *you*. You are overreaching. To me you shall not ask a request. Rather I, in the presence of your man, ask you what is the request. Therefore, may you write about your health. When I have come down into the heart of the kingdom, all my wishes I will send to my son (Monroe 2009, 137-39).

---

[13] Singer (1999, 653–59) describes in detail the commercial nature of trade between Karkemish and Ugarit that involved prince, king, officials, and merchants.

It appears that a cautious father, traveling abroad, advises his son who is at home in Ugarit about what is proper to broadcast in letters that might be intercepted. Presumably, before setting out into foreign territory needs are assessed and the venture planned. Once in the field, if messages are to be sent back home, it is the agent in the field, aware of local conditions encountered, who decides what is wise to put on a tablet as a request from home. Loosely disseminated information about wants and needs could jeopardize the merchant's ability to justify his prices while appearing fair.

Scribal training in Mesopotamia was often a private enterprise conducted in small, domestic settings, the *eduba* ("tablet house" or school) being more a socioeconomic construct than a definite building (Veldhuis 1997). Scribes and translators found employment in the major centers of the LBA world, and are especially well documented at Ugarit, where there were several private *eduba*s like the one in Rapanu's house, and apparently none in the palace (Van Soldt 1995). Several of Ugarit's mercantile households possessed a functional literacy that was the product of a scribal curriculum that emphasized correspondence and calculation, the same skills taught to merchants in the Maritime Republics of Italy (Hyde 1993, 116-17; Monroe 2009, 141-45). Indeed, it is hard to imagine the information networks, hence the market, functioning without these skills. For such reasons literacy is key to understanding the role of wealthy entrepreneurs in Bronze Age society (Pearce 1995). It opened the way to office, which rewarded one with a steady supply of capital, information, and influence, all desired components for conducting a continual, rational pursuit of profit. The question of maritime mercantile literacy is still open but tantalizingly suggested by the writing boards found at Uluburun (Pulak 2008, 367-68) and by an ambiguous Ugaritic text (RS 94.2406) sent by the Queen to the city while she was "on the sea," "on the coast," or "on the day," according to how one reads the problematical phrase, *bi yammi* (Pardee and Bordreuil 2009, Text 31; Dietrich and Loretz 2009).

Laws protecting private property and governing trader conduct might arguably be classed as political, though this presumes the law was handed down by cultic or dynastic authority and not agreed upon through social practice and communal acceptance. This is largely unknowable, but the reasons for some laws are crystal-clear: maritime trade in a riverine kingdom like Assyria depended on orderly functioning of waterways, so the Middle Assyrian law code includes right-of-way rules such as this, which appear far too detailed to be symbolic alone:

¶2a If a boat either drifts down from upstream or crosses over from the opposite bank, and either rams and sinks a fully laden boat or rams and [sinks] an empty boat moored at the bank, whatever equipment is lost [...] the rammed boat [...] (Roth 1997, 189).

POLITICAL RELATIONS

Relations between professional traders and the crown appear to have varied from kingdom to kingdom in the LBA, as do the quantity and quality of textual evidence. In the Aegean there is really no pertinent textual evidence for the trader-state relationship besides Homer, which one may cautiously take as indicating a social distaste for commerce, at least among the elites aspiring to the ideal of "guest-friendship." In Hatti little is known outside of references at Ugarit to "merchant of Ura," "merchant of the Sun," and "merchant of Hatti," in all of which the Akkadian *tamkaru* is the term for "merchant." As Vargyas (1985, 77) has shown, the activities of the Ura merchants represent trade independent of the redistributive center, a trade that included price fluctuations, credit, and profit and loss. This view may be balanced against competing notions of a strictly redistributive Hittite economy, such as Klengel's (1986). Hittite laws protected merchants with huge fines (100 mina of silver, death) for robbing or killing them (Hoffner 1997, 19). Merchants were known by official title of *unatallash* in Hittite, written logographically in cuneiform as *dam-gar*, which was the spelling for merchant (*tamkaru*) in Akkadian texts also.

A similar scenario emerges from the limited pictorial and textual evidence from Egypt. The Egyptian trader, known to scribes as *shwty*, owned his own capital and boats, and conducted his own entrepreneurial affairs in addition to serving as trade-agent while clearly not rising to levels of wealth or independence achieved by his Syrian or Assyrian counterparts (Castle 1992; Kemp 2006, 332-33; Monroe 2009, 189-92). Earlier conceptions of Egyptian economy allowed little room for entrepreneurial traders (Reineke 1979), though more recent scholarship has even a monetary system and credit in New Kingdom Egypt (Menu and Gasse 2001). Pictorial scenes in Theban tomb 162, Kenamun's, and 17,

Nebamun's, (Wachsmann 1998, figs. 3.2 and 3.7) tell us that Egyptian officials welcomed foreign traders, and suggest that foreign traders may have handled some of Egypt's foreign trade, creating what Menu and Gasse call an "uneasy interdependence" (2001, 429). Officials registered cargoes, charged taxes and arranged quarters and meetings for those who came to do business in Egypt, either with the state or private individuals. The harbor was administered by an overseer and his agents, not unlike the harbors on the Syro-Palestinian coast.

In Assur there was probably some administration of the bronze trade through high officials. Babu-aha-iddina, the Assyrian chancellor under Shalmaneser I (1273-44), received tin from a trader named Siqi-ilani (*KAJ* 274), whose business included importing wood from Canaan (Monroe 2009, 81). The chancellor accompanied a copper shipment to another town and there oversaw the weighing out of the metal with official weights he had brought for the task (*KAJ* 178). Urad-Sherua's archive also shows buying, selling, and lending of metals by four generations of Assyrian officials. As noted already by Saporetti (1977), much of the Middle Assyrian entrepreneurship was conducted by those lacking the title *tamkaru*, as were those in Old Assyrian sources, but the *tamkaru*-merchants appear to have had something like a monopoly on the lucrative tin trade and related credit industry. Three high officials were involved in trade, including the acquiring and loaning of tin. Babu-aha-iddina is the best documented and most influential of these three officials who controlled stores of tremendous wealth. Despite these commercial ties to high officials, interaction directly with royalty is not well documented in MA sources. Fortunes of Assyrian merchants could shift with changing alliances and enmities. Later in the 13th century the Hittite king decreed a blockade against Assyrian merchants reaching the coast via Amurru (more below). And in the Tukulti-Ninurta Epic (Foster 1993, 209-29) Kassite merchants are seized as part of the Assyrian-Babylonian conflict roiling at the time (1243-07). Yet by the late 12th century, as seen in *MARV* 23 (Freydank 1976), Hittite merchants and their access to Lebanese goods appear welcome at the palace in Assur:

> 132 talents and 24 minas of cedar (oil) that merchants from the land of Hatti brought here. By the palace, by the hand of Apliya, chief steward, it is charged to Babu-shuma-erish, son of Qibi-Ashur. As an offering for burning it is given to him (Monroe 2009, 200).

Trader-state relations are most fully documented in Akkadian and Ugaritic texts from Ugarit. They are fairly complex and copious, and presented more fully elsewhere (Monroe 2009, 151-89). Some wealthy *tamkaru*-merchants were recorded as royally "endowed" (*mandattu*) with silver, while less well-heeled traders were literally "of his foot" or "on foot" (*sha shepishu*), as opposed to on ship or horseback, it would seem. Lowest in the hierarchy of traders, as viewed by the administration, were merchant's representatives or assistants (*bidaluma*). Several merchants received land grants, sometimes with a service obligation called *pilku*; others were accepted into a *mudu*-ship denoting something like "associate" or being in the royal confidence. Since Liverani's (1962) early and Marxian analysis of trader-state relations at Ugarit portraying the *tamkaru* as a royal dependent, many scholars have recognized a wider range of roles including royal agent, independent trader, and foreign merchant, plus other untitled individuals who engaged in maritime and terrestrial ventures (Astour 1972, Vargyas 1986), while others still view Ugarit as a two-sector society wherein royals and their dependents, including merchants, are structurally-functionally opposed to the free peasantry (Vita 1999; Heltzer 1999). How state business was administered is still vaguely understood, though it would seem that the governor/prefect, the *shakin(nu)*, oversaw maritime trade through a harbor overseer, and oversaw titled merchants (*tamkaru*) generally via a merchant overseer, while a herald working for the palace collected duty from those bringing foreign trade and perhaps others. The governor, not the king, also seems to have overseen the tax-collector (*makisu*) who collected tax (*miksu*) from merchants. Kings of Ugarit made no visible effort to monopolize trade, instead taxing it to share in its profits and using royal grants to foster it and increase the kingdom's productivity. Even with the nominal oversight by the secular governor, there was little administrative control over traders' activities, no "merchants of the king" in Ugarit, and little if any documentation or orders requested by or filled for the palace by merchants. The dynastic, semi-divine king was thus officially and *traditionally* separated from commerce; but he was certainly interested and involved in trade indirectly and through his staff.

Trader-state relations at Ugarit can thus be summarized as symbiotic or interdependent. To illustrate with a few examples, one may first look at the tension inscribed in the letter RS 20.023 (*Ug*. 5 N 54). Therein Rapanu was late in supplying Urtenu the prefect with something required for a venture, and so Urtenu asks rather rhetorically,

> Since the tasks of the venture you do not understand, why do you delay my going down the road? Is it thus fine in your opinion that there is no wine or oil reserves or salt? (Monroe 2009, 133, lines 9-15).

It is not clear what Rapanu failed to provide, though donkeys is a strong possibility given his dossier. One gathers from this how the prefect is closely involved in provisioning the city, and how Ugarit depends on Rapanu's service—a picture antithetical to the notion of merchants as strictly royal dependents. A second and well-known example is the legal text RS 16.238+254 (*PRU* 3:107), which exempted the ship owner Sinaranu from the usual customs or duty imposed on foreign trade:

> From this day forth Ammistamru (II), son of Niqmepa, king of Ugarit frees from claim Sinaranu, son of Sigina. As Shapshu (the sun-god) is clear, he is clear. His grain, his beer and his oil need not enter the palace. His ship is free from claim. If his ship comes from Kapturi (Crete), he will bring his gift to the king, and the herald will not enter into his house. On account of the king, his lord, Sinaranu has worked hard, and his household is caring for children. May Ba'al, lord of Mt. Hazi, destroy whoever disputes these words ... (Monroe 2009, 165-67).

This is one of the most informative texts from the entire Bronze Age on the subject of maritime trade, and unfortunately unique. In spelling out the implications of the exception granted, we are told what was surely the rule, that ships coming from abroad were inspected and taxed at some unspecified rate. As if the king had to justify this exemption, the lines near the end explain Sinaranu's virtues, just the sort of moralism one would expect in a society where trade was balanced by tradition. That Sinaranu could extract this consideration from the king speaks to the value of his business to the crown, both in terms of material and certainly information. A second legal text records Sinaranu purchasing a number of properties including those of his father; he pays the king 5000 shekels of silver in total (one of the largest transactions recorded in Bronze Age texts), but the phrasing in each of the dozen or more transactions and in the summation carefully casts it all as an exchange of gifts, as in lines 50-52: "This gift is that which Niqmepa [son of Niqmaddu, king of Ugarit], gave to Sinaranu son of Sigina. First, the king gave; secondly, for silver received (Sinaranu) took (it)" (Monroe 2009, 259-62). Kings were supposed to be above the corruption of commerce, so here a hugely profitable sale was cloaked in a diaphanous film of gift exchange.

Power to grant exemptions from import taxes rested solely with the king, though one sees a request for similar tax exemption directed to the prefect/governor by an influential merchant and official at Karkemish named Ebina'e in RS 17.078 (*PRU* 4:196–97):

> Herewith I have sent my man to my son [the prefect].
> Whatever he needs he shall take on (his) word. Let no
> one obstruct him in any way. Let not the tax collector
> collect his tax. Until he is settled there [at Ugarit], attend
> him well (Monroe 2009, 185-86).

To another trader named Zulannu, the prefect was "my brother," and the two were dealing in such valuable items as gold, raw glass, finished bronzes, iron weaponry, clothes, and horses (RS 17.144; *PRU* 6 6; Monroe 2009, 187). Takuhlinu is a special case, representing perhaps one of the best documented examples of an individual climbing the social ladder via trade and office to the highest non-dynastic post in the land. As Singer (1983) reconstructed his dossier, Takuhlinu was wealthy enough to pay 1000 shekels of silver for an estate with olives and vines; he bought the status of "associate" or *mudu* of the king; his posts included palace guard, courtier, overseer of international affairs at Karkemish, and eventually prefect or *shakinnu*. In one text he is granted an entire town to be rebuilt at his own expense, literally "from his silver, from his copper, from all he has" (RS 15.114; *PRU* 3:112–13; Monroe 2009, 258). What is more interesting from a trader's perspective, however, is that the town in question is exempted from *pilku*-obligations in the same decree. Thus Takuhlinu stood to gain a source of production upon which he could capitalize to a greater than ordinary degree. He is not the only figure at Ugarit (or Assyria) wherein trade and state are so intertwined, but in perhaps no other figure are they so inextricably entangled. Despite the supposed omnipotence of the ancient Near Eastern king, in this case it was good to know, or be, the prefect.

Royals could foster trade with investment or stem it with legal-military prohibition. We saw above that merchants of Ura (who were under Hittite jurisdiction) were restricted in their lend-and-land-grab operation in Ugarit. And despite the generally favorable conditions following the Egyptian-Hittite peace of ca. 1259, international enmities still existed that might result in embargoes on specific goods or merchants. The best known LBA embargo was a condition of the vassal treaty imposed upon Shaushgamuwa of Amurru (Phoenicia, roughly) by Tudhaliya IV of Hatti:

> Since the King of Assyria is My Majesty's enemy, he shall be your enemy. Your merchant shall not go to Assyria, and you shall not allow his merchant into your land. He shall not pass through your land. But if he comes into your land, seize him and send him off to My Majesty ... No ship [of] Ahhiyawa may go to him ... (Beckman 1996, no. 17).

This was not an embargo on Ahhiyawan (i.e., Mycenaean) shipping, nor was it necessarily a prohibition on all Assyrian trade along the lucrative Phoenician coast. It was, however, an economic thrust at the Assyrian palace, whose agents would be cut off from vital trade in Cypriot copper and various coastal commodities. Non-royal traders, or those dealing in non-strategic goods (copper, tin, horses or other military *materiel*), may not have been included in the embargo (Monroe 2009, 180-81, 220). The same Tudhaliya ordered Ammistamru II of Ugarit to prevent Hittite or Egyptian messengers from taking horses to Egypt. Two copies of the decree were found at Ugarit, RS 17.450A (*PRU* 4:144) and RS 20.252 D (*PRU* 6 179), one from a palace archive, the other from Rapanu's house. So despite the peace and brotherly relations with Hatti's old enemy Egypt, Tudhaliya's caution is redolent of a détente between superpowers.

Under normal, peaceful conditions the state played an important role in facilitating trade by enforcing laws and treaties that reduced risk and transport costs. The same sort of principles and conduct that inspired the notably commercial Code of Hammurabi and later Middle Assyrian Laws (Roth 1997) were upheld in the juridical texts we have from Ugarit regarding murder, theft and other violence against merchants. Interfering with merchants carried heavy penalties: men of Ugarit must pay 180 shekels of silver for the murder of a merchant in Tarhuntasha (a Cilician territory between Ugarit and Hatti; RS 17.042 = *PRU* 4:171), and an accord between Ugarit and Karkemish (RS 17.146 = *PRU* 4:154) sets the penalty for killing an endowed merchant at 180 shekels of silver plus value of his goods. It seems that any molestation of foreign merchants resulted in an international incident adjudicated by the Hittite Queen or other royal (Monroe 2009, 173-80). Perhaps it was only symbolic but the penalty in the Hittite laws (Hoffner 1997, §5) for killing a merchant was higher than any penalty imposed in a preserved lawsuit: 100 mina or 4000 shekels of silver, plus lost goods and costs of burial. The monetary penalty closest to that sum in an actual lawsuit involving merchants is preserved on RS 17.229, where the perpetrator and host community are punished together:

> Talimmu the merchant said: "My merchants were killed in Apsuna." And Talimmu and the sons [i.e., citizens] of Apsuna came for judgment and have been judged. Those who made the blood and the sons of Apsuna [shall pay to Talimmu] one talent of silver (*PRU* 4:106).

Maritime cases show that customs and laws were in place to cover losses from wreckage and prevent the unscrupulous from defrauding the system. What are preserved are probably the exceptional cases that required royal or international arbitration. Such was the case when the foreign captain named Shukku crashed another's ship into the quay at Ugarit and had to appear in court before the Hittite crown (RS 17.133 = *PRU* 4:118-19):

> His majesty thus decided their case: the chief of the sailors of Ugarit shall swear (an oath), and his ship with his goods that were set aboard his ship, Shukku shall reimburse (Monroe 2009, 179; Beckman 1996, no. 34).

Kings also get involved in the matter of a salvaged shipwreck in an Ugaritic letter sent to the king of Ugarit by the king of Tyre (RS 18.031 = *KTU* 2.38; Pardee 2002, 3.45H; Monroe 2009, 98-99):

> Your ship that you sent to Egypt, died in a mighty storm close to Tyre. It was recovered, and the "salvage master"/captain[14] took all the grain from their jars. But I have taken all their grain, all their people, and all their belongings from the captain, and I have returned it all to them. And (now) your ship is being taken care of in Akko, stripped, so may my brother not take anything to his heart.

This is one of a number of LBA letters that may concern grain shortages and relief efforts. It is also an exceptional instance of direct royal involvement in trade, which highlights the rule that they were typically more interested in access than ownership when it came to the means of exchange. Here one sees another international incident being resolved by royal intervention. None of the actual principals are named, and the awkward title "salvage master"/captain is likely the result of linguistic and/or terminological differences between Ugarit and Tyre. It would certainly not be in either king's economic or political interest to stand completely ignorant or aloof from the business of his own house. Traditionally (i.e. symbolically and ideologically) however, the king could not be an entrepreneur; it would hardly be surprising if native nautical terms were unknown in either palace. The palace was a complex organization whose business was conducted by officials below the king.

BLOOD RELATIONS — FAMILY AND ETHNICITY

Texts from Assyria, Emar, and Ugarit show that commercial knowledge and skills were passed from father to son, and that risk and rewards were shared by family members, including women. Four letters from Urtenu's archive at Ugarit are key. Three (*RSO* 7 31, 32, and 33) were sent between Urtenu of Ugarit and Dagan-belu of Emar and show the sons of both men employed in the trade running between these two strategic towns, one on the Mediterranean coast and the other directly east sitting on the western bank of the Euphrates. In RS 34.134 (RSO 7 31) Dagan-belu exhorts his Ugaritan partner,

---

[14] There is considerable ambiguity and discussion over what is precisely meant by Ugaritic *rb tmtt*, more literally "chief of the crew," or just "captain." Much seems lost in translation from a southerly Phoenician dialect.

Do not hold back your son there; send him off so he may come. And when he comes, give to him, your son, alum, lapis lazuli-colored wool, blue wool, and a woven linen garment, my brother, so that he may bring (them) (Monroe 2009, 137).

In another letter RS 34.173 (*RSO* 7 33) Dagan-belu assures Urtenu that his son is well-cared for, lazy even, in Emar: "Ever your son, until Spring, sat while I sealed the tablet sacks" (Monroe 2009, 62). And we saw above in *RSO* 7 36 the son of an Ugaritan merchant named Tuna being scolded about the proper methods of correspondence with a business agent in the field.

Paintings in Theban tombs 17 and 162 (Nebamun's and Kenamun's) show that wives and children accompanied some Syrian merchants on their ventures abroad; they were probably more than just accompaniment, playing crucial roles in whatever negotiations, diplomacy or socializing took place. At Ugarit adoptions were used to consolidate wealth in families and create familial relationships among members of household firms. "Brother" often meant "colleague," an example of commercial and traditional structures entangling in the entrepreneurial sphere of practice (Monroe 2009, 205-13).

Gauging the weight of ethnic trader affiliation in the LBA is extremely problematic. Noting the importance of both "etic" (instrumental, constructed, circumstantial, externally imposed) and "emic" (basic, primordial, culturally inherent, self-defined) aspects of ethnicity, I follow Eriksen's broad definition since it can be mapped onto textual evidence: "aspects of relationships between groups which consider themselves, and are regarded by others, as being culturally distinct" (1993, 4). Textual markers of foreign or Other-ness, such as gentilics or other markers of foreign citizenship, are abundant. From those determinations one would like to assess whether LBA traders practiced strategies for solving the cross-culturally observed "trader's dilemma" (Evers 1994) common also to groups known as "middleman minorities" (Zenner 1991); briefly these five strategies were immigration, ethnic identification/formation, accumulation of cultural capital (assimilation), cash-and-carry trade, and depersonalization or disembedding of exchange transactions (Evers 1994, 10). The trader's dilemma was not strictly an ethnic phenomenon but appears to reflect the socioeconomic conditions of traders generally; thus it is worth considering in some detail as the meager evidence allows.

Perhaps not immigration, but at least trans-residentiality can be seen where foreign traders lived in administered or physically separated/ marginalized spaces. In residence at Ugarit were Cypriotes, Egyptians, Emarians, landless folk called (H)apiru, and probably merchants from Ura (a city somewhere in coastal Cilicia). At Emar there lived a judge noted as "a man of the land of Sidon" (*TBR* 94), perhaps there to legit-imize dealings of the merchant community or *karu* in that key town where Mesopotamian traders left the Euphrates and headed overland to the Mediterranean. Not surprisingly, foreign weights appear in Emar texts, belonging to folk from Amurru and the northerly and/or upland Subareans (Monroe 2009, 215-19). In the Memphis harbor community called *Prw-nfr* traders spoke Hurrian, or a Syro-Palestinian dialect assoc-iated with what the Egyptians called *H3rw* (Redford 1992, 228). A Linear B tablet from Knossos (KN Db 1105+) lists a shepherd who came from Memphis or Egypt (*A3-ku-pi-ti-jo*; Palaima 1991, 280). Excava-tions on Crete suggest foreign traders lived at Khania and Kommos (Hallager 1983; Shaw 2006, 113-43). If we accept the Early Iron Age (early 11th cent.) report or tale of Wen-Amun (Lichtheim 2006, 224–230) as evidence, foreign traders camped in the harbor district at Byblos, some as long as seventeen years. Ugarit of course had more than one harbor and probably more than one *karu*, though the texts mention it as if it were a single location or institution. The Ugaritic text *KTU* 4.102 appears to be a census listing residents of various households in a place called "Cyprus–town" or "town of Cyprus." One can only assume that there lived a group of Cypriotes, unless this was a census of an actual Cypriote town across the sea, such as Enkomi.

Defining ethnic identity against a perceived Other was the second solution to the trader's dilemma. One may follow E.S. Sherratt (1990) or Malkin (1998) in making judicious use of Homeric sources that speak to these and other LBA socioeconomic matters. Later Greek iden-tity formation has been discussed by Winter (1995) in terms of a dis-comfort with a growing mercantilism, which the Greeks illustrated often with Phoenician examples that provided the necessary contrast for their own emerging heroic ideal.[15] Malkin's (2011) application of network dy-

---

[15] Besides the oft-cited passages that supposedly slur Phoenicians, such as *Od*. 15.415–19, one may point to the taunting of Odysseus while a guest of the Phaeacians: "No, stranger, I would not say you were like a man skilled in contests of the many sorts that exist among men, but are like one who is used to a ship with many oarlocks, a leader of sailors who are also merchantmen, with his mind on a load, an overseer of cargoes, and

namics to Archaic and later Greece shows in theory how traders in the LBA could have created "middle grounds" where identity was negotiated between traders and others co-residing in liminal places founded to facilitate exchange. Indeed, Malkin provocatively demonstrates how Greek identity formed not in the core *poleis* like Athens but in the emporia, colonies and trading posts where transplanted people had to define themselves in the context of local languages, beliefs and material practices. This turns not only conventional thinking about Greek civilization on its head but the notion that early trade was epiphenomenal or of slight cultural consequence.

Archaeology can show the accumulation of cultural capital by traders. Some of the most spectacular houses excavated at Ugarit were owned by local entrepreneurs and officials who engaged in business on the side (Yabninu, Urtenu, Rapanu, and Rashap-abu). Actually, in the cases of these individuals known to us through architecture and text, one cannot be certain if the office facilitated the business, or that they were granted the office after having proven themselves in business and thus became more useful to the crown. If the latter holds any water, then the titles acquired by successful entrepreneurs would constitute perhaps the most visible form of cultural capital documented. However, these cases would illustrate the value to any trader, local or ethnic, of accumulating cultural capital as an offset to the more anti-social aspects of capitalism. Shipti-Baal, on the other hand, was an Egyptian who used an Egyptian signet seal, married the king's daughter, and became the overseer of the *karu* (Vita and Galán 1997); he is probably the best documented example of an ethnic trader rising to such prominence within a host culture during the LBA, and as such his file makes for a curious inversion of the biblical Joseph story, itself a meditation on the power of the transplanted Other. One may conclude that certain foreign merchants could hold office and wield considerable commercial power, with the right connections (Monroe 2009, 135-36, 163).

Cash and carry, or petty trade, is expectedly not well documented; by definition it involves minimal or no administration. While Egyptian satire alludes to small-scale itinerant traders "carrying goods from one town to another as they supply him who has not, although the tax-people carry gold..." (Castle 1992, 256-57), drier sources say little. There were probably many merchants like Shukuna of Ugarit (RS 19.020

---

of gain got by greed. You do not resemble an athlete" (*Od.* 8.159–64); the villain or foil is not the Phoenician *per se* but the practice of capitalism.

= *PRU* 6 156) who combined selling of luxury goods like purple wool and "Ashdodian garments" with everyday dairy and fish. Archaeologically there are countless examples of anonymous petty trade, including the shipwreck at Cape Gelidonya, relic of a nine to ten meter Phoenician or Syrian tramper, fully equipped for bronze-making, engaged in a continual buying and selling along the Eastern Mediterranean littoral (Bass 1995).

Last, in terms of the trader's dilemma, is the disembedding or depersonalization of transactions. One first understands that no transactions were completely disembedded except in a manner relative to local tradition. Depersonalization took place when moral aspects of a transaction were transferred from the immediate transactors to outside, impartial parties. This was certainly a function of weights—unassuming little stones establishing legitimacy in prices and equivalences, and carrying the authority of merchant, town, kingdom, and ultimately divine arbiters of justice and truth such as Thoth or Shamash. For those not willing to conduct business purely on oaths or faith, standardized city-weights and *karu*-weights were available to keep people honest with independent and impersonal confirmations. Several texts from Ugarit contain price negotiations involving the prefect (e.g. *PRU* 6 6, *PRU* 7A and B, *PRU* 4:214, and *KTU* 4.337), the official most responsible for the kingdom's interaction with foreign merchants. The prefect Urtenu's house, a large ashlar, two-storey mansion known for decades as *le palais sud*, produced more texts (over six hundred) than any building at Ugarit besides the combined archives of the palatial complex itself. Urtenu had ties to Sidon, Byblos, Beirut, Tyre and Cyprus; and his firm was also engaged in wine and oil trading with Egypt and Hatti. According to Bordreuil and Pardee (2010) Urtenu was a member of a "merchant oligarchy that governed the realm." The length of his career is indicated by the mention of three pharaohs in his archives—Seti I, Ramesses II, and Merneptah, who together reigned during most of the 13th century. From the perspective of the many foreign merchants dealing with him, he was effecttively "the State," and in that role the more modest trader or non-trader would conceivably have viewed him, or any of the harbor officials, tax collectors, or better-organized and literate merchants involved in Ugarit's trade, with suspicion and envy—classic hallmarks of the trader's condition.

Perhaps the impersonal, calculating methods and organization of Levantine harbor cities were remembered in the exaggerated Homeric portrayal of Levantine traders as dishonorable, wily and detrimental. As a case of oppositional ethnicity it seems plausible that the poet portrayed the manners of the Hellenic aristocratic household as a place where, unlike its eastern counterpart, officials would not be required because of honor and obligation. This kind of ethos fits too neatly into a grander theory that Mycenaeans left their foreign trade to Levantine thalassocrats.[16] What seems more plausible is an aggregative ethnic relationship wherein Greeks saw a good deal of themselves in their Levantine neighbors (Malkin 1998, 17-19, 27, 60). The reason, then, why trade is so poorly documented in Aegean sources, is not because Mycenaeans were too honor-bound to trade capitalistically, as Finley (1973) thought, but that little is well documented in Mycenaean texts; indeed Linear B is such a poor script for recording a behavior as complex as trade, that it was barely even attempted (Palaima 1991, 276).

The other, or another, side of the ethnic trader's role in LBA society is how they were accessed by the established loci of wealth and power. Because archives tend to reflect elite interests, it comes as no surprise to find many examples where local entrepreneurs act as middlemen between local and extra-local capital. An entrepreneurial married couple at Emar dealt with traders bearing Assyrian and Babylonian names (*Emar* 6.3 25) and were possibly running an exchange house. Nobody benefitted more from ethnic traders than the prefect of Ugarit, who dealt with traders from virtually everywhere. Sinaranu, the merchant who obtained royal grants and exemption for his Crete shipping, obviously positioned himself well, as did Shipti-Baal. Two other merchants got exemptions for trade with Egypt, Hatti and elsewhere (*PRU* 3: 165–6). At Assur the merchants Siqi-ilani and Ahu-tab connected officials like Babu-aha-iddina with tin and items brought from Canaan. Hittite and Egyptian kings and officials relied heavily upon the expertise of foreign seafaring merchants, as is clear from several sources (Monroe 2009, 220-24), and the Nauri Inscription in particular notes "foreign merchants" (*shwtyw n khaswt*) being attached to the Osiris temple at Abydos (Castle 1992, 243-44).

Unlike Egyptian kings and officials who did label merchants as "foreign," the urban entrepreneurs appear to have accommodated rather

---

[16] This is the implication of Finley's (1973) seminal study, which saw early Greek economics as a primitive endeavor involving weak technologies and non-commercial, status-oriented motivations. Current scholarship, by contrast, considers a wider range of economic modalities, including markets, in the Aegean sphere (Parkinson et al. 2013).

than divided themselves from outsiders, so terms like "other," "alien" and "stranger" are not found in their correspondence. Instead they identified people as *man from Town X, brother, father,* and *son.* Even kings writing to each other and their vassals used terms such as *friend* or *enemy*, but not alien- or Other-ness. These concepts mostly transcend political borders and depend on constructed relationships shaped by a combination of trade and tradition. The only documented way in which traders exploited their own foreign-ness, and it still requires some inference, was in the ability to practice usury without concern for social judgment. This seems to be what the merchants of Ura were about (at least in the documentation); there is no decree forbidding similar actions of local merchants, presumably because such predatory activities would not have been allowed as normal practice.

It would appear that Levantine traders, especially those at Ugarit in our period, proved adept at solving the "trader's dilemma." The political benefits of this solution were arguably great: most of the Eastern Mediterranean littoral was never dominated or administered by the core powers to the oppressive degree endured by many inland populations. Coastal cities mobilized the capital necessary to purchase relative autonomy in the midst of aggressive territorial empires. This success of foreign traders spelled an ironic role for the "Great Kings" and their agents when operating in the liminal zones beyond their cores. When the Mesopotamian world-system declined around 1750 and had to reorganize around the emergence ca. 1500 of an Eastern Mediterranean system based on Cypriot copper production (Sherratt and Sherratt 1991, 368–73), the formerly peripheral Levant became "home field" for what Braudel (1982) called *les jeux de l'échange.* As the exchange networks of Levantines and their contacts spread, along with the capitalistic modes of accumulation that created the networks, producing and consuming sectors of society would have felt the changing winds also. A class of entrepreneurs and their associates was growing, and some of these people may have identified more with that class than with ethnic, nationalistic or political interests.

CLASS AND CAPITAL

Discussions of most socioeconomic aspects of ancient states are still dominated by the 19th to early 20th century intellectual streams of Marx and Weber, a remarkable phenomenon given that neither had a solid evidentiary basis for ancient Near Eastern studies, and Marx's theoretical orientation was inherently unsympathetic to traders. Marxian influence is abundant in the interpretation of archives from Ugarit and Assyria (e.g., Liverani 1962; Heltzer 1999, 1978 *inter alia;* Vita 1999), where lexical terms denoting political and/or military rank found in much-abbreviated administrative lists are used as class markers. This fundamental bias wrongly assumes the administration to have closely administered the bulk of trade. Weber did not derive political interests of status groups (cf. Marx's classes) from their relationship to the means of production (1976, 42–65), and his methodology can serve as a counter-weight to Assyriological and archaeological trends that reify Marxian priority of production in all material relations—production, exchange, and consumption.[17]

As to LBA means of production, wealthier merchants in Assyria and Ugarit had not only access but ownership also. They produced wine and oil, possibly salt, and came to own manorial estates through several avenues: royal service contracts; price-based purchase from a ruler; purchase from individual(s); and inheritance. In Assyria, Ugarit, and Egypt officials used their positions for personal gain, though it is difficult to tell whether the office or the wealth came first. Traders paid the king of Ugarit large amounts of silver for land, concessions, and exemptions, profiting the king immediately and giving the traders investments in production for exchange (Monroe 2009, 253-65). Besides the mercantile elite, anyone employed by a trading firm or estate was tied, however loosely, to that particular means of production and thus possibly shared interests with others tied to similar households in the city or kingdom. Thus one may reconstruct an entrepreneurial sphere of land owners, donkey owners, artisans, employees, servants, terrestrial and maritime

---

[17] At the turn of the 20th century little was known, archaeologically or textually, of ancient trade and the importance of families and other independent participants. Thus Weber concluded that private trade was primitive, allowing patrimonial elites to dominate political economies through their temples and palaces. Meanwhile Near Eastern archaeology and Assyriology have uncovered enough evidence to state, as Van de Mieroop (1997, 179, 193) that "craftsmen worked both independently and in institutional workshops throughout the history of Mesopotamia; [...] connection between trade and manufacture was a crucial aspect of the urban economy." Most scholars looking at Bronze Age political economy generally (e.g., Sherratt and Sherratt 1991) hold that private production, labor and exchange constituted a much bigger portion of the ancient economy than Weber could have realized, i.e. that practically all economies are mixed economies that combine the production and consumption "agendas" of Weber and Sombart.

shippers, boatbuilders, etc., whose mode of accumulation depended upon the activity of households involved in buying or selling goods or services. Such a sphere would feature hierarchies within general modes of accumulation. Those who owned land, herds or other productive resources would as a rule extract more wealth and status than those in supporting and servile roles. Meanwhile those selling goods to the firm or being employed in transport services might gain monetarily without concomitant status rewards in a local, agrarian setting. Owners of ships and donkeys would profit more than the hired sailor or caravaneer; and skilled professionals such as shipwrights, captains, trade-agents and *tamkaru*-merchants would certainly take more than their various assistants and unskilled laborers. Sons, daughters, and servants might all be classed as free labor, earning very little, though the son stood to inherit much that the servant would not.

As demonstrated by Schloen (2001), McGeough (2007), and Monroe (2009), two-sector Marxian models simply do not predict the networks of socioeconomic relations witnessed in texts or the archaeology of Late Bronze Age states, especially Ugarit. Most households and individuals cannot be fit into the sectors, making it dubious at best to determine socioeconomic or political interests along Marxian or patrimonial-manorial lines (Monroe 2009). Weber, who was far less dogmatic than Marx, presciently warned that his models, such as the patrimonial household, were ideal types simplifying a more fluid reality:

> In principle control over different combinations of consumers goods, means of production, investments, capital funds or marketable abilities constitute class statuses which are different with each variation and combination. Only persons who are completely unskilled, without property and dependent on employment without regular occupation, are in a strictly identical class status. Transitions from one class status to another vary greatly in fluidity and in the ease with which an individual can enter the class. Hence the unity of "social" classes is highly relative and variable (Weber 1947, 424–25).

As a critic of Marxian theory and its reduction of historical force into a two-sector dialectic, Weber also warned:

> The differentiation of classes on the basis of property
> alone is not "dynamic," that is, it does not necessarily
> result in class struggles or class revolutions. [...]
> However, such conflicts as that between land owners
> and outcast elements or between creditors and debtors
> [...] may lead to revolutionary conflict. Even this,
> however, need not necessarily aim at radical changes in
> economic organization. It may, on the contrary, be
> concerned in the first instance only with a redistribution
> of wealth (Weber 1947, 425–26).

This observation points us back to modes of accumulation rather than essentialistic classes as a better means of looking for causality in social history. Because a Weberian gaze is not obstructed by class, it can more easily contemplate socioeconomic agents and forces that are networked and cut through many different planes of a society. That place, or lack of place, is the domain of the trader, who builds links and nodes opportunistically between sources of information, labor, and wealth to profit the self, the family, the firm, the state, or any combination thereof.

Weber and Braudel both understood that the rise of capitalism is best charted along improvements in credit and shipbuilding. These advances were directed by those who controlled the means of exchange, not the means of production. Marx famously avoided the term *capitalism,* which accumulated meanings amorphously throughout the 20th century and its geopolitical struggles to become an unwieldy, problematical, macro-sociological concept-cluster.[18] Weber defined capitalism processsually (and perhaps tautologically), as "the pursuit of profit, and forever *renewed* profit, by means of continuous, rational, capitalistic enterprise" (1996 [1904–5], 17); he recognized that it existed long before the Industrial Revolution, for which capitalism was more a cause than product. His "capitalistic enterprise" is "one which rests on the expectation of profit by the utilization of opportunities for exchange, that is on (formally) peaceful chances of profit" (ibid.).

The LBA textual evidence contains a number of cases where the pursuit of profit looks not only rational and continuous but wisely redundant. The wealthiest Ugarit merchants combined modes of accumulation,

---

[18] Johnson (1996) is especially helpful here.

dealing in both goods and services, and secured privileges and palatial homes for their families and dependents while minimizing the risks of over-specialization. Other *tamkaru*-merchants and untitled traders surely emulated the elite by combining strategies, one day purchasing for the palace or prefect, and another selling his own goods. Similarly, an owner of productive agrarian installations might increase his or her profit by acquiring the means of exchange, as Rapanu appears to have done in the equine trade. A household owning its own transport animals, or its own ship(s) like Sinaranu's family, had multiple streams of wealth but increased risks as well. The Uluburun shipwreck most likely illustrates combined accumulation strategies; though the social organization of the traders aboard is not readily apparent, the consensus is of a royal venture with the merchants doing private business on the side, or vice versa (Pulak 2008; Monroe 2010). From Uluburun it is also easy to see how over-investing in just the transportation side of trade could be disastrous. The texts do not document trader bankruptcies, but properties and offices at Ugarit were occasionally "lifted" or dispossessed by the king and given to somebody else, perhaps due to loan default. As Braudel wrote, owning the means of production is risk-intense and has historically led traders to opt for access rather than ownership of the means of exchange (1984, 64–65; 1982, 212). Most traders living in Ugarit or similar *cosmopoleis* of the East Mediterranean (Byblos, Tyre, Kition, Pylos, Knossos, Memphis, etc.) probably did the same and achieved a less visible standard of wealth than what is witnessed by the pseudo-palaces and archives of Rapanu, Rašap-abu, Urtenu, and Yabninu. In summarizing evidence for a merchant class (or better, cluster of related modes of accumulation) at Ugarit, the evidence tends to support Astour's main conclusions:

> It would be erroneous to visualize the Ugaritic merchants according to the pattern of medieval Europe or even of the Greek city-states [...] that is, as an energetic middle class, growing in wealth but kept in an inferior social and political position by a landed aristocracy of mounted warriors which despised business and trade. [...] In Ugarit, the big merchants were the upper class—they owned the largest land estates, they surrounded the throne as advisors and administrators,

and they served in the elite corps of the army (Astour 1972, 26).

I would say that Astour's "upper class" was only part of an entrepreneurial sphere of activities including several groups who shared similar relations to the means of exchange and production. Some of these groups played vital and pivotal roles in the socioeconomic development of Eastern Mediterranean polities. As such their activities carry further implications for understanding the inevitable transformations and collapse of the LBA world (Monroe 2009, 271-73).

"If capitalism is thrown out the door, it comes in through the window," wrote Braudel (1982, 231) after demonstrating how foreign traders gained substantial access to means of production five hundred years prior to the Industrial Revolution (ibid., 212). The Iron Age Phoenicians have been invoked as the earliest instance of merchants dominating a state economy (Braudel 1984, 119; Chase-Dunn and Hall 1997, 112, 156; Liverani 1995, 53). More recent histories of Phoenicians would imply that such dominance began much earlier, certainly in the Middle Bronze Age and most probably in the Early Bronze Age or mid-third millennium BCE when Phoenician urban culture began (Aubet 2001; Markoe 2000). What was called "Phoenician" later was already a well-established way of life and mode of accumulation in the LBA. Capitalism is rarely considered as a process in the Bronze Age due to the insistence by some that capitalism is a system of government or world order rather than a process or strategy for wealth accumulation. By viewing capitalizing as a practice, one gains a better understanding not only of the very deep roots of Capitalism, writ large, but of those LBA traders who were never told that capitalism had not yet been invented.

Looking at the above relations in the broader context of world systems, peer-polity interactions, or intersocietal networks affords a view of the impact of trade. While the most common complaint regarding world-systems is that it is overly deterministic and dualistic, or fails to account for agency, this misperception is arguably the fault of readers who refuse to dissociate the term from Wallerstein's (1974) particular application to the modern world. Others, such as Stein (1999, 42-3), have recognized how well even Wallerstein's model fits the LBA situation of competing empires. Capitalizing activities conducted within intersocietal networks or world-systems theoretically expose societies to a host of transformative processes that can only be summarized here: subsistence economies would have been reduced as production for the market (in either prestige or common items) increased; accelerated and broadened metals trading and smelting, increased shipbuilding, and elite emulation all intensified the exploitation of timber, reducing local environments accordingly; legal, military, and political control by the imperial powers did not extend to the sea, creating a viable niche for piracy, kidnapping, and murder, all of which are in evidence; capitalism drew rural resources into town where capital concentrated, a process mirrored archaeologically by rural reduction and patterns of cities surrounded by small, satellite villages at Ugarit, Pylos, Hazor, and Hattusha; urban concentration theoretically raised the chances of plague, for which there is limited textual evidence in the Amarna letters (Moran 1992, EA 35); urban concentrations of wealth would attract landless people, some of whom may have joined marauders like the Hapiru and Sea Peoples (and Achaeans at Troy?) instead (Monroe 2009, 293-96). These six or more deleterious effects of capitalism made the intersocietal exchange network a fragile system to rely upon for the metals and other goods needed to maintain a dynastic kingdom. With increasing aridity and access to grain becoming more critical, the effects of a violent migration like the Sea Peoples multiplied into interregional collapse of an interdependent elite or palatial system. As a multi-centered world system, the Eastern Mediterranean had no central means of coping with any of these negative processes; in mythical terms, LBA capitalism was a bit Polyphemic—powerful, yes, but withdrawn and lacking much depth perception.

THE IMMATERIAL WORLD: LIMINAL RELATIONS

Braudel understood that semi-peripheries were social and geographic spaces wherein traders set the rules of exchange. This gives the trader historical and transformative energy (1982, 25; 1984, 30), but it is still a material perspective that may neglect important contours of the Bronze Age trader's worldview and the world's view of him or her. One way to make an intersocietal or world-systems view of the trader more reflective of the fluid, ambiguous context of the trader is to weigh texts and material remains that subtly suggest cognitive, ritual, phenomenological, i.e. immaterial, aspects of trader relations. While poorly documented and thinly theorized, these liminal relations may be as important as material relations in reconstructing the social context of trade, especially maritime trade.

Following Westerdahl's (2005) application of liminality to the world of early Scandinavian seafaring, Turner's (1969) conception of the *ritual process* and *anti-structure* can help theorize what was experienced in harbor communities, ships, caravans, and trading diasporas where traders, like Turner's liminal passengers, could be perceived as powerful, corrupt and dangerous. Turner (1969, 128–30) argued that no society can function without the tension between structure and *anti-structure*, a tension worked out in a liminal temporal-spatial locus, or transformative threshold where social rules or structure are relaxed, or even inverted, conferring power and autonomy on the passengers through ritualized activities and relationship formations that Turner called *communitas*. Theoretically, intersocietal networks should exhibit similar liminalities because they are still social systems. In material terms Turner's structure was concrete and his anti-structure and communitas fluid; by this metaphor, in the Eastern Mediterranean LBA the landed empires were rigid, the networks of traders more fluid.

Much of the LBA world of trade was literally fluid, connected via the sea or rivers, so that it would seem appropriate to attend to immaterial aspects of water. Eliade (1987 [1959]) and more recently Mills (2002) have drawn attention to a cross-cultural pattern wherein liminal agents heroically confront watery chaos and disturb the status quo in the process. Examples of Mills' "mythologem" of the liminal hero from the Eastern Mediterranean-Near Eastern world include Gilgamesh's quest over land and water for fame and immortality, Achilles facing the Scamandros river-god, Odysseus against Poseidon, Jacob wrestling the Jabbok river, and various aspects of the Exodus story.[19] Mary Helms (1998; 1988), also greatly influenced by Turner, sees liminal experience as a key means to power and prestige, often acquired by foreign travel and the knowledge gained therefrom. According to Kristiansen and Larsson (2005, 43, citing Helms often), "Bronze Age society was obsessed with travel and esoteric knowledge brought home from outside, making travel and long-distance trade ritualized activities that contributed to elite status formations and thus to the complexity of the times."

As Westerdahl (2005) argues, ships are liminal agents whose operation may be as ritualized as it is technical. As demonstrated by Monroe (2011) the Uluburun shipwreck may be taken as a complex

---

[19] To these one might add the Egyptian tales of Sinuhe, the Shipwrecked Sailor, The Two Brothers, and Wenamun, all of which involve transformations and watery boundaries.

artifact representing a diversity of ethnicities, lost in a fluid space beyond the structures of power, and thus a relic of liminal agency and *communitas*. Though not addressing liminality specifically, Pulak (2008) attributes ritual function aboard the Uluburun ship to an assemblage of related objects: four faience ram-head cups (rhyta) and a companion female-headed cup (Pulak 2008, 340–41); four gold Syro-Canaanite pendants with rayed stars (350–52); a gold pendant with nude female (347–48); and the gilt bronze nude female figure (345–46). The last, probably representing a goddess, could have provided the material focus for ritualized placation of an immaterial spirit representing the sea, a ritual carried out with libations involving the rhyta. The pendants listed, and similar items onboard, likely represent Asherah, Anat, Astarte, Shapshu/Shamash, Baal-Hadad and or other deities associated with the sea, storms and the sun. Pulak suspects that the number of Syro-Canaanite merchants represented by personal belongings (four) matches the four rhtya because "the cups and statuette were used in shipboard rituals intended to ensure a safe and productive voyage" (Pulak 2008, 341). Thus the sacred technology of the immaterial functioned redundantly alongside the profane, rational, material technology that ensured the safety and success of their venture, e.g., weights to bargain, the over-built hull of thick cedar planking, many extra anchors (twenty-four!), careful stowage of dense items low in the hold, and the laws, correspondence, and other relations hidden from view but connected to planning and protection.

The cognitive landscape of the Uluburun mariners (and all maritime traders) was a fluid one with shifting boundaries and constant threat of annihilation in water, a particular source of terror that resounds in ancient myth, folklore and modern cinema (Monroe 2011, 89, Bachelard 1999 [1949]). Ritual equipment, with identifications appropriately ambiguous, connected the mariners to the immaterial realm of Asherah and Baal or whoever made them feel a bit safer while at the utter mercy of wind, water, and possibly hostile shores. In his Tale or Report, Wen-Amun relied heavily, and ultimately with success, upon the notion that he was an agent of Amun, an idea legitimized by his portable statue or "Amun-of-the-Road" (Lichtheim 2006, 225). This practice is also hinted at in Pap. Lansing:

> The ships' crews of every (commercial) house have
> received their load(s) so that they may depart from

Egypt to Djahy [Syria-Canaan]. Each man's god is with
him. Not one of them (dares) say: "We shall see Egypt
again" (Caminos 1954, 384–89).

Mariner's cults on shore, identified with votive anchors or ship graffiti,
have been located at Ugarit and Kition in the LBA; and coastal shrines
found at numerous sites along the Levantine coast testify to the particular
anxieties facing maritime folk (Brody 1999).[20]

I conclude on a more hopeful note, sounding the only LBA text
that specifies the sort of aid the gods were expected to provide for the
anxious trader on foot or afloat. A Middle Assyrian hymn to the sun-god
Shamash includes these lines:

> You give support to the traveler whose j[ourney] is
>   trying,
> To the seafarer in dread of the waves you lend [aid],
> You are wont to g[uide] the roamer (?) on unexplored
>   routes,
> You always guide [on the ro]ad who turn towards
>   [Shamash]
> You rescued from the flashflood the [mer]chant bearing
>   his purse,
> You bring up the one gone down to the deep, you set
>   wings upon him,
> You reveal havens in sea and [wastelan]ds.[21]

CONCLUSION

Networks of trader relations are perilous to reconstruct; lacunae and ambiguities perforate the topic generally as they do the hymn above.
Nevertheless the larger picture of Late Bronze Age trade reveals rulers
and merchants, together with their families, partners and various
customers, connected in material and immaterial webs. Objects, people,
and perceptions all limited what the trader could do. Donkeys, ships, pro-

---

[20] The anchorage at Tel Nami, Israel (Artzy 1995) is but one example of this particularly
liminal setting. A small site with no agricultural catchment, it still produced numerous
prestigious metal items. The wealthiest grave excavated produced the equipment of a
priest who plausibly oversaw a small shrine overlooking the sea.

[21] Foster 1993, 539.

duction chains, legalities, social norms, calculations, scribes, archives, weights and silver, kidnappings, murder, piracy, storms, rocky shores and rogue waves—even the most daring venturer (and his god) had much to deal with. There was also much to gain, especially in a world overflowing with the exigencies of charismatic status. One would not confuse a Bronze Age kingdom with a modern economic system, but the professional pursuit of profit in evidence illustrates how capitalism's tangled roots descend from Industrial Age topsoil and Medieval and Hellenistic clays to find deep Bronze Age wellsprings.

The heterarchical nature of maritime trade in particular has been underestimated. Not simply the province of kings and their royal fleets, it drew land empires into relations of dependency and currency organized by experts inhabiting the liminal world of shorelines. In a material sense the sea trader entangled everyone, not only in the chrematic, commodifying web of silver but the deep, dark blue of the Mediterranean and its myriad alien shores. All it carried—wealth, information, invasion— would have arrived like the waves of nature's most creative, chaotic element. The person who could manage that force, through material and immaterial means, was a more powerful agent than hegemony or history has apprehended.

II

TRADERS IN THE ARCHAIC AND CLASSICAL GREEK KOINE[1]

David W. Tandy
University of Leeds

In the study of the ancient Greek economy generally, the Finley ortho-doxy (e.g., 1973), which emphasized subsistence and status, was inspired by Hasebroek (1928 ≈ 1933) and Polanyi (1944; Polanyi et al. 1957), and persisted after Finley's death in 1986. It is only recently giving way to a New Institutionalist approach that focuses on description, on institutions and measurement, eminently successful examples of which are Scheidel et al. (2007), whose breadth and expertise certainly makes it the necessary starting point for approaching any aspect of the ancient econ-omy, and Bresson (2007/08), which focuses on Greek urban centers and emporia. Morley (2007), in spite of its concision, is a very good intro-duction to ancient trade, as is Möller's chapter on trade in the Classical period in Scheidel et al. (2007). To ensure that this chapter gets minim-ally distracted away from proper trade (and instead into questions of production, consumption, and development) I will organize it around the traders themselves by asking, "Who moved goods in the Archaic and Classical periods?" As we shall see, conclusions are difficult to come to, for the nature of the evidence is such that ambiguities abound. While the Homeric epics seem to be purposely skewing the trade narrative to disguise the identities of traders, the *aristoi* of the classical period, in keeping with their commitment to avoiding the appearance of depen-dence, kept trade at arm's length by restricting themselves to the finan-cial side of things only. It may be said in advance, however, that in the Archaic period trade (in its various senses) seems to have been domi-nated by elite individuals, while in the Classical period trade, especially in grains (which come to predominate the trade volume), was undertaken mostly by independent shippers who were to a large extent dependent on financing from wealthy investors. States were involved in regulating

---

[1] All errors herein survived the efforts to prevent them by P. Devine, E.M. Harris, P.S. Horky, B.M. Lavelle, D.E. Lavigne, and J. Stiebert. Gratitude to seminar participants at Manchester and Durham for their comments and corrections on portions of this. Editor Tim Howe saved readers from many (if not all) low moments.

trade around its edges, but among the most important things states did—this was certainly the case at Athens—was to provide efficient support mechanisms for exchange and attractive arenas for the settlement of disputes among both shippers and investors.

It is useful to emphasize near the start that a very small percentage of the local Greek economies was taken up by trade, likely no more than two per cent (Cartledge 1983, 11; 1998, 6); this is true for the entire pre-industrial world. By trade I mean the activity whose practitioners consider it their livelihood when they are undertaking it, to be distinguished from the micro-regional cabotage or tramping undertaken by small timers, brought to the van recently by *The Corrupting Sea* (Horden and Purcell 2000) and succinctly captured by Neville Morley's phrase, "the constant 'background noise' of short hop mixed trading" (Morley 2007, 77). This small role played by trade underlines how little most Greeks in most Greek communities had to do with exchange beyond their immediate vicinities and how difficult economic growth must have been. Nevertheless, economic growth would have been nearly impossible without trade, as arithmetic prevents economies without outlets from growing, not to mention the important role of trade in cultural expansion and exchange, be that measured in spices or ideas.

ARCHAIC PERIOD

EARLY IRON AGE ARCHAEOLOGICAL EVIDENCE

There is no ambiguity any longer about the darkness of the Early Iron Age: the isolation and cultural regression of the Balkan peninsula were for years overstated by scholars,[2] and greater continuity between Bronze Age and the Archaic period is now becoming recognized.[3] This does not discount the profound effect on the Greek world of the Bronze Age Catastrophe (Drews 1993) that began in c. 1200, but it is clear now that there was much more than darkness visible between 1050 and the mid 9th century. While until twenty years ago the evidence seemed to point to Euboeans first out on the sea-lanes with Phoenicians no earlier than the late 9th century, now we see that Euboean materials manufactured in the eleventh and tenth centuries are turning up throughout the eastern

---

[2] Snodgrass (1971); (1980 succinctly at 35-36); Desborough (1972, esp. 329ff); Murray (1980, 16-20); (1993, 8-15); Hall (2004, 59-66).
[3] Papadopoulos (1993); Snodgrass (2000, xxiii-xxxiv); Lemos (2000a, 2007a).

Mediterranean, on Cyprus (Amathous) and in the Levant, at Çatal Hüyük and Ras al Bassit in the north and at Tyre, Tel Hadar and Tel Dor in the south (Lemos 2002a, 228; map 229), while Phoenician materials are turning up on Cyprus (Aubet 2001, 51), Lefkandi on Euboea (Popham et al. 1982b, 217-220), and at Kommos on Crete (Bikai 2000; Stampolidis and Kotsonas 2006). Although scholars tend to attribute the former's distribution to actions by Euboeans and the latter's to actions by Phoenicians, we cannot tell who the traders are, only that the goods have been moved from west to east and from east to west.

In addition to the (limited) movements of these materials, Greek eastward and Asian westward, ancient traditions had it that many Greeks were soon on the move, most notably to Ionia and Aeolis (although the latter appears now to be a mirage (Rose 2008; Parker 2008) and the former may eventually suffer a similar fate[4]); in general, migrations are off the archaeologists' radar (van Dommelen 2012).

But there is formidable evidence that people were moving goods around the Mediterranean. The "Heroon" was deemed a spectacular discovery when it was first unearthed on Toumba hill at Lefkandi on Euboea by a developer's bulldozer in 1981. After thirty years there has been no consensus reached as to its full meaning. Dated to about 950 BC, the Heroon is a long narrow structure (160 feet by 30 feet) that covered more than twice the area of any contemporary building. In one of the two shafts dug into the building's floor were found four sacrificed horses; in the other were found the cremated remains of a male adult, his ashes contained in a 100-year-old bronze amphora manufactured in Cyprus with a bronze bowl acting as a lid. There were textiles in the amphora, a robe of some sort; next to the amphora lay an iron sword, a spearhead, a razor, and a whetstone: this was the tomb of a warrior. Next to the warrior was found a woman's skeleton adorned with gold jewellery, some of which was of Near Eastern manufacture and at least 650 years old.[5]

I intentionally restrict my inquiry into the Heroon to the foreign objects found—the 100-year-old amphora from Cyprus and the 650-year-old necklace from even further east. We may surmise that the latter came to Greece at the time of manufacture and was a family heirloom, but it

---

[4] Vanschoonwinkel (2006) and Lemos (2007b) review the literary traditions and material records for Ionic, Aeolic, and Dorian migrations, independently demonstrating that the literary and archaeological evidence are not in agreement.

[5] For the amphora, see full description by Catling in Popham et al. (1993, 71-96); for the necklace, see Popham et al. (1993, 81-96).

also may have arrived, which the amphora certainly did, in the last hundred years. This is a warrior with foreign connections of some sort.

The Heroon was covered over by a tumulus and subsequently the contiguous area began to be used as a cemetery, a sign, perhaps, that in the burial of the Hero we are witnessing the birth of the soon-to-be-dominant aristocracy, as certain Lefkandians brought an end to a big-man/*basileus* society and established a new elite of *aristoi*.

In this cemetery, Tomb 79 dates from the second quarter of the 9th century, a hundred years after the Heroon, which is located a scant few meters away. The man buried in 79 was an important person, cremated and his bones placed in a bronze cauldron with lid—the only other similar deposition in the Dark Age is in the Heroon. Among the burial goods in 79: an impressive krater, two very fine nearly identical EG II oinochoai (which date the burial), a "killed" iron sword, a spearpoint and arrowheads (all iron), two iron knives and a bronze grater,[6] as well as two contemporary Phoenician bichrome jugs and a seal of the North Syria type dating back to about 1800 BCE, almost a thousand years before, an heirloom or good-luck charm reminiscent of the necklace buried with the Hero's wife. In addition to all that, the burial contained several incomplete sets of balance weights denominated in the three major standards used in Phoenician ports, the Babylonian standard based on a shekel of 8.4 grams, the Syrian standard of 9.4 g, and the Palestinian standard of 10.4 g (Kroll 2008, 39).

Who was this versatile and prepared weigher? Popham and Lemos, the excavators, called him a Euboean warrior-trader; other opinions have been forthcoming,[7] but Nino Luraghi (2006) seems to have it right that Mr. 79 was a pirate-trader, emphasizing the fine line between trader and pirate that has been discussed by Sally Humphreys.[8] It is important to recognize that the weights indicate that his activities were fully inte-

---

[6] The grater, not dissimilar to the modern kitchen device, appears to be present to indicate that the man was a "heroic" wine drinker: see *Il.* 11.638-640 and essential discussion in Ridgway (1997).

[7] John Papadopoulos (1997) opined that he was a Phoenician, Carla Antonaccio (2002) that he was a *proxenos* resident at Lefkandi, acting in the interests of eastern merchants; Lemos (2002b) makes sensible arguments for why we should conclude that the buried man is a Lefkandian (albeit possibly an easterner fully integrated into the community, perhaps by marriage).

[8] Humphreys (1978, 167). This fine line, to which I will return below, is nowhere better discerned than in the single ship design of the period, oar-driven transportation for soldiers and cargo.

grated into the broader world within which he travelled. Whether or not he was particularly rich or successful, the man buried in 79 was engaged with the discourse that drove the movements of goods across the Aegean and eastern Mediterranean wave-tops. The three standards of weights were in use in the eastern Mediterranean from the mid-second millennium forward; the merchant's weights in Toumba 79 "happen to be the only balance weights that survive in Aegean Greece from between c. 1200 and the sixth century BC" (Kroll 2008, 36).

We now have the recently excavated Family Tomb no. 1 from Achziv on the Phoenician coast, which contains burial goods of the latter half of the 10th century that offer an uncanny parallel to those in Toumba 79.[9] The two men buried at Achziv are almost certainly Phoenician, and the man at Toumba not so clearly Greek, but above all the parallels allow us to discern even more fully the partnership of Phoenicians and Euboeans, for there are times, such as this one, when we cannot even tell these people apart. These were highwaymen in the strictest sense, out on the sea-lanes to make their livings, by trade or by piracy, depending on the circumstances.

The Lefkandi warrior trader offers us some insights into the 9th century while simultaneously illustrating the difficulty of reading the archaeological evidence for trade in the EIA. Is this warrior-trader one of the descendants of the *aristoi* who buried the Hero a hundred years before and now are out on the sea-lanes pursuing wealth, caring only about themselves, their ἑταῖροι, and their οἶκος? There is no polis in sight at Lefkandi.

HOMER

The Homeric epics refer to many luxury items that come to the Aegean from the exotic East: fine dyed textiles and the output of admired metal workers, including cauldrons, mixing bowls, and tripods. But there is no consistent explanation for who was responsible for transporting these

---

[9] For the tomb at Achziv see Mazar (2004). Nijboer (2008) draws attention to the many parallels and similarities between Toumba 79 and the two men buried at Achziv Family Tomb 1; he also concedes the differences, such as the several attributes of Toumba 79 shared with other Toumba burials (e.g., the grater). Of the twenty-two stone objects in the Achziv tomb (Mazar 2004, 128-9), many appear to be weights, but none corresponds to any of the three standards found in Toumba 79. This additional difference—one of sophistication?—between the two burials does not undermine the obvious parallels.

luxury goods into the Aegean; the only constant is that Phoenicians were regularly in the picture.[10] Metals are the cargo on one occasion (*Od.* 1.184); wine is moved by ship from Lemnos and Thrace.[11] But no staples are being moved in the epics: all production is consumed locally.[12]

Homerists will recognize that the man interred in Toumba 79 is in fact the archaeological embodiment of the object of the question posed by Nestor to Telemachus and Mentes, by Polyphemus to Odysseus and his *hetairoi*, and by Apollo to the Cretan sailors who will serve him at Delphi (*Od.* 3.71-74 = 9.252-255= *h.Ap.* 452-455):

ὦ ξεῖνοι, τίνες ἐστέ; πόθεν πλεῖθ' ὑγρὰ κέλευθα;
ἦ τι κατὰ πρῆξιν ἦ μαψιδίως ἀλάλησθε
οἷά τε ληϊστῆρες ὑπεὶρ ἅλα, τοί τ' ἀλόωνται
ψυχὰς παρθέμενοι, κακὸν ἀλλοδαποῖσι φέροντες;

Visitors, who are you? From where do
you sail the wet roads? Are you <u>on a
specific task</u> or do you wander
aimlessly <u>the way pirates do</u> over the
sea, the ones who wander by putting
their lives at risk, as they bring trouble
to foreign people?

Scholars have been arguing forever about who the traders are in the world of Homer's audience. The later standard word for trader,

---

[10] A few examples will suffice. Menelaus regifts to Telemachus a mixing bowl he received when he was visiting Phaidimos, basileus of Sidon on his way home (*Od.* 4.615-619); a fine metal cup was given to Thoas of Lemnos by Phoenicians who brought it there (*Il.* 23.740-745); the embroidered robes that the Trojan women fetch to dedicate to Athena were made by Phoenician women who were brought to Troy by Paris (*Il.* 6.289-292).

[11] There are daily wine deliveries to Troy from Thrace (*Il.* 9.71-72: νῆες ἡμάτιαι); Odysseus got his super-strong wine from Ismarus (*Od.* 9.196-200). Jason's son Euneos brings wine to Troy from Lemnos at the end of *Iliad* 7. There is an οἶνος Πράμνειος (*vel* πράμνειος: *Il.* 11.639; *Od.* 10.235) that defies determination, be the modifier geographical or descriptive of some other property of the wine.

[12] At *Od.* 14.335, Thesprotians sailed towards Doulichion πολύπυρον, but this hardly means that they were sailing there for a shipload of grain (*pace* Knorringa 1926, 9).

ἔμπορος, in Homer means a traveler on another person's ship.[13] One word for trader in Homer one time is πρηκτήρ (*Od.* 8.162) when Euryalos taunts Odysseus in Phaeacia, but it is context-specific, like κατὰ πρῆξιν in the question above, and πρηκτήρ doesn't mean trader in its only other use in Homer (*Il.* 9.443). Terminology aside, the primary traders in the poems seem to be the Phoenicians, who are also kidnappers and slavers; of course, this is no surprise. There are also Taphians, who seem to be similar to Greeks—in fact they may serve as substitutes for absent Greek traders; Mentes the Taphian moving a cargo of iron in *Odyssey* 1 parallels precisely what Greeks are doing in fact in the 8th century (Tandy 1997, 62-72). In addition to trading, the Taphians, whose home island of Taphos has no location, are active as kidnappers and slavers. In his lies, Odysseus speaks of Cretans as traders, raiders and slavers; in his lie in *Odyssey* 14, Odysseus resembles the warrior-trader in Toumba 79. Any Greeks? In the only market in the *Iliad* (at the end of book 7), Euneos, the son of Jason and Hypsipyle, comes to Troy from Lemnos and makes a substantial payment to the Atreidai to gain access to the market there, where he exchanges wine for what he can get from the pre-monetized Achaeans. But the hellenicity of this Lemnian is quite suspect—Lemnos, in Homer, was home to the Sintians before others arrived (*Il.* 1.594); Homer calls the Sintians ἀγριόφωνοι "wild talkers" (*Od.* 8.294); it is on Lemnos that the mysterious "Etruscan" inscription was found in 1885, and new pre-Greek inscriptions have followed (de Simone 2009); Herodotus (6.140) narrates that non-Greek Pelasgians were still resident there in ca. 500 when the Athenian general Miltiades arrived; no Lemnian fights with the Achaeans at Troy. Homeric Lemnians are hardly Greeks—the payment to the Atreidai was a strategy learned from the Phoenicians two generations before when Phoenicians gave Euenos' grandfather Thoas a cup in exchange for access to Lemnian markets (*Il.* 23.745).[14] The heroes at Troy do not buy and sell

---

[13] The meaning "trader" does not survive before Semonides 16.2 ἠλειφόμην μύροισι καὶ θυώμασιν/καὶ βακκάρι· καὶ γάρ τις ἔμπορος παρῆν), the context of which seems to require it.

[14] One other payment for market access may be that made to King Alcinous on Scheria by unnamed sailors, who give him a female slave whom they bought or kidnapped at a place called Apeire, which has no location (*Od.* 7.8-10).

things apart from slaves. They raid, of course, even taking pride in their raiding.[15] But Greeks don't trade in the epics.

There is an air of mystery or secrecy to Homeric trade. The Phoenicians who camp out for a year at the island of Syria (*Od.* 15.403: location unknown[16]) selling ἀθύρματα, "trinkets," to the locals while plotting the kidnapping of Prince Eumaeus, for whom they find a buyer in Laertes of Ithaca, who had enough possessions (κτέατα) to purchase him (15.483). (The Phoenician woman who betrayed Eumaeus had herself been kidnapped by Taphians and sold to Eumaeus' father on Syria [*Od.* 15.427-429].) Phoenicians and Taphians may be scoundrels but they have access to the best houses in Greece and elsewhere. I would emphasize that it is not just a matter of there being no proper Greeks who trade in the epics; trade itself is exceptionally rare in the epics; non-Phoenicians who practice trade are also markedly mysterious, the Taphians and the Lemnians. This aura of mystery and the repeated geographical indeterminacy connected to trade is the clearest indication that the poet is manipulating things to disguise something very important (Redfield 1986, 31; Tandy 1997, 12).

Attempts to unravel that mystery by proposing by what social/economic mechanisms goods were moved in the world of Homer's audience are open to charges of speculation. Were the *aristoi* themselves moving goods? Is it possible to discern trade as distinct from piracy/raiding, as we saw in the Homeric question above? Bravo (1977) argues that wealthy nobles sent out their dependants to do their trading and/or financed such trips through loans (collateralized by land) made to impoverished nobles. Mele (1979), whose *prexis/ergon* commerce distinction I will take up below, believed that the epics supported aristocratic trade by negatively painting the non-aristocratic trade of, e.g., the Phoenicians. There is no clear evidence in Homer that the aristocrats undertook their own trading but there is no indication either that they did not or could not. What nearly all scholars who have taken up this question recently agree on is that Homer (for whatever reason) is being incomplete in his cover-

---

[15] There is no more impressive raid than that undertaken by Nestor in the generation before the Trojan War, when a raid into the territory of Elis yielded fifty herds each of cattle, sheep, swine, and goats, as well as 150 mares, many with foals (*Il.* 11.677-681).

[16] Scholars have tried to downplay the impossibility of Syria being an island by appealing to the possibility that the Syria episode is a dim memory of the *Mycenaean* presence at al Mina (Lorimer 1950, 83, applauded by Hoekstra in Heubeck and Hoekstra 1989, *ad Od.* 15.403), while looking the other way at the description of the place as an island (νῆσος).

age of this topic, whether that is intentional disanimadversion or something more innocent. Mele's explanation acknowledges this incompleteness and is straightforward; my own explanation (Tandy 1997) was that the *aristoi* for whom Homer was composing were active in the acquisition of metals, especially iron, from distant sources so that they would not be themselves dependant on local resources for their position in the expanding aristocratically dominated economy. Thus the poet accomplishes the separation of the *aristoi* from the trade narrative by implicating others in it and obscuring details of it.

ARCHAEOLOGY: NINTH TO SEVENTH CENTURIES

The picture of the ninth and eighth centuries hasn't changed terribly much in the last thirty years. Euboeans are out in their ships following the lead of the Phoenicians in earnest in the 9th century. This is reflected well by the warrior interred in Toumba 79 and his *Doppelgänger* at Achziv. By 800, Euboeans are active at Pithekoussai in the west and at al Mina in the east. At Pithekoussai, it has finally become clear that a large percentage, perhaps one third, of the settlers there are non-Greek.[17] At al Mina, the role played by the Euboeans remains unresolved—traders? mercenaries? permanent residents?—but their presence is not in question.[18] By the mid 8th century, there are Euboeans and other Greeks travelling all over the sea, creating settlements on Sicily, southern Italy and the northwest Aegean, called *apoikiai* by Thucydides (1.2.6 and *passim*), and although all these "homes away from home" became similar in their narratives in the passage of time, they must have been individually distinct at their starts. In the 7th century we see further expansion in the west (mostly from *apoikiai* there, but also Phocaeans to the mouth of the Rhone) and also into eastern Thrace, Thasos, the Troad, both Propontides, the west coast of the Black Sea and a bit of the Adriatic, plus Libya

---

[17] Jonathan Hall puts it well: "Pithekoussai on the island of Ischia was a mixed settlement, albeit one in which the Euboean presence was dominant" (2004, 35; see literature in note 1).

[18] Boardman (1999) makes a case that through al Mina, the northern Syrians in fact played a larger role in their partnership with the Euboeans than did the Phoenicians in theirs. Nor, of course, were these the only Greeks players, as virtually identical Cypriot graffiti from about 700 on a SOS amphora at Mende in Thrace and a vase at Policoro in southern Italy are possibly suggestive of the activity of Cypriot ἔμποροι (Vokotopoulou and Christidis 1995).

(Cyrene) and Naucratis on the Nile. In the 6th century there is a filling out of the Black Sea and Adriatic littorals. Apart from the occasional resettlement (e.g., Thurii at Sybaris) or Athenian cleruchy, this is essentially the end of the "movement." (The new non-imperial settlements in the fifth and fourth centuries are very few. Damastion from Aegina after 431 and Pharos from Paros (perhaps with help from Syracuse) in 385, both in Illyria, come to mind.)[19]

It remains unsettled what drove or lured the Greeks out into their sea. Were these individual or state initiatives? Trade driven? Land shortage? Shortage of quality land as a result of population increase? Large increase? Small increase? These are all probably speculations, interesting ones. What among all of this was trade and who were the traders? At the start of the expansion, the traders were after metals; by the 5th century, enormous merchant-boats stuffed with grains were crowding into each other on their way back from Sicily and the Black Sea.

For recent scholarship, see Möller (2000) on Naucratis, Bresson (2002) and Demetriou (2012) on *emporia*. Irad Malkin has made an important contribution to our understanding of "colonization" by applying network theory to the colonial landscape.[20] Gocha Tsetskhladze (e.g., 2006/08) has inherited the mantle of Mr. Colonization from the late John Graham (1983[1964]; 2001), as he oversees and contributes to a growing body of work on the Greek expansion, especially in the Black Sea area. Robin Osborne, eschewing literary material whenever possible, has become a voice to reckon with on early trade (e.g., 1996, 2007). Jonathan Hall, who has written the best comprehensive book on the Archaic period (2007), has in his narrative no place for the excitements of Mytilene that we find in sources as otherwise reliable as Hellanicus and Aristotle because there is no material evidence that might corroborate the literary material. All of this reflects a general shift that is occurring in the field of early Greek studies from a dependency on literary sources to a firm starting point with the material record, as well as an additional shift, this one away from colonization towards colonialism, a shift that began in earnest with the appearance of the papers in Descoeudres (1990), and has

---

[19] The most convenient and accessible survey of the *apoikiai* is Boardman (1999), which can be supplemented by Ridgway (2012 with bibliography there). For most individual sites a very reliable starting point is Hansen and Nielsen (2004).

[20] Malkin (2011); see also the issue of *Mediterranean Historical Review* earlier devoted to network theory, Malkin et al. (2007).

continued through, for example, the essays in Hurst and Owen 2005, which further argue for the need to move away from the emphasis on foundations and foundation dates. Nicholas Purcell (1990; 1997; 2004; 2005a; 2005b) sees all colonial activity as an effort to find outlets to which and later from which to distribute surplus production, a position that coheres well with the idea that since the cities of Old Greece needed outlets for their livelihoods, the colonial histories were invented to enable that (Purcell 1990).

HESIOD AND OTHER VOICES

Hesiod has advice on ἐμπορίη and ναυτιλίη, but he himself is not going anywhere as an ἔμπορος. The distinction between the (relatively) well-focused and organized *prexis* commerce as practiced by Homeric traders and *ergon* commerce as practiced by Hesiod and his neighbours, was introduced by Alfonso Mele and developed further by others, who argued that Hesiod's trade is one *ergon* among many *erga* (Mele 1979; Tandy 1997, 75, 212-214). Hesiod is full of advice on trade: don't put too much cargo in your wagon, the axle may break and you lose your freight (692-3); don't put all your material on board ship, keep most of it at home (689-90); praise a small boat but put your cargo in a big one (643). It is relevant that Hesiod expresses no interest in where this cargo may be going, but it is emphatically not going to Thespiai or Askra. Although he himself is not on board, Hesiod's *ergon* trade resembles nothing else more than the cabotage that is the background noise of the Mediterranean, and there is precious little, and very likely zero, overlap in a Venn diagram that combines trade in Homer and what Hesiod describes.

 Can the testimony and testimonia of the lyric poets help? In the mid 7th century, Archilochus went to Thasos in service to his native Paros, where he served as a merchant marine trading and fighting on land and sea. His political metaphors of the ship at sea reveal comfort with the language of the sailor.[21] There is no sign that he had anything to do with the legendary Thasos wine industry that we can easily discern after 500 (see below). Fr. 93a indicates that he is working for a state or collective enterprise and reveals an example of *prexis* commerce, albeit inseparable from its military context. Alcaeus of Mytilene is clearly a sailor, as his

---

[21] Frr. 4, 24.8, 105, 106; discussion in Tandy (2004). Archilochus' sister's husband was lost at sea (fr. 13).

poems betray, nowhere more clearly than in the relatively new and neglected end parts of fr. 208 (ἀσυννέτημμι τῶν ἀνέμων στάσιν).[22]
Alcaeus was said to have traded wine in Egypt, perhaps at the port of
trade at Naucratis, which had been started up by 625. Sappho's brother
Charaxus, until recently suspected not to have existed, was out trading, to
judge by the newest Sappho papyrus (Obbink 2014).[23] Plutarch tells us in
the *Life of Solon* (2.7) that in addition to Solon himself Protis the oikist
of Massalia practiced trade, as did Thales, Hippocrates and even Plato.[24]
Dionysius of Halicarnassus relates (3.46.3) that Demaratus the Bacchiad,
father of Tarquinius Priscus of Etruria, was a trader. It looks as if narratives of prominent figures tend to take this shape, which may undercut
the accuracy of the specific pictures that these narratives offer.[25]

The Hebrew Bible and Assyrian records refer to Greek mercenaries (and other specialist laborers) in service from the 9th century forward (see Niemeyer 2001; Sullivan 2011). Archilochus may have served
as a mercenary in the south, in Egypt or the Near East.[26] Alcaeus' and his
brother Antimenidas' mercenary work included service to the Lydians in
Anatolia and perhaps to the Babylonians or their enemies in the Levant.[27]
Mercenary service has at its heart substantial transfers of wealth, be it on
behalf of a victorious employer or for a mercenary when he gets paid or
gets to loot; as a result, any study of early Greek trade, or the broader
economy, or economic development, has to take mercenarianism into

---

[22] Also frr. 33.4, 73.1-6, 118.2, 124.7, and the Hymn to the Dioscuri, fr. 34. On the end of
208 and on Alcaeus' use of the expert vocabulary of the sailor, see discussion in Tandy
(2004).

[23] Joel Lidov (2002) has made clear that Herodotus' account of Charaxus' relationship at
Naukratis with Rhodopis, as narrated in Herodotus (2.135), is a 5th century invention. But
the newest Sappho (Obbink 2014) supports Herodotus' statement that Charaxus was
trading in the south. Sappho knows nautical language, but as for her trader husband, the
only testimonium that contains any specifics refers to him as Kerkylas, trading out of
Andros, that is, Willy-Man from the Isle of Man (Suda, s.v. Σαπφώ).

[24] Solon is also said to have traveled κατ' ἐμπορίαν at *Ath. Pol.* 11.1.

[25] In most of these cases, the narrative does not develop until the 4th century and even
much later, conceivably part of an effort of soften the criticism of later traders.

[26] Archilochus *qua* mercenary: frr. 15, 216; Tandy (2004); Lavelle (2009).

[27] Fr. 69 seems to indicate that Alcaeus served as a mercenary for the Lydians. The action
(a παράταξις) at Gephyra (perhaps located in Ionia: Forrest *apud* Huxley (1965, 205);
perhaps on the banks of the Halys; there are communities by this name attested on the
Axios in Thrace (*Barr.* 50 C3) and the Orontes in Syria (*Barr.* 67 C4) or at a bridge
during his second exile (*P.Oxy.* 2506 fr. 98 = SLG 282) may well be the same sort of
service. His brother Antimenidas worked for the Babylonians (fr. 350) and was with
Alcaeus in Lydian service according to *P.Oxy.* 2506 fr. 102 = SLG 283.

account. Two examples will illustrate this. Pedon of Priene, a precise contemporary of Alcaeus and Antimenidas, served as mercenary to Psammetichus II (r. 595-589), and left this inscription on an Egyptian statue that he brought home:

Πηδῶμ μ᾽ ἀνέθηκε-
ν ὠμφίννεω ἐξ Αἰγ-
γύπτώγαγὼν ῥῶι βα-
σιλεὺς ἔδωρ᾽ ὠιγύπ-
τιος Ψαμμήτιχο-
ς ἀριστήια ψίλιο-
ν τε χρύσεογ καὶ
πόλιν ἀρετῆς ἕ-
νεκα.

Pedon son of Amphinneus
dedicated me having carried
me from Egypt, to whom
the Egyptian king Psammetichus
gave as rewards a gold bracelet
and a city for his fine performance.

Add to this example pieces of horse equipment manufactured during the reign of King Hazael of Damascus in the 9th century that bear the identical inscription: a blinker piece in an 8th century stratum at Eretria and a nose piece at Samos in an early 6th century context—contemporary with Alcaeus. These harness pieces, accompanied at both locations by additional pieces of horse equipment, must have been booty from the sack of Damascus by the Assyrians in 732, subsequently acquired by others, perhaps also by plunder, who took them westward later.[28]

What does seem clear is that nearly all of these trading persons in poetry and the later testimonia have one thing in common: they are away from home. It seems that the exiled persons we *do* hear from would have had limited opportunities for incomes except trade. Alcaeus (and

---

[28] On the Pedon inscription see discussion in Ampolo and Bresciani (1988). On the Hazael inscription and harness pieces see Bron and Lemaire (1989); Eph'al and Naveh (1989). The harness piece from Samos is well seen in Burkert (1992, 18, fig.2); Kyrieleis surmises that the nose-piece from Samos and the blinker piece from Eretria "could well have belonged to the same set of trappings for a four-horse team" (1993, 148).

other poets as well as craftsmen) may have had access to performance arrangements abroad, but non-performers and non-craftsmen would have been dependent on *xenoi*, perhaps easily arranged, but not for all the disenfranchised. It does not surprise me that trade is the activity of those who are locked out.[29]

OTHER ARCHAIC TRADERS (LITERARY AND ARCHAEOLOGICAL)

Herodotus (4.152) tells us of Colaeus, a ναύκληρος who on the eve of the foundation of Cyrene in about 630, was blown to Tartessos and to a fortune for his Samian crew, who resemble a *hetaireia*,[30] and so the Samian ship resembles Homeric ships that trade or steal depending on the relative strength of parties. Given the large amount of foreign pottery found at Naucratis (established no later than 625), it is difficult to imagine that it is not present because of the large amount of trade of being undertaken, presumably but not necessarily by professional traders. Finally to identify truly professional traders we need look no further than Sostratus of Aegina, son of Laodamas, to whose success Herodotus compares Colaeus' and whose existence has been verified by the discovery at Gravisca, the port of Tarquinia, of a fragment of an anchor inscribed (Torelli 1971): ᾽Απόλονος Αἰγινάτα ἐμί· Σόστρατος ἐποίεσε ηο[, "I belong to Aeginetan Apollo; Sostratus made (me), the son of [."

This Sostratus may also be responsible for the many potmarks ΣΟ, as Johnston argued (1972; list in Johnston 1979, 80-83). His ubiquity (if the approximately 100 potmarks marked ΣΟ refer to him) and notoriety (as he is still remembered by Herodotus) mark him as a full-time, successful trader, which cannot be said of the many others whose names are mentioned in later writers or found in inscriptions. For example, the son of Peisistratus in Archilochus 93a looks more like a marine than a mariner,[31] and the presumed traders at Naucratis, whether found in

---

[29] Another option: Nancy Winter (2002) makes a good case for material evidence of Bacchiad exiles from Corinth plying their roofing business in Etruria, Corcyra, and Sicily during the Kypselid tyranny (c. 657-582).

[30] Both Möller (2000, 55) and Reed (2003, 64-65) refer to Colaeus' crew as ἑταῖροι, but Herodotus does not say this. That οἱ Σάμιοι made the dedication at the Heraion at the end of the voyage makes the crew look like a ἑταίρεια, but "the Samians" may instead be a reference to the assembly at Samos, who may have sponsored the expedition to begin with.

[31] πάϊς Πεισιστράτου/ἄνδρας ..(.)ωλεῦγτας αὐλὸν καὶ λύρην ἀνήγαγεν/ἐς Θάσον φύσι Θρέϊξιν δῶρ' ἔχων ἀκήρατον/χρυσόν, οἰκείωι δὲ κέρδει ξύν' ἐποίησαν κακά: "the

inscriptions[32] there or in later narratives,[33] are not certainly fulltime traders or successful at trade. It seems both reasonable and instructive to consider Sostratus comparable to Mr. 79 at Lefkandi (above), and although the circumstantial evidence would suggest that the later trader was the more organized and busy of the two, the earlier trader's weights reflects a much wider geographical cast of his activities, and a greater versatility.

A discussion of professional traders lets me turn to other evidence for institutionalized aspects of trade. From the end of the 8th into the 6th century archaeologists have been able to isolate the presence of what are aptly called SOS amphoras, transport containers that were prduced mostly in Attica, presumably for olive oil export (although other agricultural product would have been moved in these containers), of similar shape and decoration and many with the tell-tale squiggly SOS written on the neck, although the absence of any effort to regularize the capacity of the amphoras makes it difficult to imagine that there developed any savings in transaction costs that would come from customer satisfaction with amphora volume.[34] Nevertheless, the effort to routinize the appearance of the amphoras, what one scholar calls an effort at "brand recognition" (Osborne 2007, 285), may reflect an understanding on the part of those responsible for trade of the importance of gaining tactical and financial advantage through meeting the expectations of customers. Thus the SOS amphoras probably indicate that there are professional traders out there—we just can't get a clear look at them or hear their voices, unless we are willing to professionalize the Archilochi and Alcaei.

Sostratus, whether or not the potmarks refer to him, seems from the anchor to have been involved in shipping material into Etruria from the east, and may have arranged many consignments of Attic Black

---

son of Peisistratus brought men . . . on the pipe and lyre carrying gifts for the native Thracians, pure gold, and he made a public disaster with his personal gain"; the context is one of military conflict between Parians and Thracians.

[32] Discussed by Möller (2000, 54ff).

[33] Such as those discussed above: Charaxus, Solon, Alcaeus, and so on.

[34] Johnston surmises that from the 8th century forward there may have been an effort to have the capacity more or less equal to one Attic *metretes* of 12 *choai* (Johnston and Jones 1978, 134-135), but "more or less" doesn't really cover the range of capacities and seems to sidestep the whole issue of the difficulties that arise from both an inconsistency of capacity and an inability to see that inconsistency, well illustrated by Greene and Lawall (2005/06).

Figure pottery. Robin Osborne, in his enduring 1996 article on the narrow distributions of this BF pottery in Etruria, most notably from the workshop of the Athenian Nicosthenes, argues that he can discern a world of interconnected markets in those distributions in the second half of the 6th century. Whether or not he is right about the significance of the distributions,[35] it is certainly the case that someone was shipping a lot of finished work from Nicosthenes' factory to Etruria, perhaps in specially dedicated cargoes, carried by ships consigned for that very purpose, some of it in the care of people like Sostratus.

I have made several passing references to Naucratis, located on the Canopic (westernmost) branch of the Nile, 83 km. southeast of Alexandria. It was first settled perhaps as early as 650s (Lloyd *apud* Asheri et al. 2007, 373); the archaeological record indicates Greeks present no later than 625 (ceramic evidence in Möller 2000, appendix 1). Herodotus tells us that the Hellenion there was built jointly by Ionians from Chios, Teos, and Phokaia, Dorians from Rhodes, Cnidus, Halicarnassus, and Phaselis, and by Aeolians from Mytilene; additional structures were built by Aeginetans, Samians, and Milesians (Hdt. 2.178). Ten of these twelve groups can be supported archaeologically.[36] Naucratis was a port of call for Sappho's brother Charaxos (*P.Oxy.* 1800.1), for his countryman Alcaeus (Strabo 1.2.30), as well as for Solon (*Ath.Pol.* 11.1), and remained a vigorous *emporion* right through the arrival of the Persians in the 540s; it probably became a proper polis only after Alexander (Bresson 2000, chs. 1-2; Bowden 1996). The Greek traders must have been bringing in silver for the most part (to pay mercenaries) and perhaps wine and olive oil; what they took out was grains (although not until the Classical period), linens for clothing and ropes, and papyrus for rope and (later) writing material (Möller 2000, 211-212). The earliest ceramic material is Corinthian, followed by

---

[35] Boardman (2002, 5, n.23) questions Osborne's conclusions about the significance of the absolute numbers of the Black Figure pots delivered to Etruria without considering the overall distribution of Black Figure pottery during the period studied.

[36] See Möller (2000, esp. 166-81). Halicarnassus and Phaselis are not archaeologically present at Naucratis, but archaic Phaselis is nearly invisible epigraphically and Halicarnassus seems to be involved on the seatops in the first half of the 6th century, as we see from the Pabuç Burnu wreck that dates to the first half of the 6th century (Greene at al. 2008, esp. Table 1). The earliest inscriptions at Naucratis are synchronous with Greek inscriptions at Abu Simbel (c. 592) and with the archaeological remains of the Greek barracks at Tell Defennah.

Middle Wild Goat and Athenian Black Figure. The first Eastern Greeks at Naucratis no doubt brought the Wild Goat, and the Corinthian and Athenian wares were plausibly brought by Aeginetans, who made no fine wares of their own (Möller 2000, 123), which would put Sostratus' trading predecessors in the south long before he was working in Etruria.

Draco's Homicide Law of the last quarter of the 7th century refers to border or frontier markets (ἀγοραὶ ἐφορίαι: Dem. 23.37-39), presumably for surplus agricultural production from Attica; we know nothing more about them (though Hopper (1961, 214, 216 n. 241) offers discussion). Hipparchus son of Peisistratus may have built roads for overland trade,[37] but we have no certain evidence of this and we cannot hear the voices of the overland traders.

Solon and Peisistratus both instituted laws that may have encouraged particular patterns of production in Attika, but it is difficult to see how precisely those policies would have affected the activities of traders. Solon made a law forbidding the export of any agricultural product besides olive oil (and perhaps figs) (Plut. *Solon* 24.1); Peisistratus levied a 5% tax on agricultural production (Thuc. 6.54; [Arist.], *Ath. Pol.* 16.4), which ought to be read as a reflection of high levels of surplus production rather than their cause.[38]

CLASSICAL PERIOD

I begin this section by repeating that formal, non-cabotage trade would have accounted for up to only 2% of domestic economic activity, but also that this less-than-2% would have been the only portion of the overall economic structure of Classical Greece that would have provided opportunities for growth. So, again, a warning on the small role trade played but also a reminder that any economic development that occurred in the Classical period probably happened within the world of long-distance trade.

---

[37] That is the inference drawn from [Plato], *Hipparchus* 228d-229b; see discussion of road markers in Larson (2000, 213-214).

[38] Plutarch is not sure of himself (παρέχει δ᾽ ἀπορίαν καὶ ὁ τῶν δημοποιήτων νόμος) but reports that Solon encouraged men who had lost their citizenship elsewhere to join the Athenian community ἐπὶ τέχνῃ, to ply their trades there (*Solon* 24.4), but neither Plutarch nor other later sources known to me mention Solonian action to encourage traders to come to Athens.

The goods that moved most voluminously in the Classical period were grains, timber and extracted minerals and metals, and slaves; of these, grains were by far the predominant cargo.[39] The most important and fullest recent overviews of Greek traders in the Classical period are Reed 2003, Moreno 2007b, and Engen 2010, to which I will refer regularly below.[40] (Excellent in its concision is Austin 1994, 558-562.)

No state was self-sufficient in grain every single year.[41] There was a need to import grains at Corinth and other Peloponnesian states in the 410s;[42] Argos and Corinth were, after Athens, recipients of the most grain aid from Cyrene in the 320s.[43] Athenian anxiety about grain imports led to making it illegal for Athenian ships to carry grain to any port save Peiraieus, of which there is a single documented violation when an Athenian ship was caught taking a shipment to Corinth.[44] Warfare, especially in the 4th century, created shortages all over Greece.[45] We can add that some states specialized in non-grain production (e.g., Phlious

---

[39] Möller (2007, 362-67). The 5th century comic poet Hermippus provides a lengthy (and funny) list of imports, including specialty foods and spices, but also raw materials as well as manufactured items (Hermippus fr. 63; Athen. 1.27e-28a; see brief discussion in Kallet 2007, 83). I will not rehearse the arguments about fine wares, whether they were primarily containers or valued in their own right. For a snapshot of the debate over whether decorated pots were themselves significant commodities, see Boardman (1987; 1988 (yes)); Gill (1988; 1991 (no)). While the presence of piggy-backed fine wares may have meant that there was a specific port of call for their delivery, the pots would never have been the primary economic purpose of the ship carrying them: see Möller (2007, 366).

[40] At the risk of oversimplification: Reed's approach is a devout defense of Hasebroek. Moreno, whose book is the most complete and up-to-date coverage of the Athenian grain trade, presents himself as the Anti-Hasebroek, asserting that wealthy Athenians were deeply involved with funding the Athenian grain trade, with legislation pertaining to it, and with the allotment of honors. Engen (2010) tries earnestly to find a middle way between economistic approaches and those that emphasize the embeddedness of the economy, and to a large degree he succeeds, by showing the blurring of honor and profit in the self-presentation of those in the grain trade.

[41] Austin (1994, 558).

[42] Thucydides 3.86.

[43] In Rhodes and Osborne (2003, 96) a list of 41 recipients of 805,000 *medimnoi* of grain as shortage-relief in 330-326 from Cyrene, Athens received 100,000, Alexander's mother Olympias in Epirus 60,000, then 50,000 each went to Argos, Larisa, Corinth, and Alexander's sister Cleopatra. The other 35 groups received on average less than 13,000 *medimnoi*.

[44] Lycurg., *In Leocratem* 27. See further below.

[45] For example, Thebes was unable to bring in a crop two years running in the 370s, but was ordinarily self-sufficient (Xen., *Hell.* 5.4.56).

devoted itself to viticulture); others, land-poor, turned to trade (e.g., Aegina); Mantinea's poverty of good bottomland led to a cessation of horse breeding.[46] Megara's land was under specialty crops (onions, garlic, apples, and pomegranates) and sheep for the highly successful woollens industry.[47] It should be no surprise that Athens was a net importer, but the sheer volume of imported grain into Athens is marked (Moreno 2007b, 207-208, 315).[48] Conversely, only Thessaly and Euboea in Old Greece were said to be exporters of grains,[49] and one should note further that the export frequencies and volumes are indeterminate.

Boats leaving Athens were either empty, intent on fetching a cargo for delivery back to Athens, or carrying specialty agricultural products (olives, olive oil, wine) or silver from the mines at Laureion (Knorringa 1926, 132-139). Again, it is unlikely that fine pottery was ever a predominant cargo, although both it and other manufactures no doubt filled open spaces in outgoing ships.

First, the landscape: At Athens the two major markets were at Peiraieus and the agora. (There had been frontier markets in the 7th century but these had become a dim memory by the fourth.) At the suggestion of Themistocles, the Athenians began developing (through fortification) Peiraieus and her three harbors in 493/2—until this project the Phaleron harbor and beach had served as port for Athens (Hdt 6.116; Thuc. 1.93). That they had not acted sooner helps us understand that there was no need for expansion in order to accommodate any increase in grain imports: the Phaleron harbor was unable to accommodate the heavy, deep-drafting merchant ships filled with grains, so the completion of the Peiraieus upgrade, completed most likely in the 470s,[50] may be a terminus post quem for any upward spike in grain importation. Moreno

---

[46] References in Austin (1994, 559); Burford (1994, 677).

[47] Legon (1981, 87, 89).

[48] "For you of course know this, that we consume imported grain the most of all peoples" ἴστε γὰρ δήπου τοῦθ', ὅτι πλείστῳ τῶν πάντων ἀνθρώπων ἡμεῖς ἐπεισάκτῳ σίτῳ χρώμεθα (Dem. 20.31). One instructive event was the seizure in 340 by Philip of either 180 or 230 grain-bearing ships as they prepared to head south to Athens from Hieron on the east side of the Bosporus, carrying probably between 500,000 and 800,000 *medimnoi* all told (Didymus, *Demosthenes* 10.34-11.5; see discussion in Bresson 1994, 47-50 = 2000, 131-133; Whitby 1998, 119-120; Moreno 2007a, 207 n. 298).

[49] See Jardé (1925, 194 and notes 1 and 2 there), who reminds us that Euboea was exporting to Athens and was virtually part of the Athenian economy in the sixth through fourth centuries.

[50] There is no reason to doubt Diodorus' (11.41) dating of the completion to 477/6.

shows that Athenian imperial locations on the Aegean littoral and islands were the primary source for grains in the 5th century (2007, 339-340). The archaeology of the Black Sea littoral from Thrace to Olbia indicates "a degree of political and military unrest that is incompatible with seeing the area as a major source of grain in the 490s and 480s" (Moreno 2007b, 161);[51] in fact, in all likelihood, imports from the Black Sea can only have commenced in earnest after the establishment of the Bosporan kingdom in c. 438 (Tsetskhladze 2008). Regular shipments from Egypt do not begin before the end of the 5th century (Thuc. 4.53; 8.35); regular shipments of grains from Sicily *to Athens* are not documented until the mid 4th century ([Dem.] 32; 56.9), although there may have been regular shipments to the Peloponnesus in the 5th century (Thuc. 3.86); we have a record of one large shipment from the Po Valley in the late 5th century (before 409: Lys. 32.25) a large cache of Attic Red-Figure fine ware at Spina on the Po (Moreno 2007b, 343), but no indication of regularity.

What about quantity of imports into Athens? Up to half of a normal year's imports would have been grains.[52] Peter Garnsey computed the total arable of Attika and reckoned that Athens did not need to import grains from abroad in a normal year.[53] Alfonso Moreno has turned such computations on end by showing that by the 5th century Attic production of grains could only meet 30% of the population's requirements (2007, 10, Table 1). Michael Whitby (1998, 121) is able to make an effective argument that there were years in the 4th century when the Athenians imported so much grain that Peiraieus may have been the leading *exporter* of grain in the Aegean world.

Who were the traders, how were their cargoes financed, and how were states involved in the business of trading? Hasebroek's shadow has

---

[51] This means that the ships sailing south at the Hellespont in 494 (Hdt. 6.5, 26) and 480 ("heading towards Aegina and the Peloponnesus" Hdt. 7.147) were *probably* not on a routine route or heavily laden with grains, although it is also fair to observe that these were unlikely to be the first ships ever to sail south from the Black Sea with agricultural product, and the latter ships are σιταγωγά, "grain-carrying." On balance? Red herrings.

[52] A better way to put it would be that at least half of a year's imports in a normal year were non-grains, both processed foods and non-food items. This is the inference from Isocrates (*Peace* 20-21), who expected revenues to double when things returned to normal after the Social War, in 355. If grains have been coming in at their regular levels but nothing else was arriving, then 50% of a normal year's trade was non-grain (McKechnie 1989, 185-186).

[53] Garnsey (1988, 104). Osborne (1987) made similar calculations, concluding that Athens normally never imported grain; he has retracted this position (2004, 140). On this important issue, see discussion on modeling in Moreno (2007b, chapter 1).

proved a long and persistent one, dominating the discourse over the best method for studying the players in the Athenian grain trade. Followed by Finley and most others, he limned a classical Athenian economy in which a great divide can be discerned between impoverished, non-citizen traders and wealthy, non-trading citizen-consumers. Hasebroek overstated his case when he said, "In Classical Greece the class of regular traders. . . consisted almost entirely of resident foreigners. . . There was scarcely a single merchant of citizen status" (1933, 101). Reed concludes that most traders in Peiraieus were "not only foreign. . . but non-resident as well" (Reed 2003, 44; cf. 28-29). It is difficult to argue with this conclusion, although one may ask what has been accomplished by it. Ste. Croix had taken Hasebroek to task on this very point (1972, 393), imagining instead an international community of traders, at home nowhere and everywhere (1972, 266).

For Hasebroek, trade was undertaken exclusively by capital-less ναύκληροι. Reed (2003) indulges in Hasebroek's categories, obsessing over the question of traders' wealth. He has assiduously collected all references to ἔμποροι and ναύκληροι, which the reader can manipulate as she sees fit, whether concerned especially about the wealth/poverty issues or not, but it is unclear how this brings us any closer to understanding who the traders were. For that, we need to turn to finance.

The Athenian trade was financed by bottomry loans made by Athenians and non-Athenians. These loans, usually at very high interest rates (routinely over 20% (or even 30%[54]) compared to the 12% rate on a conventional (non-maritime) loan), were repaid by the shipowner upon delivery of the cargo, the ship itself was the collateral, and the lender lost nearly all if the ship and its cargo were lost. Bottomry loans have been frequently, although not accurately, termed a form of insurance, which they resemble.[55] Most of the evidence for this financial instrument is the Demosthenic corpus (32-36, 45, 56); the earliest surviving reference to bottomry is a fragment from Eupolis' *Marikas*, produced in 421 (Harvey 1976). It seems necessary that bottomry loans (and the opportunity to invest in them) became prominent only when the grain trade took off, the

---

[54] Since the interest rate was paid for the duration of the loan rather than at an annual rate, an exceptionally speedy completion of a delivery, in a few weeks instead of months, could make the annual interest easily exceed 100%. See Ste. Croix (1974, 46).

[55] Millett (1983, 44-45) argues that bottomry loans resemble better consumption loans, as they tended to cover only half the cargo and thus the other half would not be "insured."

terminus post quem for which would be the development of Peiraieus in the 470s (see above).

While Hasebroek remains substantially correct to the extent that there are no prominent Athenians who were shipowners or retailers, it is very easy to see that many prominent Athenians were made rich by investing in long-distance trade, among them the orators Demosthenes and Aeschines. (Andocides in fact *did* act as a trader, *when he was in exile* (c. 412-403),[56] which is in line with the archaic evidence discussed above.) The conclusion one is forced into now is that there were many prominent Athenians involved in various ways in the grain trade and they became wealthier from it.[57] The difficulty in perception is due to the efforts by the prominent to distance themselves in the public eye from this activity. The financiers worked hard to separate themselves from their "business," and were perhaps especially successful at deluding those who have studied them.[58]

---

[56] I owe this observation to Ste. Croix (1972, 267).

[57] Moreno's position (2007b, 192) may overstate things: "[A]n Athenian elite was involved in every aspect of its city's grain supply, from the personal and lucrative level of lending money or receiving and selling grain (Andocides, Demosthenes, Aeschines, Philocrates), to the official and empowering faculties of proposing a grain-tax law (Agyrrhius senior), preserving or moving Spartocid honours (Demosthenes, Androtion, Agyrrhius junior), or establishing cleruchies and protecting the Hellespontine sailing routes (Timotheus)." But this is a more productive position to take than nearly to ignore the financiers altogether. Engen (2011) also makes this abundantly clear in a recent essay on the hidden economy of Athens, offering a clear analysis of the affairs of Demosthenes' father.

[58] Hasebroek and his descendants, including Polanyi, have misunderstood Aristotle (see Meikle 1995, 58-59) on καπηλική—for Aristotle was not criticizing just the retailers jostling in the Peiraieus and agora because they were entering into exchanges with the narrow focus on maximizing a cash outcome—*anyone* engaged in M—C—M' exchange—that is, in the quest to maximize cash for its own sake—was subject to the same criticism. For Aristotle, in χρηματιστική, natural exchange aims at use value (or getting useful things), while unnatural χρηματιστική aims at exchange value (or getting money) and includes many things (among them καπηλική) (after Meikle 1995, 47). The practitioners of καπηλική include Demosthenes and Aeschines, already mentioned above, as well as the prominent 5th century Athenian politician Cleon (Moreno 2007b, 229-235), Darius I of Persia (Hdt. 3.89.30), and, perhaps most obviously (because he was caught out), Cleomenes, Alexander's satrap in Alexandria, who accumulated wealth of 8,000 talents (Diod. Sic. 18.14.1) by manipulating the international grain market ([Dem.] 56.7-8), while also controlling the grain trade within and out of Egypt itself and stripping wealth from the temples there ([Arist.], *Oec.* 1252a16-23; 1252b22-25; Howe 2013; Baynham 2015).

How did states get involved with trade and traders? It is accurate to say that neither Athens nor any other state had its own merchant fleet, nor did any state have a trade policy that extended beyond its own people and residents (Ste. Croix 1972, 393-96). We know, however, that in Athens in the Classical period there were in place δίκαι ἐμπορικαί, special commercial maritime courts, which treated non-citizens and citizens equally and did their business of dispute settlement rapidly. The courts were characterized by "supranationality of access, rapidity of process, rigor of procedure and enforcement of judgments" (Cohen 2005, 300).[59] As Demosthenes tells it, the courts existed for the settlement of disputes among ἔμποροι and ναύκληροι that arose over shipments into and out of Athens and for which there was a written contract;[60] thus we have commercial courts that exclusively served traders and must have been a great inducement to bring goods to and from Athens.[61] The courts met each month in the winter (that is, generally the non-sailing time) to assign dates for cases (Dem. 33.23). The efficiency and transaction-cost containment that the courts offered must have been an inducement to take goods to and from Athens (Thür forthcoming). It is likely that such courts existed in other poleis.

In addition to these efficient places of recourse, there were political actions that could attract traders into ports and could encourage particular behaviours. The assembly at Teos in about 470 passed this action:

ὅστις ἐς γῆν τὴν Τηίην κ-
ωλύει σῖτον ἐσάγεσθαι
ἢ τέχνηι ἢ μηχανῆι ἢ κατ-
ὰ θάλασσαν ἢ κατ' ἤπειρο-
ν ἢ ἐσαχθέντα ἀνωθεοίη,
ἀπόλλυσθαι καὶ αὐτ-
ὸν καὶ γένος τὸ κένο.

---

[59] Cohen (2005, 297-301) is an excellent and precise overview of the *dikai emporikai*; Cohen (1973) is fuller.
[60] Dem. 32.1: οἱ νόμοι κελεύουσιν, ὦ ἄνδρες δικασταί, τὰς δίκας εἶναι τοῖς ναυκλήροις καὶ τοῖς ἐμπόροις τῶν Ἀθήναζε καὶ τῶν Ἀθήνηθεν συμβολαίων, καὶ περὶ ὧν ἂν ὦσι συγγραφαί.
[61] In the Demosthenic corpus, 21.176 refers to a case litigated in this court, and 32-35, 37, and 56 are speeches delivered in (apparently) actual cases being tried; also, Hyperides 3 involves a dispute about a contract involving an exchange entirely on land.

> Whoever interferes with grain being
> imported into Teian territory by any
> means at all, whether by sea or land, or
> exports (*or* pushes up the price of)
> what has been imported: may
> destruction visit both him and his
> family.[62]

Presumably the Teian assembly thought that this action would bring in more traders with more grain.

We can compare laws at Athens, preserved in Demosthenes and Lycurgus, that forbade Athenians from underwriting bottomry loans for grain cargoes that would be delivered to any port other than the Peiraieus ([Dem.] 35.51; cf. Lycurg., *In Leocratem* 27) and forbade any Athenian from transporting grain to any other port than the Peiraieus ([Dem.] 34.37; cf. [Dem.] 35.50), any violation of which offered the death penalty (see Garnsey 1988, 139-140). Two laws at Thasos dating ca. 425-415 seek to protect growers and consumers against local retailers and regional wholesalers. The laws empowered "fruit-reckoners" (καρπολόγοι) to collect taxes and tariffs within the wine industry, protected local growers (γεωργοί) from unscrupulous traders (ἔμποροι), restricted futures contracts, and forbade the movement by Thasian ships of non-Thasian wine within a broad patch of the northern Aegean stretching from Athos to Cape Pacheia south of Ainos (*SEG* 36, 790-792 = Salviat 1986:147-150, 152-153, 181-187).

But the assembly acted in pro-trader wise with other actions, for example in general the law passed ensuring the purity of silver coinage in 375/4 (Rhodes and Osborne 2003, 25) would have drawn traders to Athens because of the reduction in transaction costs it offered.[63] Similarly, actions on behalf of specific groups would have encouraged traders to come to Peiraieus: (i) a special arrangement passed in 374/3 required that the cleruchies at Lemnos, Imbros, and Skyros pay their taxes to Athens in grains (Rhodes and Osborne 2003, 26), which presumably would have benefitted traders and Athenian underwriters who may have had inside tracks to bidding on the shipments, and (ii) a decree passed by the assembly in 333/2 that permitted traders from

---

[62] Meiggs and Lewis (1969, 30A.6-12).
[63] For a recent discussion see Ober (2008, ch. 6).

Kition on Cyprus to purchase land and build a sanctuary to Aphrodite. Permission to non-citizens to purchase land was exceedingly rare, and the motive in this case appears to be strictly to curry the good will of Cypriot traders, as was the case at least once in the past when the assembly had done the same for Egyptian traders: "it is resolved by the *demos* to give to the traders of the Kitians the right to purchase a property on which they will build their sanctuary for Aphrodite, just as also the Egyptians have founded the sanctuary of Isis" (Rhodes and Osborne 2003, 91.38-45).[64] It is difficult to categorize the land grants for worship and the other broad inducements[65] differently from the honors granted to ναύκληροι for their euergetism, to which I now turn by way of conclusion.

Darel Tai Engen (2010) has done the discipline a great service by his collocation and study of the honors given to traders by the Athenian assembly. He has collected 34 inscriptions dating between c. 414-412 and 310/09 that honor individuals, 25 of which are extant, nine inferred from inscriptions or from judicial speeches or in one case Athenaeus. Among the honored actions: outright gifts of cargoes of timber and grain, deliveries of grain at reduced or established prices, and a gift of cash to purchase grain. The honors given for these benefactions include gold crowns, *asylia* (protection from property seizure), *ateleia* (exemption from taxes), *enktesis* (the right to own land and a dwelling on it), and even citizenship. Honorands are metics and foreigners (*xenoi*, including Bosporan royalty); he concludes that Athenians are not among the honorands and that the ratio of Greeks to non-Greeks is a reflection of the ratio in the trading population rather than any bias in favor of Greeks. His analysis is of great service, although, practically speaking, there is also great value in the rich database that he has created for others to sift though (and the same can be said for Reed's (2003) work). Obviously this honoring practice could encourage others to act similarly towards the Athenian *demos* (Luraghi 2010), but it is very unlikely that honors ever preceded euergesia.[66]

---

[64] Garland (1987, 109) lists the many foreign divinities worshipped in Peiraieus, many as early as the fifth and fourth centuries and perhaps under circumstances not dissimilar to the Egyptians' and the Kitians'.

[65] Reed (2003, 44-46) offers a list of other inducements to foreign traders, but overlooks the silver coinage legislation.

[66] Domingo Gygax (2003) argues that euergetistic actions were indeed a response to pressure brought to bear on the elite stratum by the persistent issuing of honors by the *demos*, all of it operating within a landscape of gift exchange; this clearly works well

Retailers were subject not only to much regulation[67] but also to the same criticism (e.g., Arist., *Pol.* 1257b40-1258b7) leveled at the practitioners of καπηλική, but we saw above that Aristotle was not criticizing only the retailers down in the markets, but all those across the status-spectrum. What all these κάπηλοι have in common is not the accumulation of wealth but the acquisition of money for its own sake narrowly. This charge was why wealthy Athenians distanced themselves from the world of trade, although it is clear that many were deeply involved. Another way of accomplishing this distancing or separation was to have other persons working in their interests (Moreno 2007b, 281, 290; Bravo 1977; Wilson 1997/98), but these were not examples of agency in any legal sense (made very clear by Harris 2013).

There is a curious parallel between these efforts of *aristoi* financiers of the classical period and those of the *aristoi* of the Homeric world. The archaic *aristoi* sought to mask their involvement in trade because they did not want to reveal that they had acquired wealth from outside the communities of which they were the centers. The classical Athenian *aristoi*, unwilling to be perceived either as in any way dependent on others or as undignified seekers of money for its own sake, restricted their involvement to the financing of trade in and out of Peiraieus. There is a poignancy that the *dikai emporikai* at Athens, which provided transaction-cost controls and other advantages to those investing in trade, thankfully also provide us with the transparency that allows a clear view of trade in classical Athens.

---

within citizen groups, at Athens and elsewhere, but it has less traction when the honorands are aliens.

[67] That the assembly at Athens set limits on retail mark-up on imported grains would not have had significant effect on traders bringing grains in. In addition to the limit (3.3% or 16.7%) on the retail markup of imported grains (Lys. 22.8, 12), the assembly acted to cap prices on goods later in the production process made and sold by millers and bakers ([Arist.], *Ath. Pol.* 51.3).

III

A HAND ANYTHING BUT HIDDEN: INSTITUTIONS AND MARKETS IN FIRST MILLENIUM BCE MESOPOTAMIA
Michael Kozuh
Auburn University

With regard to first-millennium BCE Mesopotamia, the evaluation of new approaches to ancient systems of economy and trade immediately runs into old problems. To put it bluntly, traders, especially private long-distance traders, exist largely in the Mesopotamian background. From the correspondence of the Assyrian court, through the business archives of entrepreneurial Babylonians, to the administrative records of large-scale Babylonian temples, we have a broad range of sources. Despite these sources, our knowledge regarding trade is minuscule relative to other economic operations. Other than wool, exactly what first-millennium Mesopotamians might have exported to the wider world remains uncertain, and the mechanisms of international trade are enigmatic at best. Our knowledge of intra-Mesopotamian trade is only slightly better. Given the current state of information, little in the two broad *koine* of first millennium Mesopotamian history[1] lends itself to useful comparisons. One might, for example, fruitfully investigate the type, content, and speed of international trade information centered on Assyria, but it is nearly impossible to do the same for Babylonia, at least in a way that elicits real comparisons between the two. For Babylonia, we can broach a variety of questions (e.g., what was the role of the state in ending the career of a prominent business family) that find no parallels in evidence from Assyria. Compounding the problem is the field's general ambivalence toward economic modeling (Bedford 2005; Jursa 2010, 15ff.), which does not lend itself to a rich historiographic tradition on this topic. This lack of basic information about trade may be due to the purview of our sources; it is also possible that traders wrote in Aramaic on parchment and thus their records are largely lost to time. Whatever the reason, and notwithstanding the state of evidence, scholars

---

[1] The two phases of common culture, which this volume has chosen to call after the Greek models, *koine*, are roughly Assyrian in northern Mesopotamia during the first half of the millennium and Babylonian in southern Mesopotamia from the mid-first millennium through the Macedonian conquest.

ascribe a tremendous amount of importance to trade in the ancient Near East.

In what follows, I will try to unite Assyria and Babylonia in a conceptual model by way of the New Institutional Economics (henceforth, NIE), concentrating specifically on the work of P. F. Bang. To do this, this chapter examines the role of Mesopotamian institutions—primarily temple and state—in giving shape to the economy. Although Finley cast Near Eastern institutions into the economic shadows (Finley 1985, 28), scholars of the ancient Near East regularly grapple with this issue. For this reason NIE is so useful since it either calls many assumptions (some explicit, some tacit) into question or helps bring them into line.

While there is much scholarship on this topic, I find Bang's criticism of market equilibrium as a model for the ancient economy particularly valuable (developed in Bang 2004; Bang 2006). Referencing the Mediterranean, Bang disputes the notion that ancient markets would naturally reach an equilibrium shaped by supply and demand, where goods and services came to be parceled out across an integrated expanse according to market forces (Bang 2006, 56ff.). Casting doubt on the idea that "ecological need" (i.e., that unsustainable peasant autarky in any given area of the Mediterranean engendered markets of exchange) was a primary mover of markets, Bang instead argues that peasant autarky was of secondary concern to the desires of social, governmental, and religious institutions. Indeed, he goes as far to say that

> [w]hile social elites could not, in the long run, afford to be completely indifferent to the well-being of agricultural producers, they had no interest in the most desirable ecological equilibrium from the peasant point of view. Such an equilibrium ran counter to their need for siphoning off a substantial portion of production over and above the bare minimum peasant subsistence . . . Economic interdependence was not simply a reflection of organic, Durkheimian co-operation. Exploitation and conflicting interests were also a prominent part of the process (Bang 2006, 57).

For Bang, institutions play vital roles in markets; in some ways, markets are entirely dependent upon them. Concentrating on information inefficiencies (e.g., the fragmentation of markets and slowness of the flow of information between them), logistical problems (in transport), and ecological uncertainty, Bang demonstrates how the economy of the Roman empire was "anything but [a] level and even playing field" (Bang 2006, 58f.). Instead, it was one shaped and dominated by asymmetries in information, frictions, and logistical problems that consistently prevented market equilibrium.

Moreover, Bang insists that there is no reason to assume that institutions worked to make markets more efficient. In fact, state agents could work to keep markets fragmented and slow moving. This existed not only at the level of customs or tolls but also in state actions against merchants (with price controls or flooding the market). We will return to this below, but for now it is important to consider how institutions could bring markets together. This issue is not well developed in Bang's writing, but he makes this important point:

> in the pre-industrial world closer integration of economic resources and tighter co-ordination of markets, in particular, depended on a hand anything but hidden. It took very tangible and overt forms of organisational power to tie supply and demand across locations into a more stable relationship where markets would be more closely integrated and behave more uniformly. It is in this context that the many mercantilist privileges and attempts to promote commercial interests, often backed by armed force, in early modern Europe take on a crucial importance. They enabled merchants to a much higher degree than hitherto to overcome local resistance and connect separate markets in more stable and permanent ways. These policies were part of the centralising state's strategy of breaking down local particularisms and mobilising an ever expanding share of social resources to meet its own quickly growing requirements (Bang 2006, 74).

Bang's aim here is to expose a critique of the common understanding of Smithian *laissez faire*. Indeed, while Romans (and Assyrians, and Babylonians, and Persians) recognized the benefits of trade within their empires, these benefits never developed into a functional ideology. Instead,

> they were justifiable primarily in terms of the ability of merchants to complement the needs of local societies by making available goods which were otherwise lacking . . . The main concern was not the uninhibited operation of markets, but whether supplies were made available to consumers, mostly urban, while the right of local aristocracies to control the agricultural surplus still had to be maintained (Bang 2006, 76).

In other words, Bang changes the perspective on what one might call the benefits of empire. It is well known, of course, that empires open roads and other means of communication and connect distant peoples. The protection and security of the roads and waterways has been a trope of empire since Lugalzagezzi. Yet what exactly did those now-safe interconnections link up? Bang criticizes the prevalent notion that, having connected disparate markets together, empire then allowed for the laws of supply and demand to run their course under its aegis. Instead, empire connected markets under a distinct set of political aims: to move goods from the periphery to urban consumers (usually in the core), and, in so doing, not to upset any political power balances.

Indeed, Bang's criticism lays bare a longstanding assumption in ancient Near Eastern studies, which usually takes one of two forms. In the first, it is sometimes assumed that adverse political conditions kept a substantial and ever-present merchant class in abeyance, waiting for the opportunity to take advantage of better conditions to ply their wares in distant lands. Upon the removal of those political roadblocks the merchant classes of various societies then interlinked and we then find large-scale networked trade. The second, which I think is more prevalent, assumes almost the opposite—that networked, long-distance trade existed in some form or another at all times, and empires (or politics in general) worked simply to redirect or influence it as best they could. Stable and supportive political conditions brought traders in, while unstable or predatory political conditions forced them to change their routes and circumvent certain areas. Under this assumption, politics shaped an ever-present network of trade.

Generally speaking, while these perspectives must contain some truth, they offer insufficient explanatory power. It is no longer tenable to assume that a segment of society (or indeed a part of every human activity) exists solely in the economic sphere, and, if it were not for meddlesome political arrangements, would go about its business of trucking and bartering. By separating *homo economicus* from *homo politicus*, such assumptions retain a view of Neoclassical economics that has undergone substantial modification in a variety of disciplines, from economics to anthropology (Graeber 2011). From another perspective, Bang argues scholars face the conundrum of a source discourse that was suspicious of, if not outright hostile to, trade and merchants, but they also find the widespread existence of markets and commercialism in the Mediterranean world (Bang 2009, 101). For the Ancient Near East, we do not see hostility to trade and business in first millennium Mesopotamia (Jursa 2002, 203f.). Instead, our conundrum is how to integrate basic assumptions about long distance trade with the fact that, although we have tens of thousands of economic texts at our disposal, there is little evidence for robust, ever-present international trade networks. The first millennium cuneiform record is indeed biased toward institutions, yet even then we have to deal with the fact that those institutions only rarely exchanged with international traders. Even in the well-documented private sphere, evidence for trading ventures outside of Mesopotamia is sparse (Jursa 2010, 208f.; Waerzeggers 2010).

THE NEO-ASSYRIAN EMPIRE

Aiming to recapture the greatness of the Middle Assyrian Empire (c. 1365 – 1076 B.C.E.), kings of the Neo-Assyrian Empire dominated the Near East for the better part of two centuries. Historians divide Assyrian hegemony into two phases (Kuhrt 1995, 473f.): in the first (934-823 B.C.E.) the Assyrians sought to reestablish the borders of the empire carved out by their Middle Assyrian predecessors, mostly over neighboring peoples; after a period of instability, the second phase (745 - c. 610 B.C.E.) eventually brought Assyrians to world empire: from the Persian Gulf to Central Anatolia, and from Armenia to Egypt.

The sources for the Assyrian empire are numerous and diverse, many of them generated by the Assyrian court.[2] Of primary importance

---

[2] A beginning bibliography for the second phase of Neo-Assyrian history can be found at: http://www.ucl.ac.uk/sargon/bibliography/

are the royal annals and inscriptions, which recount the military exploits and empire building of Assyrian kings. There are complex historiographical issues involved in using these sources to reconstruct Assyrian history (see Kuhrt 1995, 474f.), yet they nonetheless remain an invaluable resource. Secondly, for the latter half of Neo-Assyrian history we have a substantial quantity of court correspondence at our disposal (over 2300 letters), in addition Egyptian, biblical, Phoenician, and Babylonian sources provide an outsider's perspective on the empire.

Most authorities agree that Assyria came to ascendency partly in its effort to control the trade routes that crisscrossed the Assyrian heartland (e.g., Jankowska 1973; Tadmor 1975; Cole 1996, 70; Radner 2004),[3] although the early Neo-Assyrian kings themselves couched their imperialism in defensive maneuvering against hostile Arameans. It is less clear (at least historiographically) why the Assyrians strove to control trade routes. Discussions of trade under the Assyrian empire seem to operate under one of two assumptions: either that the Assyrians simply sought to take in goods from subject nations (Diakonoff 1968; Oppenheim 1968; Liverani 1979; Kuhrt 1995, 535ff.), in effect working to make all trade routes end in the Assyrian heartland;[4] or that the Assyrians strove to control and profit from traders on the routes themselves through things like taxes and tariffs, extracting revenue from trader networks that would have continued to operate with or without imperial supervision (Postgate 1979; Gibson 1991; Cole 1996; some combine these two assumptions, e.g., Jankowska 1973).

Radner gives the most comprehensive discussion on Assyrian trade (Radner 2004). She argues that the Assyrians tied trade and politics so closely together that it is best to speak of Assyrian *Handelspolitik*. Fundamentally, she follows Tadmor in arguing that the Assyrians moved from a network empire—that is, one that worked to solidify control over various nodal points, whose relationship to trade remains unclear (Liverani 1988, 86ff.)—to the more commonly known territorial empire. This process and transformation, which were never brought to completion empire-wide, puts Assyrian attitudes toward trade into stark relief. For her, early Assyrian demands for tribute (*mandattu*) from non-Assyrians were not simple imperial extractions to benefit a core elite, but

---

[3] Brief skeptical thoughts on the relationship between Assyria and trade are found in Grayson (1976, 135); Lanfranchi (2003, 97f.).

[4] Oppenheim's argument (1968, 36f.), that there is much gray area between "trade" and "tribute" belongs here.

instead payments for Assyrian protection and the benefits of empire (Radner 2004, 155). In other words, the Assyrians demanded gifts and tribute in exchange for the fact that Assyrian infrastructure, blood, and treasure went, *inter alia*, into the building and maintaining of trade routes in northern Mesopotamia.

Justifications of this sort are, of course, common in the history of world empires, where extraction from the periphery to the core requires infrastructure, bureaucracy, and a distinct ideology that stresses the universal benefits of empire to the conquered (for the Assyrian ideology, see Radner 2004, 155f.). Indeed, Radner maintains that as Assyrian imperial expansion came up against peoples long connected into networks of trade, mostly to the south and west (namely, Carchemish, Babylonia, Egypt, and Phoenicia), the Assyrians shifted the tribute-as-protection ideology into the next gear. Sparing the main centers of international trade—despite undertaking military activity in the vicinity—the Assyrians then demanded clientship from the conquered. In these cases, the Assyrians offered major trading cities protection and access to the routes controlled by the Assyrians. This was done in exchange for taxes and materials needed for military power and state building, which was then funneled to the heartland by royal Assyrian merchants, a process Radner labels "symbiosis through control."

Often the Assyrians set up a new trade-town (*kāru*, on these see below) near long-standing centers of international trade in order to facilitate the process of symbiosis. As the Assyrian empire grew, however, the independence of these trading centers was called into question; Sargon II annexed multi-cultural, polyglot Carcamesh in 717, which then put the Phoenician trading centers of Tyre and Sidon in Assyria's sights. With no desire (or ability) to build up its own Mediterranean navy, the Assyrians played favorites; Sidon was destroyed in 677, and in its place the Assyrians established a trade town (*kāru*), which they used to monitor and deal with the remaining city of Tyre. The well-known treaty between the Assyrian king Esarhaddon and Ba'al, king of Tyre, gave the Assyrians access to the Mediterranean coast, allowed them to claim Ba'al's shipwrecked vessels in "Assyrian territory" on the Mediterranean, and listed the ports of trade that Esarhaddon permitted Ba'al to use (Parpola and Watanabe 1988, 25ff. for a translation of the treaty).

Despite the relationship between trade and the rise of the Assyria, we know little about the independent Assyrian trader. The royal merchant, connected to the king at times by blood, given the power to negotiate on behalf of the empire, and supplied with troops, is well known (Elat 1987; Radner 1999). Radner rightly likens Assyrian royal merchants to Drake, Columbus, and Cortez, in that they were

> equipped with military and diplomatic competences by the ruler of a world empire . . . [to] travel along well-known routes, reestablish almost forgotten ones and discover new ones, their ultimate goal being to get what their monarch needed to rule the country: slaves, horses, metals and luxury goods of any kind (Radner 1999, 103).

Yet it is only recently that private trading ventures have been identified in Neo-Assyrian records at all (Postgate 1979, 205ff; Radner 1999, 109ff.). It seems fairly certain that the Assyrian kings did not strive to control trade routes in order to give Assyrian-flagged private caravans an advantage.

As should be clear by this point, the surviving evidence for Assyrian trade makes it very difficult to frame the Assyrians as promoting trade by simply removing the barriers between markets and letting distant merchant classes develop them organically. When we put the divergent and admittedly patchy bits of information together, we find an empire born on the crossroads of major connection routes, one that justified its control over other peoples as protection, one that dealt with major cities at nodal points of trade routes outside of its control with sophistication and, at least at first, a sort of deference. Yet at the same time we find very little evidence that the resulting effect was the freeing up of a merchant class to go and ply its wares in now-liberated and –networked markets. On the contrary, we find most merchants connected to the imperial machine, working mainly to find ways by which they could supply the heartland with the tools, supplies, and paraphernalia of empire.

Indeed, Bang's argument that the coordination of distant markets depended upon a "hand anything but hidden"—i.e., that markets came together only through the conscious actions of powerful institutions— echoes one aspect in the historiography of Assyrian trade, which is somewhat awkwardly termed "forcible exchange." This approach, with its roots in Marxist thought, argues that the Assyrians engaged in "predator commerce" (Graslin-Thomé 2009, 175ff.) in order to fulfill the needs of the growing Assyrian center from its unwilling or uninterested neighbors. The main proponent of this philosophy is Diakonoff

(Diakonoff 1968, 29ff.), who argues that the Neo-Assyrian empire at first aimed simply to loot trading and industrial cities (what he calls "'forcible exchange' in its purest form") in the interests of an urban and royal elite. Jankowska tempers this idea somewhat, arguing (after some analytical gymnastics) in effect that the different zones of economic activity in the Near East rendered organic integration impossible. Large-scale, inter-regional exchange could only "be the effect of a mode of exchange based on extra-economic coercion" (Jankowska 1973, 275).

The notion of forcible exchange gave rise to criticism and revision (Oppenheim 1968; Graslin-Thomé 2009, 373ff.); if nothing else, as noted by Graslin-Thomé, it melds pretty well with Assyrian propaganda, but its doctrinaire inflexibility becomes evident when measured against the day-to-day evidence for Assyrian trade. But at times that day-to-day evidence can bring forcible exchange back to the front. In a remarkable letter from the Assyrian king Assurbanipal to the "Elders of Elam," the king attempts to get them to turn over a rebel Chaldean whom he suspects they are sheltering. The end of the letter has the king trying to convince the elders that hiding the rebel is the sole cause of Assyria's enmity toward Elam:

> First of all, why (else) would I myself persecute your country? If it were some sort of trading post [= kāru] of precious stone(s), I would say "Let me seize it and add it to my land" or "Let me take horses and mules from its midst and add them to my forces" or I would say "It is a place of silver and gold, let me impose tribute upon them" or 'there are things worthy of kingship in its midst." But there is nothing of the sort in it (Waters 2002).

Assurbanipal's quote here almost perfectly aligns Radner's symbiosis through control with Diakonoff's forcible exchange: if Elam had trade routes, the Assyrians would take them over; if it had goods, the Assyrians would appropriate them outright.

More enlightening, I think, is the work done by people influenced by Diakonoff's ideas. Over a series of articles, Elat argued for a more nuanced understanding of forced exchange (Elat 1978; Elat 1987; Elat 1991; Elat 1998). He seems to take Diakonoff's basic suppositions for granted, but then works through Assyria's trade relations with peripheral peoples. These people either rivaled Assyria in might and population (Egypt) or were unassailable because technology or culture put them out of Assyria's immediate reach (e.g., the Arabs with dromedary-run Arabian trade or the Phoenicians with their sea-born Mediterranean trade). Elat discusses how, during the reign of Sargon II, Assyria set up a trading town on the newly formed border between the empire and Egypt (Elat 1978). It is with reference to this trading town that we find the most tantalizing quote from an Assyrian royal inscription on trade:

> I [= Sargon] opened the sealed h[ar]bor of Egypt, mingled Assyrians and Egyptians together and made them trade with each other. (Fuchs 1994, 88, lines 17-18 – translation from Na'aman 2005, 281).

Indeed, the Assyrians conducted their much-remarked-upon relations with the Phoenicians at Tyre and Sidon through trading towns. In a famous letter (ND 2715) from an imperial official to the Assyrian king, the official reports on the business of Assyrian trading towns on the Mediterranean, stating that he is taxing lumber being cut by locals and monitoring tax collection in general (Saggs 1955; Yamada 2005, 69). Yamada shows how the Assyrians set up trading towns on the frontiers of the empire as it grew, either by building on virgin soil or by repurposing a conquered town (Yamada, 2005). Each trading town essentially served as the entrepôt through which provincial goods, either as tribute or trade, made their way to the Assyrian heartland, in accordance with agreements between Assyria and the host province. Yet, as far as we understand the surviving documents, there was nothing predatory about these agreements; while they certainly reflect the superior position of Assyria, nothing indicates that Assyria sought to bleed its vassals dry. Instead, they reflect Radner's symbiosis through control—i.e., that Assyria sought to preserve the networks of trade controlled by major trade cities, until political or imperial pressure forced them to do otherwise.

Yet even with the new focus on Assyrian trading towns, it is difficult to dismiss forced exchange completely. As Graslin-Thomé notes, Assyrian texts certainly put the ability to force the movement of goods to Assyria before any mention of movement through trade. Indeed, in perhaps the most generous take on Assyrian methods, Graslin-Thomé, turning the notion of Assyria at the crossroads of trade routes on its head, puts forward the idea that perhaps the Assyrians actually had ill-developed institutions to deal with the trade crisscrossing their land. Rather than developing sophisticated methods of controlling trade—in other words, rather than developing an Assyrian Carchemish or Sidon—the Assyrians developed their military and chose to offer protection-through-alliances in return for foreign goods (Graslin-Thomé 2009, 373ff.).

There is much to recommend in Graslin-Thomé's ideas (cf. Bang, 2007, 39ff.). Among other things, Graslin-Thomé's observations help to explain why, for an empire that many assume was built on or around trade, there seems to have been very little actual trade infrastructure or market sophistication at the Assyrian core (especially considering the role of trade in early Assyrian history). Moreover, her take sets up a scenario by which one can understand why those areas on the periphery of the Assyrian empire bloomed in the wake of Assyrian collapse, while those closest to the center imploded. For Graslin-Thomé, peripheral areas were forced to innovate in order to meet Assyrian demands, while innovation stalled in the center as novel and exotic goods flowed in from outside the empire. This idea has roots in Assyriological thought and is attractive at face value, thought it needs to be contemplated against some of the literature on pre-industrial economic and technological innovation (see, for example, the thoughts in Mokyr 1990). Among other things, I am not convinced that we can classify Neo-Assyrian Mesopotamia as lacking innovation.

Finally, issues of trade and the creation of a Near Eastern *koine* under the Assyrian empire must take mass deportation into consideration. Starting in large-scale with the reign of Tiglath-Pileasar III, the Assyrians relocated massive numbers of people throughout the empire as a method of imperial control (Oded 1979; Na'aman and Zadok 1988).[5] They resettled most deportees in Assyria proper, putting them to work on various building projects in the main capital cities (Oded 1979, 28; Postgate 1979). Others they brought to ransacked cities and towns in order to jump-start the local economy (Oded 1979, 62f.). Finally, the Assyrians resettled people on agriculturally barren or disregarded areas in order to restore ravaged land, to increase the Assyrian presence in sparsely populated areas of the empire, or to bring under cultivation

---

[5] Oded puts the number as high as 4.5 million deportees (Oded 1979, 20).

strategically important locations. As is often stressed, the Assyrians did not subject their deportees to death marches. Letters between those in charge of deportations reflect a concern for the health and well-being of the deportees under their control (Radner 2011). Throughout the empire the deportees joined with the local population, resulting in interesting forms of cultural mixing and acculturation.

Although we have yet to come to terms with the effect of the mass deportations on the culture and history of the ancient Near East, the simple fact that Assyrian kings moved multitudes of "those living by the sea to the mountains, and those living in the mountains to the sea," as their royal inscriptions often state, must have profoundly transformed Near Eastern *koine*. To take an obvious example from the Assyrian heartland, early Neo-Assyrian kings counted the deportees not as slaves or anonymous imperial labor but "as though they were Assyrian" (Oded 1979; Postgate 1989; Machinist 1993). By deporting a variety of Arameans and other west Semitic speakers into Assyria, the Aramaic language began to take hold. As a result, "Assyria was faced with the paradoxical fact that, as the empire expanded and more and more people were made Assyrian, the conquered people were making Assyria less and less Assyrian culturally and linguistically" (Beaulieu 2006, 188). Tadmor and Garelli have noted increasing use of Aramaic and Arameans in the Assyrian court, bureaucracy, and culture starting in the eighth century (Tadmor 1982; Garelli 1984; Tadmor 1991). Changes of this sort must have occurred anywhere the Assyrians placed deportees, in every aspect of life. We see another aspect of this expressly stated in the Book of Kings, where the writer mentions a nearby village of deportees (2 Kings 17: 26ff):

> Each national group made its own gods in the several
> towns where they settled, and set them up in the shrines
> the people of Samaria had made at the high places ...
> They worshiped the lord, but they also appointed all
> sorts of their own people to officiate for them as priests
> in the shrines at the high places. To this day they persist
> in their former practices. They neither worship the lord
> nor adhere to the decrees and ordinances, the laws and
> commands that the lord gave the descendants of Jacob,
> whom he named Israel...Even while these people were
> worshiping the lord they were serving their idols. To this

day their children and grandchildren continue to do as their fathers did.[6]

Indeed, were one to take an economic cross-section of the Assyrian empire at its height, arguments for flourishing trade and economic expansion would immediately present themselves: the empire put new lands under cultivation, it rebuilt and repopulated formally rebellious cities, traders moved around the empire, and trading towns on the empire's border buzzed with activity. With this in mind, some scholars have even suggested the idea of a *pax Assyriaca* (Hallo and Simpson 1997, 137; Fales 2008).

Yet a faceless cross-section would conceal a contrived new world, one crafted neither by some overall plan nor by an invisible hand, but instead by the unsystematic compulsions, demands, and decisions of empire. The resettled population was economically dependent on (and in many ways owed its continued existence to) the Assyrians. Although the resettled people may have sprouted their own "craftsmen, scholars, experts, and businessmen" (Oded 1979, 99ff.), they built economic and social networks far away from (and of a much different sort from) those of their ancestors. Indeed, connections between deportees and the people of their homeland may have created new interconnections between geographically disparate areas, while time-tested local networks fell into disuse. Under the Assyrian empire, the Near Eastern *koine* was in a state of rapid flux and reorientation.

Here, in fact, we come up against an interesting conundrum. One might assume that by ripping people from their homeland and resettling them in other parts of the empire, by setting up trading stations throughout the empire, and by using its military power to move goods to the center, the Assyrians seized the opportunity to impose some standardization on the process of moving goods over long distances. The evidence suggests otherwise. At least three different silver standards circulated under the Assyrian empire (Radner 1999, 130ff.), which suggests that there was no standardization of currency to facilitate trade, although there are hints of an imperial standard weight (Eph'al and Naveh 1993).[7] The metal standard changes from copper to silver between the eighth and the seventh centuries (Postgate 1973, 25; Müller 1997, 120), and we have no evidence for the regularization of taxes and tariffs

---

[6] New International Version translation.

[7] There is even one called a "merchant's *mina*," which is the least attested of the three.

on trade. The relationship between Assyrian road-building and trade remains unclear (Kessler 1997). Moreover, Assyrian royal propaganda (and, for that matter, court correspondence) does not often concern itself with trade; when it does, we tend to get statements like the following:

> . . . oxen, sheep, camels, and men, [the Assyrian army] carried off without number . . . I [Assurbanipal] distributed camels like sheep and caused [them] to overflow to the people of Assyria dwelling in my country. A camel for half a shekel, in half shekels of silver, they valued in front of the gate. In the sale of captives which were gathered in droves, they bartered camels and men.

and

> A fortune without number, not seen by my forefathers, I [Sargon] heaped up in my city Dur-Sharrukin, so that the exchange rate of silver in the Land of Assyria was equal to that of copper (Annals from Khorsabad 232–4 = Fuchs 1994: 130 ff., see Van der Spek 2006, translation borrows from (Tadmor 1958).

In other words, Assyrian kings did not celebrate the fact that they freed merchants to buy and sell under Assyrian jurisdiction with everybody reaping the benefit of a market at equilibrium. Nor, for that matter, did they seem to recognize themselves at the center of a rapidly changing cultural vortex, over which they had relative control. Instead, they boasted of the implementation of an imperial "trade policy" that brought abundance to the heartland of the empire and thus proved its success. To put it another way, one can safely conclude that Assyrian kings considered secondary the result of any policy that did not immediately contribute to the maintenance and perpetuation of their empire.

BABYLONIA IN THE MID-FIRST MILLENNIUM BCE

The move to lower Mesopotamia (henceforth, Babylonia) in the mid-first millennium BCE confronts us with evidence that differs considerably in origin and purview from that of the Neo-Assyrian Empire. We have little from mid-first millennium Babylonia that stems from royal archives,[8] and we lack substantial information on the military campaigns and empire building of the Neo-Babylonian and Achaemenid kings. We know even less about long distance trade (see below). Instead, the evidence stems mainly from archives—some of them immense—generated in two different spheres of economic activity. First, we have archives from the administration of Babylonian temples (especially in the cities of Uruk, Sippar, Borsippa, and Babylon itself); second, there are archives from the economic activities of private entities, which run the gamut from tablets documenting a few transactions of one family to large-scale, multi-generational business firms like the Egibis. These spheres overlap at times—for instance, in the large-scale contracting of temple property to private individuals—and the royal administration engages with each of them in various ways as well (see van Driel 1999; Beaulieu 2000; Bongenaar 2000; Joannès 2000; Jursa 2010, 282ff; Wunsch 2010).

Hence, when seeking to evaluate the relationship between institutions and the market in Babylonia we have to take a perspective that essentially upends the one we used for the Neo-Assyrian Empire. If Assyrian sources tend to highlight the heavy hand of the state in forcing markets together, Babylonian sources have us searching for the state and markets in the background. With that in mind, the analysis divides into three sections: first, it examines the function of institutions in shaping the Babylonian economy in general. Second, we investigate the ability of those institutions to end the careers of prominent economic players in Babylonia. Third, it explores institutional role in high-level bulk wool transactions, which may have formed the basis of Babylonian exports.

Politically, the mid-first millennium BCE is the period of the Neo-Babylonian and Persian (Achaemenid) Empires. Generally speaking, the numbers of cuneiform tablets from both the private and temple spheres of the economy begin to increase with the onset of the Neo-Babylonian empire, peak during the latter part of the 6th century, which is roughly the switch between the two empires, and then start to peter out during the reigns of the Persians Darius I (522-486) and Xerxes (486-465). Between Xerxes and Darius III we have significantly less information; most of what we know from that period is dominated by information from the Murashu archive (see below). Temple texts pick up

---

[8] See (Pedersén 2005) for preliminary remarks on one royal archive.

again with the Macedonian conquest, but they do not concern the analysis here.

It is difficult to get an accurate count of the immense number of texts stemming from the resurgence of documented Babylonian economic activity in the mid-first millennium BCE . There are, for example, estimates of over 25,000 texts from the Ebabbar temple of Sippar dating to this period (Jursa 2005, 117f.)—most of these are short administrative texts (that is, they document the movement of goods and personnel within the temple itself); the Eanna temple of the southern Babylonian city of Uruk produced an archive that has left us with between 8,000 and 9,000 texts (Beaulieu 2003). In contrast, texts in archives associated with the Ezida temple of Borsippa number around 3,500 texts (Waerzeggers 2010, 15f.). For private archives, the Egibi/Nur-Sin archive numbers at least 1,700 texts (Wunsch 2003) and the Murashu archive has over 700 (Stolper 1985, 1). At least a dozen smaller archives have over 100 tablets each (Jursa 2005, 60ff.). All told, we have tens of thousands of texts documenting economic activity in mid-first millennium BCE Babylonia.

Until recently, this immense body of evidence made it nearly impossible to analyze the Babylonian economy with any precision. The majority of texts were unpublished, so scholarly attention understandably took piecemeal approaches to the material. Assyriologists had enough difficulty acquiring a full appreciation of one archive, much less attempting a meta-assessment of the Babylonian economy. This situation began to change in the mid-1990s; by the early 2000s Michael Jursa of the University of Vienna put together the START-project (a.k.a. Wirtschaftsgeschichte Babyloniens im ersten Jahrtausend v. Chr). Under the auspices of his project, he assembled a team of scholars to read and catalogue unpublished texts for use in an internal database. The Vienna group has published scores of monographs and articles, but their humbly-titled *Aspects of the Economic History of Babylonia in the First Millennium BC*, a nearly 900 page tome, brings their achievements together. It is difficult to overstate the accomplishment of this study—the product of nearly a decade's worth of work, written by a team of scholars, and not beholden to any particular theory (Jursa 2010, 15ff.). With access to huge caches of unpublished material, the book establishes the first real foothold in the analysis of Babylonian economy. It marks the point of departure for this paper.

Despite a sizeable amount of documentation and newfound elucidation, we still struggle with basic framing. As we approach the question of institutions shaping the Babylonian economy, what stands out is that in Babylonia the beginning of large-scale economic text generation, and thus presumably increased economic activity, is more or less co-terminous with the onset of the Neo-Babylonian Empire. The causation between an empire centered in Babylon and ensuing economic activity seems obvious at first glance, yet direct interaction between the state and the principals of most archives, especially large temple archives, is not all that frequent (MacGinnis 1994; Abraham 2004; Kleber 2008). Moreover, explicit documented activity around the more obvious economic aspects of empire, such as the collection and storing of tribute, mustering of soldiers, or the settling of deportees, is relatively un-common as well. One must find cause and effect elsewhere.

In one of the few attempts to address this issue, van Driel argues that the royal administration set the framework of institutional economic stability in Babylonia by defending the land from outsiders and providing for cultic rites in major Babylonian temples (van Driel 2000). Jursa emphasizes stability as well, putting it in the context of the NIE's "'optimality band' . . . where the government is neither too grasping nor too weak" (quoting Jones 1988, 187; cf. the discussion in Jursa 2010, 56ff) and highlighting the role of urban elites. Continuing with the temples, van Driel further argued that, because the crown brought stability and provisioned the cult, Babylonian temples are best understood as "tool[s] of the royal administration" (van Driel 2000, 6). In addition to needing state protection, he contends that temples could not operate without royal supervision due to weakly aligned personnel bases. But by propping up these large temple institutions, with their multiple levels of personnel and control over large amounts of resources, the crown essentially set up a situation in which local power bases would form against royal interests (and in favor of local ones). The crown, in turn, appointed watchdogs in the temple who over time integrated into the temple's bureaucracy, blurring the line between temple and state. As a result, van Driel sees royal administration in Babylonia—with its own weaknesses (van Driel 2000, 7)—as protecting and priming the pump of the other large-scale Mesopotamian institutions, both drawing parts of them closer to the royal sphere while, at the same time, encouraging the formation of local sympathies.

The crown's function in setting the stage for the private economy is more difficult to assess in Van Driel's work. He cryptically refers to Babylonian entrepreneurs as "hangers on," but does not explain further (van Driel 2000, 3). In general, for some private archives, we find direct connections to the administration of royal land and/or the land-for-service sector (Jursa 2010, 197ff.). In these cases, at least part of the operations of the archive holders had a direct institutional background. Some private entrepreneurs also leased large-scale tracts of temple land under a program that itself had connections to the court (Jursa 2010, 194f.). On the other hand, the Egibis only established their royal connections *after* their success in shipping commodities, although these connections were instrumental to their later growth (Wunsch 2003, 236ff.). Other archives show only minor connections to royal land or other governmental work; many small archives show no institutional connections at all.

In general, then, the rise in economic documentation with the onset of the Neo-Babylonian Empire correlates in both direct and indirect ways to the establishment of political control in Babylonia, and this continued into the Persian period. Clearly (some?) temples benefitted directly from Neo-Babylonian/Achaemenid rule, and some entrepreneurs had direct access to crown functionaries. Perhaps anticipating long-term stability and contractual enforcement, others also began to take the kinds of actions that required a written witness: long-term investments in infrastructure and agriculture, the planting and management of cash crops meant for urban consumption (especially date palms), long-term and large-scale leasing of land and other capital, arrangements for urban housing, wills, documentation of prebendal rights, and so on. In the end, it is unclear where to draw the line between phenomenon and epi-phenomenon.

The main problem with placing too much correlative confidence in stability is that it is vague; it leaves enough gray area to put blind faith in notions of the coordinated formation of markets. In other words, one might argue that having set the framework of economic stability in Babylonia, the state unleashed an economy dictated by supply, demand, and price within that framework. Bang is clearly critical of this notion, but it is worth investigating its merit for mid-first millennium Babylonia. Jursa establishes without a doubt that local prices are market prices, reflecting supply and demand (Jursa 2005; Jursa 2010, 734ff.); first millennium Babylonia is certainly not in a command or redistributive economy. Moreover, Jursa adamantly argues that the western edge of Babylonia—from the waist of the Tigris and Euphrates down to the Sealand—should be seen as a "fairly" or "comparatively integrated" economy, centered on the Euphrates River. He gives four reasons for this integration (Jursa 2010, 62ff.): that goods and communications flowed easily and cheaply on the Euphrates; that craftsmen and craft goods moved around the Euphrates corridor (that, in effect, cities were not just centers of consumption, but also centers of production); that temple administrators saw the Euphrates corridor as their economic horizon, from which even bulky agricultural goods could be shipped to them; and that transport costs were dealt with as a routine matter. There is also no doubt that people in one market of Babylonia were aware of higher and lower prices for goods in other ones, and Jursa makes it abundantly clear that the cash economies of the Ebabbar and Eanna temples precluded only local consumption; they had to be interconnected to the wider Babylonian world to fulfill their ritual responsibilities.

As integrated as Babylonia may have been, the problem is that these criteria fail to address price stability, which is a key concept of market integration (Bang 2006, 69ff.). This is why Jursa stresses that the western corridor was "comparatively integrated," but for now (Jursa 2010, 793) we simply do not know if the corridor was integrated enough that high prices at, say, the southern end of the corridor affected the plans of businessmen at the north end to bring the market back to a Euphrates-wide equilibrium. While monetary inflation after 550BCE was Babylonia-wide (Jursa 2010, 734ff), perhaps unsurprisingly (cf. Bang 2006, 58ff.) references to markets in letters tend to mention their failure: either bereft or too full of commodities.

Another way to gauge institutional power in Babylonia is to explore the role of the state in denying access to the documented economy. For this, we can turn to the end of archives—the process by which various economic players in Babylonia finished (at least one phase of) their business dealings. Generally speaking, we often do not know why archives came to an end. There are no obvious instances of an archive-holder's enterprises collapsing as a result of bad business decisions. This may be partly due to the nature of our information, in that we might only have archives of people who invested wisely; I suspect that we simply do not know enough to recognize bad investment decisions in the documentation. There are, though, two instances where major archives close for somewhat understandable reasons. We can use those instances to contemplate the role of institutions in making or breaking various economic players.

As had long been noted with curiosity, many archives of cuneiform business tablets, especially from northern Babylonia, end in the second year of Xerxes' reign (484 BCE). Early on, scholars attempted to date the end of those archives to a series of revolts against Xerxes mentioned by Greek historians (Briant 2002, 544ff.); later the historicity of those revolts were called into question (Kuhrt and Sherwin-White 1987). However, in an influential article, Waerzeggers revived the debate and argued that, in fact, one can date the revolts conclusively to the summer of Xerxes's second year, and that a series of business archives come to an end at almost exactly the time of the revolts. She emphasizes the widespread nature of the end of these archives in northern Babylonia (Waerzeggers 2003/4, 157). Indeed, some of the archives are of business families that kept records over multiple generations—for example, the famous Egibi and Re'i alpi family archives. The huge archive of the Ebabbar temple of Sippar comes to an end in 484 as well.

There are commonalities, however, apart from the coincidental endings of the archives. The archives are either the administrative records of a temple, the archives of urban elites connected to northern Babylonian temples, or (at least in the case of the Egibis) those of elites connected to governmental administrators (Waerzeggers 2003/4, 158). On the other hand, the archives that continue on past the second year of Xerxes either were in southern Babylonia or belonged to the people she calls *homines novi*; that is, not the traditional, temple-bound aristocrats (the class of people Jursa calls "rentiers"), but businessmen (Jursa's "entrepreneurs") who were connected with the new Persian power through the business of empire. She argues, then, that Xerxes worked to break the power of the "Babylonian elites who played a leading role in the religious and civic ... administration of northern Babylonian cities since pre-Achaemenid times," while promoting the segment of society that was "pro-Persian, and in economic terms [described] as dependent on the Persian nobility in Babylonia for its livelihood" (Waerzeggers 2003/4, 160).

The argument has held up well; it has indeed been sharpened (cf., Kessler 2004; van der Spek 2006, Baker 2008, Jursa 2013, but see also Henkelman 2011). Yet we remain in the dark as to exactly how and why these archives came to an end. On the one hand, the sharp break in Xerxes' second year is dramatic; when associated with the revolts and Xerxes' rumored destruction of Babylonian temples, this break lends itself to ideas of temples being laid to waste, the archives smoldering in the temple ruins. On the other hand, we know these archives ended in a deliberate process of sorting out and purging—that is, scribes did not abandon them as they fled their desks with temples aflame. Instead, we have what we call "dead" archives. The archives as we know them consist of texts that the archive holders deliberately purged and set aside, presumably because the transactions thereupon no longer held relevance. They moved title documents and other relevant texts to a "live" archive (van Driel 1998; Jursa 2005, 148f.). Why this sorting out happened is not understood (Waerzeggers 2003/4, 162; Jursa 2004; Jursa 2013), but seems to reflect an orderly transition as political winds began to shift in favor new groups—in this case, groups connected in some way to the new Persian regimes.

Even if this version of the end of archives seems less exciting than the pervious understanding, it still represents a radical break. Xerxes' policy toward northern Babylonian temples "deprived the old aristocracy instantly of income, prestige, and access to power" (Waerzeggers 2003/4, 162). Indeed, with the exception of the Egibis, the holders of these archives belonged to what Jursa calls the "rentier" class of Babylonian society (Jursa 2010, 282ff). Attached to the temples through various offices, and concerned with stability, rentiers had a limited economic horizon. They worked to preserve their paternal estate; they invested in land (rather than contracting), built up (usually priestly) offices in their portfolios, and if they became engaged in trading businesses it was through their agents. In other words, they had portfolios *designed* to survive things like political fallout and turmoil.

One wonders, then, whether we can connect the abandonment of their archives more deeply to the revolts. Two poles frame the debate for why we think people wrote cuneiform business documents (Jursa 2004, 146f.): one pole argues that the documents served a police function, working mainly to keep track of obligations; the other pole argues that people kept accounts in order to have material for prognostication and future planning. Perhaps this end of archives stems from a higher-level police function of the documents—that, in effect, the documents removed from the archives were those that showed both complicity in the revolts and title to property that was to be confiscated and redistributed on account of that complicity.[9] Either way, the end of archives under

---

[9] In parallel, we think that the Eanna archive, which ended early in the reign of Darius, comes to us as the result of the temple dealing notorious thief and troublemaker (van

Xerxes seems to show the crown limiting the access of the rentier class to the documented economy.

One finds the social flip side to Xerxes' end of archives in the end of the Murashu firm during the latter half of the fifth century. The Murashus were clearly in the entrepreneurial class of Babylonia, as they leased land from military settlers around the city of Nippur, which they then sublet to tenants of the firm (along with agricultural capital in seed and draft animals). The firm also made loans against pledges of property (Stolper 1985, 27f.). For the Murashus, the succession crisis of Darius II precipitated the end of their tenure in Babylonia. According to Stolper, the timing of the crisis caused many small landholders to turn to the firm for extraordinary mortgages in 423 BCE in order to obtain cash to equip themselves in the struggle. The result was a large number of mortgages in the firm's archives dating to around that year. The Murashus survived the crisis, but Stolper speculates that the firm's position between the crown and its soldiers attracted negative attention; hence the crown withdrew its patronage, which spelled the end of the firm (Stolper 1985, 155f.). Even if one sympathizes with van Driel's alternative inter-pretation, that the reason we have so many mortgage texts around 423 BCE stems from an imperial forgiveness of debts (van Driel 1989; Jursa 2004), the point remains the same: the Murashus were a firm of traders, instrumental to the local economy, who were pushed out by decisions and actions of the crown.

In other words, the end of archives shows us that the crown had enough control over the documented economy to spell the end of major players, in all walks of Babylonian economic life. While this may be self-evident—indeed, it is a basic act of political control—it also moves us beyond the notion that the crown simply provided stability to an economic environment that then operated and developed organically. As I see them, the actions taken in Xerxes' second year were quite *destabilizing*, as he removed people with generations of handed-down experience and institutional memory from positions of control; much the same can be said for the end of the Murashu firm. If we are hunting for the limits of the "optimality band," I think that removing major players from the economy is an explicit example of a government being "too grasping."

Driel 1998, 67f.); see as well some of the speculations in Stolper and Jones (2008) on the formation of the Persepolis Fortification archive during the reign of Darius.

Returning to fill out van Driel's argument, we run the risk of either resting too comfortably in vagueness or making unsubstantiated claims. There is no doubt that the Neo-Babylonian and Achaemenid empires brought stability to Babylonia, thus heightening economic activity. They also brought political control, and the rise in documentation may partially reflect the fact that there was now a powerful authority, with regional sympathies, encouraging the use of cuneiform records and enforcing the agreements written therein (or, indeed, using them to prove cases against conspirators). Moreover, it is also evident that some of that new economic activity directly stemmed from royal business; a substantial part of economic activity was related to the activities of the temples, but how that activity was born through political stability still needs elucidation. To push this further, it also seems certain that participation in the documented economy required good political standing, which was true for the two broad economic classes (rentier and entrepreneur). The wrong political decision could spell the end of generations of familial investment and inherited expertise.

Frankly, though, the purview of the documentation makes it difficult to assemble a strong case for institutional control over the Babylonian economy in the sense that Bang intends. As tantalizing as this theory may seem, we do not understand the beginning of archives, and it is possible that a good deal of our documentation just stems from what happens to be a document-prolific time, regardless of political stability. Moreover, we do not know enough to explain why the years leading up to the second year of Xerxes were so prolific while the level of later documentation drops off. Indeed, stability alone cannot account for the pre-Xerxes proliferation; the longest-serving Achaemenid kings follow Xerxes, and Babylonia itself was relatively stable between the reign of Darius I and the Wars of the Diadochi.

We can locate certain institutional control in one crucial area. Generally speaking, we know very little about Babylonian exports; what we can say with confidence is that there is very little native to Mesopotamia that lent itself to international trade. Most authorities accept the notion that resource-poor Babylonia used wool and textiles as its main export products, with other native produce too bulky to justify long-distance transport costs. This makes wool interesting in itself, but it carries further ramifications for the use of silver in Babylonia, which Jursa has recently taken up afresh. We know neither the provenance of

Babylonian silver nor the method by which it made its way to Babylonia (van Driel 2002, 328); for at least some of the silver, most assume some version of the Old Assyrian model, in which Mesopotamian textiles and (foreign) tin were traded for Anatolian silver, was in operation in first millennium Babylonia, although we have no evidence for it.

Very little is known about secular Babylonian textile work, although we know quite a bit about the garments of the gods (Beaulieu 2003; Zawadzki 2006). However, we do have good evidence for large-scale raw wool production at the Eanna temple of Uruk. Jursa and Kleber's work on the Eanna wool operations reveal that the temple produced vastly more wool than it needed to satisfy its own demands. It appears the temple used this surplus wool as its main cash crop for funding other endeavors, such as paying workers engaged in state projects in Babylon, and buying sesame oil and grain. Moreover, their work demonstrates that large sums of wool changed hands between the temple and either the royal administration of Babylon or the Sealand government to the south of Uruk (Kleber 2008, 237ff.; Kleber in Jursa 2010, 595ff.).

The temple clearly had much surplus wool at its disposal; the issue rests in trying to quantify it. Unpublished scribal worksheets, unknown to (or not used by) Jursa and Kleber, give us the upper limit of the annual wool collected by the Eanna.[10] These texts record individual herd inspections at the shearing, but they add the numbers from those inspections to running totals of all the adult sheep, male lambs, and sheared wool of the season. By examining the scribal worksheets that date to the latest part of the shearing season, we gain a fairly clear estimate of the Eanna's total wool collections for a year. The latest scribal worksheets give the following totals of wool:

Text	Date (year/day/month)	Weight (talents/mina)	Weight
NCBT 318	Nebuchadnessar: 03 / 03 / III	856 talents 7 mina	28 tons
NCBT 339	Nabopolassar 20 / 04 / III	492 talents 20 mina	16 tons
NBC 4944	[Royal name broken] 10 / 02 / IV	1, 219 talents	40 tons
NBC 4818	[Royal name broken]	1,266 talents	42 tons

---

[10] See Kozuh 2014, 46ff.

	15 / 06 / IV		
NCBT 319	[Nabopolassar] 13 / 09 / IV	992 talents 15 mina	33 tons

As is expected, the temple collected a varying amount of wool each year. Since the fourth month was the end of the shearing season, we can assume that 1,300 talents (c. 43 tons) was about the most the temple could expect to collect. Years of low collection probably came in at a total of 1,100 talents (36 tons). This gives us an average collection of 1,200 talents (c. 40 tons) of wool per year at the Eanna. This is about 1/2 to 1/3 of the amount assumed by Kleber (Kleber in Jursa 2010, 595).

Kleber estimates that the temple needed no more that 150 talents per year to satisfy internal demands (Kleber in Jursa 2010, 596). I am unaware of the derivation of this number, but I see no reason to argue with it. That is a bit over 12% of the temple's average intake. If we begin with an average collection of 1,200 talents and then subtract 150 for the Eanna's internal use, that leaves us with about 1,050 talents (c. 35 tons) for the Eanna Temple to put on market — 88% of its total intake. This is a remarkable sum, but it is important to contrast it with large deliveries of wool to outside sources:

text	delivery, in minas of wool (estimated in parentheses)[11]	% of the Eanna's surplus wool	estimated sheep to produce that wool	destination
NBC 4851	(7,760)	12%	6,467	Palace
JCS 54, 117	(12,724)	20%	10,603	Sealand(?)
JCS 54, 117	(28,800)	46%	24,000	Sealand(?)
JCS 54, 117	(14,400)	23%	12,000	Sealand(?)
BIN 1 133	(23,040)	37%	19,200	Palace
NCBT 799 (Kleber 27)	(6,120)	10%	5,100	Palace
JCS 54, 103	(12,000)	19%	10,000	Sealand
YOS 6 87	12,300	20%	10,250	Sealand
PTS 2164	11,400	18%	9,500	Palace

---

[11] Estimates for amounts of wool are calculated from the price; they assume four mina of wool per shekel of silver.

PTS 2121 (Kleber 31)	9,625	15%	8,020	Sealand

There are some difficulties with these numbers; it is not clear, for example, if some of them represent one time orders or totals for the year, and it is unclear to me whether we should treat the palace and Sealand as a "royal institution" or as two separate institutions. Regardless, we cannot escape the notion that wool's production was run by large institutions that traded in bulk between each other at nearly industrial levels. Kleber makes much the same point with different metrics (Kleber in Jursa 2010, 606f.), and convincingly argues that the institutional trade dwarfs the retail and commercial trade in wool. Moreover, she is able to locate textile production in the palace (Kleber 2008, 246ff.).

Above, we struggled to find ways to conceptualize the function of institutions in the Babylonian economy. The evidence makes it difficult to take the discussion in any direction beyond van Driel's notions of royal stability and protection. However, when it comes to the one product that all authorities agree was raw material for the main Babylonian export, we find its production dominated by temple and state, trading directly with each other in huge amounts. The one peek behind the export curtain looks much like Assyria, with an active state in control of long distance trade. There is too much unknown to take this much further, but if indeed trade with textiles brought silver into Babylonia and that silver was circulated by the state through payments to soldiers— what Geoffrey Ingham calls the "military-coinage complex" (Ingham 2004, 99)—we will have to rethink van Driel's notion that the state propped up temples. We may have it reversed.

CONCLUSION

The observations of this paper are quite general, yet I think they show that NIE has potential to provide an analytical framework for the Near Eastern economy of the first millennium BCE. By highlighting the role of institutions and downplaying the economy of ecological need, NIE analysis speaks directly to our most abundant sources. Indeed, the idea that we can expect institutions both to force markets together and at the same time stall or thwart economic growth, all in the interest of the political elite, is where NIE should prove most fruitful.

For Assyria, I think a village repopulated with deportees is probably the best lens through which to contemplate traders and trading *koine* under the Assyrian empire. The inhabitants came from once-rebellious parts of the empire, and, ripped from the networks of sustenance and trade that had sustained their ancestors for innumerable generations, were resettled far from home. They remained economic players in the new empire; most notably they were conscripted into the army, serving both in combat positions and as quartermasters and suppliers in Assyrian camps. Many were put to work on imperial building projects, and others resettled in border or desolate towns to jump-start local agriculture. Yet the village was an artificial construction, often placed at a particular nodal point in the empire to solve or prevent a problem on the frontier or in the heartland.

Wherever one might stand on the continuum between Diakonoff's predator commerce and Graslin-Thomé's protection-as-trade-good, it seems uncontroversial at this point to state that the "anything but hidden" hand of the Assyrians forced far-flung markets together in idiosyncratic and procrustean ways, markets that most likely would never have linked up organically in the absence of imperial rule and large-scale deportations. Yet even if one assumes that streams of independent traders, nearly invisible to the written record, continued to trade under the Assyrians in a way that was economically robust enough to influence the Mesopotamian economy, or indeed to cause the downfall of the Assyrian empire (Gibson 1991; Radner 2004, 162f.), they were doing so on trade routes that the Assyrians reformulated and re-regulated. Traders stopped in trading towns set up by Assyria to monitor and direct commerce, traders came across villages full of people whose ancestors lived in distant parts of the empire, and, in addition to dealing with imperial tolls, traders were certainly under tremendous pressure to move their goods to Assyria at low prices. In a sense, Assyria's *Handelspolitik* pours forth textbook examples of tangible and overt forms of institutional power tying supply and demand together, in ways that, I think, we are just beginning to understand.

The NIE case for mid-first millennium Babylonia is more difficult to make. Compared to the Assyrian empire, Babylonia is not only a smaller geographical area (centered on an easily navigable river) but most of our documentation concerns the local economy. There is no doubt that cuneiform evidence for trader activity parallels the rise of politically-powerful Babylon, but the correlation between those two phenomena is not as obvious as it might seem. We rest on the crutch of assuming that political stability brought increased economic activity, but that same activity carried over unscathed through unstable political times (and, indeed, evidence for trader activity ebbs right before the most stable period of Achaemenid history). Furthermore, good evidence for the institutional role in the economy shows that, by putting major economic players out of business, the crown made destabilizing economic decisions for (it appears) political reasons. Even our evidence for the wool and textile trade is no better than a look through a keyhole; we can definitely connect major transactions in wool between the Eanna temple and the palace, but almost every step after that has to be implied.

Indeed, as attractive as NIE may be, we need to be cautious of the limits. Contrary to expectations, it may be the case that Babylonia was integrated enough to have price stability for most of the 6th century; it is also difficult to put aside the strong historiographic impulse that the Assyrians worked to manipulate trade routes that carried enough private traders to merit royal attention. Theory should always bow to evidence. At the same time, the onus rests on us to determine whether contrary evidence results from an aberrant situation or indeed calls the basic tenets of the theory into question.

IV

HELLENISTIC TRADE(RS)
J.G. Manning[1]
Yale University

...one of the excitements and disadvantages of ancient
history is that even fundamental points are disagreed.
Hopkins 1983, xxi.

PARAMETERS—SEEKING THE "HELLENISTIC" IN HELLENISTIC TRADE(RS)

In his recent study of world economic history *The Contours of the world economy, 1-2030 AD*, Angus Maddison began his account with the Roman Empire. The Hellenistic period on its own (the Roman conquest of the Mediterranean is treated briefly by Maddison (2007, 18-28)) received one third of a page (2007, 12).[2] The reasons for beginning with the Roman economy are clear: the Roman Empire at its height in the first two centuries CE was the largest and wealthiest empire of the pre-modern world, more data can be quantified, and more information is readily available in secondary analyses.[3] When the overarching narrative is less clear, when the processes of new state formation are lost in the mists of time, when the most important city of the period (Alexandria) is nearly entirely absent from the historical record, and with such great diversity in state size and organization, Hellenistic trade can be dismissed as a kind of "little tradition" compared to the "great tradition"

---

[1] I am grateful to Alain Bresson, Emanuel Mayer, and to the editor of this volume for their thoughtful comments and suggestions on earlier versions of this chapter. I am also grateful to my Yale colleagues Tim Guinnane, Naomi Lamoreaux, and Francesca Trivellato for discussions on trade in general.
[2] The Hellenistic world gets a bit more press, one page, in Smith's survey (2009) of pre-modern trade, and a chapter in Abulafia, specifically on Alexandria, (2011, Chapter 6), to name just two recent treatments in English. Abulafia, regrettably, misses out on all of the recent archaeological work at Alexandria.
[3] On quantifying the Roman economy, see Bowman and Wilson (2009), particularly Part IV.

of Roman trade, to borrow the famous concept from Robert Redfield.[4] For several reasons, a focus on Rome does capture the fact that Rome in the first two centuries CE was the largest and wealthiest state of the entire pre-modern world. But this teleology overwrites Hellenistic history with often little regard for how trade opened up the eastern Mediterranean ca. 400 BCE to ca. 200 BCE, the core period of Hellenistic history, and how this fits into the increasing political and military dominance of Rome from the end of the third century BCE.

"Hellenistic" is a term that all too frequently merely signals a pastiche, a loose conglomeration of ancient Greek and ancient Near Eastern practices and institutions, rather than anything distinctive. But this undervalues the impact of the formation of new state frameworks in ancient areas such as Egypt or Mesopotamia, the variety of Hellenistic states, and the inter-state competitiveness, that make the period distinctive. In this context, the term "Hellenistic" does not sufficiently describe what is going on in the Mediterranean basin and western Asia during the last four centuries BCE, a period in which the Greek world was linked in many ways to the Achaemenid, with Egypt remaining a vital and an important engine by and through which trade moved.

The social, political and economic history of Greek trade in the Mediterranean, especially in the last four centuries BCE, covers a much larger territory, both in terms of geography and in terms of economic institutions, and extends far beyond the traditional boundaries of classical Greek history. A better description of "Hellenistic" would center on the interaction of Greek and non-Greek populations, and the movement of people that produced institutional change and increased the intensity of exchange on all levels of the societies involved beginning in the 8th century.[5] There are, in fact, two main aspects that shaped Hellenistic institutions of trade; the legacy of Ancient Near Eastern trade, and the growing connectedness of the Mediterranean to western Asia beginning in the 4th century BCE. Consider, for example, the centuries long contact between Naukratis in Egypt and the Greek world.

The study of trade and traders is connected to almost every other aspect of Hellenistic society: the movement of soldiers and other people (individually or in groups), war, the new political structures that

---

[4] In an important volume on ancient trade, of the thirteen articles in Garnsey et al. (1983), five are dedicated to Greek trade, seven to Roman trade and only one, Dorothy Thompson's study of Nile grain trade, to the Hellenistic period.
[5] See the chapter on classical Greek trade in this volume.

established sovereignty over both ancient and new territorial space, the overlap of ancient trading patterns with new ones (connections between the Black Sea and Ptolemaic Egypt, for example), money and credit, ethnicity, religious beliefs and their diffusion, artistic and architectural styles, and changes and fluctuations in both supply and demand, just to name a few areas where trade activity involved, and had consequences for, Hellenistic societies.[6] Without attempting to circumscribe "trade" around a particular set of issues or questions, we risk "losing one's way in the infinite," as Heichelheim (1958, 3) once described the problem of analyzing ancient economies. This was simply a more poetic way of saying that economic phenomena were embedded within political, military and ideological structures of ancient societies. Importantly, the period from ca. 400 BCE on was one of *increasing* articulation of separate spheres of human action in economy, politics and religion.[7]

ISSUES, APPROACHES AND METHODS

Keith Hopkins' overview of ancient trade (1983), and the fundamental questions that he asked (1983: xxi) about trade in the "classical world" are equally valid for Hellenistic trade. Although much has been written about classical Greek (especially Athenian) and Roman trade, and while there have been some excellent theoretical treatments—Keith Hopkins' classic "Taxes and trade" studies come to mind—theory has been slow to come, as it has generally, to the ancient economy. There have been promising starts in the use of economic theory, in particular closer and more fine-grained work on institutions, largely stimulated by New Institutional Economics (NIE). Although we would do well to remember the distinctions between modern and pre-modern economies, the use of theory in understanding ancient trade is not intended to explain antiquity but to define institutions more carefully, to understand how they developed over time, and to establish how institutional structures affected performance.

The Hellenistic and Roman Mediterranean, ca. 400 BCE - 200 CE, was a part of a complex set of processes of economic expansion, what Morris (2003) refers to as "Mediterraneanization," and there is little need to make a hard break between the "Hellenistic" and "Roman" in the

---

[6] On the connections between the Black Sea and Egypt, emphasizing especially Egyptian cults and glassmaking, see Archibald (2007) and Reger (2007).

[7] On Roman expansion and trade, for example, see Marasco (1988).

third century BCE. A major center of this expansion was an Egypt that would in this period link North Africa, the Red Sea, the Indian Ocean and the Mediterranean. Hellenistic trade and traders are essential in understanding later developments in the economic history of the Mediterranean, particularly in the realm of risk. The Hellenistic period may well have been a time of higher risk, and therefore of higher transportation costs, compared to the first two centuries CE. Indeed, the highly competitive multi-state ecology, and, a non-integrated "inner sea" (i.e. the Mediterranean) would have tended to cut against another Hellenistic trend, the lowering of transaction costs. But the economic sphere of Hellenistic trade extends well beyond the Mediterranean basin and pushed ancient trade routes of the Near East deep into Central and South Asia, for which there is increasing material evidence (Ray 2003). As studies of "peripheral" areas such as the Red and Black Seas and Indian Ocean regions, for example, have increased in recent years, the overall appearance of Hellenistic trading appears even more complex. Clearly, we must include, however different was its ecology, the Indian Ocean and Red Sea trade in the context of "Hellenistic" economics. And we must credit the Ptolemies, and Greek traders in Egypt, with opening up these markets (Bresson 2005).

A more extensive treatment of the earlier context of Hellenistic trade is provided in other chapters in this volume. Here, it is important to consider the last four centuries in the Mediterranean in the context of earlier Greek trading patterns, including those connected to Phoenician, Egyptian and Achaemenid trade and new institutions such as coinage. The increasing interconnectedness of Mediterranean and Near Eastern trade as well as politics, what Polybius famously termed *symploke*, began not in the Hellenistic and early Roman periods, but much earlier, as Monroe argues in Chapter I of this volume. And the Athenian and Persian imperial frameworks played a vital role in this regard.

The Hellenistic period was a time of joining the Greek to the Achaemenid worlds—both with impressive, ancient trading histories in their own right—and the Indian Ocean to the Mediterranean. This "joining" was in large measure done by people, overwhelmingly soldiers at first, moving through and settling in territory. Much escapes our gaze, and quantifying key data, from shipwrecks, especially cargo volume (Wilson 2011, 213) and the ubiquitous amphorae, remain problematic. War and new state formation, inter-state competition, piracy and the drag of tax demands probably constrained trade. But states did attempt to lower transaction costs and foster trade; inter-city agreements of the Greek world were even more extensive and tax exemptions were often given. Understanding the balance between state-directed trade and private trade, which appears from the evidence to have increased over the course of the Hellenistic period and particularly in the last two centuries BCE, then, is of paramount importance.

The second century BCE, in some ways, marks a shift in the history of ancient Mediterranean trade.[8] The discovery of the Indian Ocean monsoon cycle, the rise of Parthia, and the increasing dominance of Rome in political and military affairs substantially altered and extended trade patterns and networks. The central problem here in analyzing trade is assessing the balance between networks, hierarchies and markets, and between state and private actors. To be sure, trade, the organization of trade, and the social status of traders, are among the most important topics, and therefore among the most discussed and bitterly debated, in the study of ancient economies. Since Hasebroek's study appeared almost a century ago (1928), most scholars have assumed that private traders played a marginal role in trade at best, as non-citizen, illiterate outsiders who relied on loans simply to survive from one transaction to the next. But as Bresson (2003) has demonstrated, this view can no longer be sustained. Private merchants were on the rise since Archaic times, they played a crucial role in supplying Athens in the Hellenistic period, and, importantly, assumed a great deal of risk that could, at times, provide them with considerable fortunes.[9]

HELLENISTIC TRADE AND THEORY

The debate about ancient trade has been framed narrowly by Moses Finley's *Ancient Economy* and framed in such a way as to demonstrate an important contrast to early modern economies.[10] Earlier, Hasebroek drew a strong contrast between medieval Italian and northern European merchants with their Greek predecessors, and found the latter wanting

---

[8] I use the term "shift" purposefully, and follow Irwin and O'Rourke's (2011) definition of shift ("...slow-moving, long-term changes in comparative advantage or shifts in the geopolitical equilibrium..."), in contrast to "shock" (a "sudden jolt" to the equilibrium caused by war, or other political event, or sudden climate impacts such as poor irrigation conditions).

[9] On the relationship between merchants and the state, see also Gabrielsen (2011).

[10] A good, brief summary of the debate can be found in Morley (2007); cf. Monroe in this volume.

(Bresson 2003, 140-41). The conclusion to be drawn here, then, is that no amount of evidence, and no theory, can be used to understand the context of ancient trade and its role in economic "development." No ancient city looked like the late medieval city that gave rise to a merchant class and capitalism, as Weber and Hasebroek concluded.[11] There are, in any case, limits to the use of theory, and the point is not merely to sound "economic" or to prove neo-classical theory right. The point, rather, is to establish more precision in describing the nature of the ancient economy and to improve, if possible, current theory. To actively describe, in other words, not to passively apply, the theory.

One crucial area of social theory that must be examined is that related to the political economy; that is, the relationships between the governance and the economic performance of Hellenistic states. Here the Mediterranean, Near Eastern and Indian Ocean worlds before 200 BCE in certain aspects appear substantially different from the world of a unified Roman Empire ca. 100 CE. The Hellenistic "Republics," Rhodes and Rome, and their private merchants, are often juxtaposed, in order to draw a contrast to the Hellenistic Kingdoms, particularly the Ptolemies and Seleukids and their state-administered trade.[12] The former came to dominate Mediterranean trade in the early third century BCE, and underlying explanations have been readily forthcoming. The data that have been frequently analyzed, the shipwrecks, the lead isotope analysis from Greenland ice cores, and meat consumption, all suggest that we are indeed in a new political framework after 200 BCE.[13]

In order to supply what is missing, however, one needs a deep historical understanding of hundreds of regions, local events and an understanding of both shifts and shocks to trade networks, and an idea of how regions were linked by the political power of the wide variety of states in the Hellenistic political ecology.[14] And that is how the study of Hellenistic trade has generally proceeded in recent years, with an emphasis on local or regional trade, e.g., trade on Delos, or in the eastern desert of Egypt, the role of merchant groups in Rhodes, and so on.

Much has been written about trade from the point of view of the institutional structure of ancient societies, and the extent of political

---

[11] Morley (2007, 7).

[12] On Rhodian governance, see below.

[13] On the data, see for example Jongman (2007).

[14] For a good example, see Oliver's study of Rhamnous (2001). On "shifts" and "shocks," I follow Irwin and O'Rourke's definition cited in n. 8.

control of trade versus the continuing pattern of long distance trade that had been a part of the eastern Mediterranean world for millennia.[15] It is not so much a matter of arguing about the existence of markets as a mode of exchange, but rather how prominent a role markets played, and how new states, and new urban centers such as Alexandria, altered pre-existing patterns. Polanyi's model in which non-market exchange was dominant until the emergence of price-setting markets in the Greek world in the fourth century BCE and profit-motivated merchants in the Hellenistic period, has been compelling, and only serves to reinforce the important processes that opened up trade after 400 BCE. To be sure, geography and social networks have been important aspects in understanding the structure of trade, but all of these—markets, geography, social networks—and the new states that were formed after 323 BCE, are important in considering how exchange patterns might have changed. Consequently, two broad theories have been advanced in recent years.

The first, World System Theory developed by Immanuel Wallerstein, has been applied by some scholars. Caution is surely in order because Wallerstein's work concentrated on the emergence of the modern capitalist system. But in that context Shipley's work discussing the theory is useful in understanding what the new networks of trade and the "distance-related effects" were (Shipley 1993, 274). The important relationship between Egypt and Rhodes comes to mind (below). Hellenistic state formation, new centers of state (military) power, and the control of peripheral areas (e.g., *contra* Shipley 1993, 283, Caria with respect to Egypt) certainly had implications for "core-periphery" extraction of resources over long distances.[16]

The second, wide-ranging theory that goes beyond Neoclassical Economics is New Institutional Economics.[17] A central concern of NIE is transaction costs, and this is beginning to be explored with respect to ancient trade, in terms of the role of states and technical improvements in shipping (Scheidel, discussed below). The value of an institutional approach to trade has been very well illustrated in Sheilagh Ogilvie's recent study of Medieval European guilds (2011) and Jessica Goldberg's study (2012) of 11th century Jewish merchants. In the Hellenistic

---

[15] A literature review of key discussion is handily provided in Horden and Purcell (2000, 612-15).
[16] A good summary can be found in Smith (2009).
[17] A good overview of NIE applied to the ancient Greek economy is given by Bresson (2007).

economies too, as later with Rome, NIE approaches have suggests new understandings of trade, and in particular institutions that promoted it while reducing costs and improving efficiency (e.g., Gabrielsen 2011, esp. 237-38, emphasizing the effect of *ateleia*, tax exemption).

Thus, the questions about ancient trade asked by earlier generations remain to be answered.[18] Indeed, the principal problems in the analysis of Hellenistic trade have come in the evaluation of the evidence of trade, how to strike the balance between private and state-driven exchange, how to connect "trade" to "market," and how to quantify trade (if we can at all)—especially in the realm of the value and the volume of cargoes—the extent of long distance trade and, finally, the shift in trading patterns over time.[19] We cannot always distinguish between state-administered trade by the Hellenistic polities through markets, and royal gifts of commodities such as grain (Bringmann 2001), or timber (Antiochus III's gift of timber to Jerusalem: Josephus, *Ant. Jud.* 12.141). New fiscal institutions introduced by the Hellenistic kingdoms, especially new methods of taxation and the use of coinage, must have facilitated both long and shorter distance, inter-state and internal trade, but precisely how we can quantify this remains elusive.

EVIDENCE

Another intractable problem has been and remains centered on the nature of the sources, which in general allow only partial answers to some of these questions. It is a particular annoyance that for the early Hellenistic period, a time in which the new ports at Alexandria, with its enormous lighthouse guiding ships, was literally the economic beacon of the Hellenistic world, our sources are so meager. It is that lumpiness, of course, which makes nearly every aspect of Hellenistic economies difficult to synthesize into anything that we might want to call "Hellenistic trade." But this is not the way forward. At a local level we have many fascinating things that might be suggestive of private trading activity.

The papyri from Egypt, for example, provide much of interest about small, local traders. On a different level, the activities of Apollonios, the finance minister of Ptolemy II, mentioned below, and

---

[18] On the basic problem of connecting pottery, the most basic archaeological remnant of exchange, with trade, see, inter alia Gill (1994).

[19] On quantification, see Bowman and Wilson (2009).

how his own trading activities, involving spices, incense and slaves, among other goods, through his personal network in Syria, has been the exception that proves the rule.[20] I have treated briefly elsewhere the case of Ptolemy, a religious recluse in the Serapeum at Saqqara outside of Memphis, whose financial dealings in textiles are well documented. Ptolemy functioned as a kind of middleman, a "Hellenistic man of affairs" (Thompson 1988, 229), in a textile operation centered in the Serapeum, a temple to the popular Apis cult, but his network was apparently extensive, extending back to his home village in the Herakleopolite nome some 80 km to the south.[21] This kind of local trading, taking advantage of local networks, small scale, short-distance selling at temples and between neighboring towns and villages, or during festivals, had been a feature of Mediterranean life everywhere from time immemorial. It was no doubt the main form of trading, and small-scale merchants and segmented trade, with consequently higher transaction costs, were no doubt quite typical of the period, if not always well documented.[22] Both Apollonios and Ptolemy, it is worth remembering, were rather closer to the 11th century Jewish merchants of the Geniza records, than to the majority of the farmers along the Nile, and comprised a small minority of those who profited from the institutional structures of Hellenistic society.[23]

None of these features of Hellenistic trade are likely to be known in any kind of detail and in any case they do not appear to be anything especially new. Other kinds of sources, e.g., inscriptions from Rhodes, might open for us a window onto long-distance trade. But to come up with a global picture that integrates long and short distance patterns of exchange, and that strikes a balance between the role of the state and the agency of individual actors, for any one period of Hellenistic history remains elusive.[24]

---

[20] Apollonios' activities are well summarized by Orrieux (1983) in a section notably titled: "Un Commerce sans Commerçants." Cf. the brief discussion below on *P. Cair. Zen.* 59012.

[21] Manning 2011.

[22] *P. Tebt.* 3.2 890 (second century BCE) perhaps gives a flavor of the small scale, local, private lending practices of a bank in the Herakleopolite nome.

[23] On the Geniza merchants, see Goldberg (2012).

[24] See Gabrielsen (2011), who emphasizes the complex and intimate relationship between states and private actors with respect to the so-called monopolies.

SHARED FRAMEWORKS — MERCHANTS AND TRADERS

If trade itself is well documented but problematic, the organization of trade and the role of traders and merchants is even more so. And yet, understanding how trade was organized is without question a key to understanding ancient economies, particularly with respect to the differential role of market exchange over time. For the Hellenistic period, and for the "ancient economy" as a whole, Finley went further, arguing that no ancient society could be characterized as having "an enormous conglomeration of interdependent markets" (1999, 22). Herodotus 1.152-153, Finley was quick to point out, described market exchange and its problems in the context of the Persian Empire. But there were changes in institutions as well as continuities. Clearly there was an expansion of trading activity in the fourth century BCE, and a concomitant rise in piracy. Italian traders ("Tyrrhenians") mentioned frequently in our sources came to dominate trade networks with respect to Rhodes and elsewhere.[25] But Hellenistic merchants and traders moved within an ancient framework of well-established ports and harbors and within pre-existing social networks. John Ma (2003) has emphasized what we might call Greek trade diasporas, which was certainly *one* constituent (and important) part of Hellenistic trade.[26] But there were also new states, and large new cities like Alexandria, as well as ancient patterns of exchange in all parts of the Mediterranean world, that lay underneath the political changes.

HELLENISTIC TRADE AND THEORY:
DEFINING TRADE IN THE ECONOMIC SPHERE

Trade is a word with many meanings in the literature. I follow Harris (2000) in understanding trade as an "exchange of goods in which a desire for profit is the motive of one party or both." In Moses Finley's influential work, no amount of evidence, not even the theorizing of Aristotle or Xenophon, was sufficient to conclude that trade was either an important or a distinct mode of exchange in the "ancient economy" since trade, especially long distance trade, was thought to have played a minor role, and the economic sphere could in no way be separated from

---

[25] De Souza (1999, 50-52). On Roman traders, see Müller and Hasenohr (2002).
[26] Cf. Davies (2001, 39-40); Shipley (1993, 282). On trade diasporas more broadly, see Pomeranz and Topik (2006).

the political and the social.[27] But this misses the important social processes set in motion particularly after the collapse of the Athenian and Persian empires during which economic action was becoming dis-embedded from other "sources of social power," to use Mann's (1986) famous phrase. But Finley's account simply did not treat Hellenistic economies as something distinctive. Thus while a "Roman" economy can be described in certain terms, and compared to classical Greece, a "Hellenistic" economy "in the sense of a continuous market-defined exchange of the whole range of goods and services throughout the eastern Mediterranean" (Davies 1984, 270) cannot, at least in Finley's view, be so described.

Rostovtzeff, in contrast, thought that trade was central to understanding Hellenistic economies, and it is still his general treatment of trade and traders that has been the foundation of most subsequent work. He divided the subject of Hellenistic trade by criteria of distance as well as by mode of transportation.[28] For the former, there was "internal" trade and "foreign" (i.e. inter-state) trade. "Internal" trade meant trade between Hellenistic states, and foreign trade was concerned with trade between Hellenistic and non-Hellenistic states. Both of these were essentially long distance exchange. One could also add internal exchange in the sense of intra-regional trade as well, emphasized effectively by Reger (2011). It was no doubt the case that regional and intra-regional trade outweighed long-distance sea-borne trade in the period. [29]

If the substantive differences between Finley and Rostovtzeff have occasionally been exaggerated (Saller 2005), the role of trade was one area where there was serious disagreement. For Rostzovtzeff, the Hellenistic period was precisely characterized by an increase in trading activity. Sea, land and river were the three basic modes of transportation, the first was the most developed and the most important mode of transport. A more ancient but continuing mode, land and river, continued of course to be important (e.g., trade on the Nile and in the eastern and

---

[27] Cf. his incisive 1970 essay. Needless to say, the primitive/modernist debate, which has now become a debate between "pessimists" and "optimists" is not only stale in my view, it is rancid, and should be discarded entirely. I do not have the space to develop arguments here, but I do so in Manning (forthcoming). Posner (1980) already declared the binary opposition "sterile" some thirty years ago.

[28] Especially as summarized in his great work on Hellenistic economies, Rostovtzeff (1941, 1238-58).

[29] The classic study of regional trade is Reger (1994). See also Reger (2011, 368).

western deserts, along the Near Eastern caravan routes).[30] The silk roads, overland and sea, are usually discussed in the context of Roman trade but were very much a Hellenistic phenomenon that were built out from old Achaemenid routes and extended, gradually, in the wake of Alexander's campaigns to connect the Greek core to the east.

Was this supposed increase the result of the creation of new Hellenistic states, or merely part of an overall trend in slow steady growth in surplus production over the course of the first millennium BCE? (Hopkins 1983, xiv-xvi). Surely it was both, if we understand Hellenistic history within the context of a greater "transformation" of the Mediterranean world. Connectivity between places was improved, driven by exploration, the wider use of coinage and the building of new roads and new ports (state-driven activities), as well as new social networks established by new communities, or "trade diasporas."[31] This expansion in volume, intensity and connectivity was, however, as Rostovtzeff argued, constrained by a prevailing mentality in Hellenistic states of self-sufficiency. Indeed, the planned economy of the Ptolemies was a central point in much of his work on Hellenistic economies although it is no longer a widely used concept. Trade was also constrained by the increasing political power of Rome and its magistrates who began to control Mediterranean trade in the second century BCE. Piracy, limited improvement in the technical aspects of sailing, political instability and internal wars within the Hellenistic states, as well as particular events (e.g. the destruction of Carthage and Corinth, the creation of Delos as a free port) all contributed to the general constraints of Hellenistic trade that would be lifted, gradually and to a certain extent, by the steady imposition of Roman imperial control of the eastern Mediterranean.

For Rostovtzeff and all who have followed him, internal and external trade in the Hellenistic world was dominated by the grain (specifically wheat) trade,[32] where supply and demand was irregular (Rathbone 1983). It certainly was and still is the best documented aspect of long-distance inter-state trade, and in particular the main sources were Egypt, Cyrene, Sicily and the Black Sea region, the main consumers

---

[30] Sidebotham's work on trade through the Red Sea port at Berenike concludes that considerable land-based trading via the eastern desert roads in both directions may lead us to think that Rostovtzeff's emphasis on long distance water routes should be re-evaluated, as it has been for Roman trade. Sidebotham (2011, 213-14).

[31] Exploration in Ptolemaic Egypt is summarized in Préaux (1939, 356-59).

[32] Casson (1954). Erdkamp (2005) for the Roman world.

Greek urban centers (Athens above all, Aegean Asia Minor towns as well).[33] And while the slave trade began to grow in importance, especially during the second century BCE, here too, supply and demand were irregular.[34] Consequently, the organization of trade was, and is still, not very well known. Rostovtzeff emphasized the centralized, state-controlled character of it, and in Ptolemaic Egypt above all other places he found much evidence. Rhodes, on the other hand, offers a view onto Greek polities in the period. Taken together, they offer us a range of evidence to understand the connections between political economies and trade as well as the role of private trading activity.

LOCATION OF TRADE—EGYPT

Egypt had been an important center of trading activity, connecting East Africa and the Red Sea, as well as the East and southwest deserts in the oases, to the Mediterranean and the Near East. Herodotus already hints at the extensive trade routes, no doubt ancient, including those in the oases, crisscrossing Egypt in the fifth century BCE. Cleomenes of Naukratis' cornering of the Egyptian grain market to take advantage of a severe economic shock in Greece continues to get a good deal of press, most of it bad, and his fate seems well earned.[35] The earlier history of trade centered in the Delta has been sketched by Möller (2000) and Pfeiffer (2010), but there is more to do with respect to Greeks in other parts of Egypt in the first millennium BCE.

The documentation of Ptolemaic trade, and how it was taxed, has been well treated by Préaux (1939, 353-71), Rostovtzeff (1941, 226-30) and Fraser (1972, 132-88). Ptolemaic evidence provides a very important lens through which trade and traders in the Hellenistic world can be understood. Grain, papyrus, glass, and spices were among the important commodities moving from Egypt to external ports. Trade entering Egyptian ports was taxed at higher rates than elsewhere in the Hellenistic world—given its location, the Ptolemies took advantage of taxing the transit trade that moved through Egypt. Such taxation is generally understood as Ptolemaic "protectionist" policy associated with the monopoly

---

[33] Black Sea: Moreno (2007a); Tsetskhladze (2008); For Athens' grain supply: Oliver (2007); Cyrene: Bresson (2011), already noting Cyrene's importance to Greek mainland in the 6th century BCE.

[34] Rostovtzeff (1941, 1259). Slave trade from the Black Sea region: Avram (2007).

[35] Ps. Aristot, *Oik*. II.2.31-34 (=1352 a-b); Dem. 56.7. Howe (2012); Baynham (2015).

system and the Ptolemaic trading/currency zone.[36] A well known document from the Zenon archive, for example, preserves a list of goods imported from Syria (some via Greek or Asia Minor ports) by Apollonios at Pelousion and shows that certain products were taxed at very high rates, up to 50% of the value of the cargo, rates much higher than other parts of the Hellenistic world.[37] Standard rates were generally lower. A 10% tax was collected on imports in the Saite period text from Naukratis, and the Ptolemies continued to tax cargoes, at higher rates, *ad valorum*.[38] A parallel is suggested by an important papyrus dated ca. 475 BCE. Therein, extensive information about cargoes loaded onto "Ionian" and Phoenician ships entering and leaving Egypt is documented. The Greek ships were the majority, but Persian fiscal practice shows important differences from the preceding Saite period. The taxes on the ships and the men were collected under Persian rule at the port of Thonis (Heracleion) *ad valorum* just as in later Ptolemaic practice.[39] And while the Ptolemies clearly built upon Persian precedent, the rise of Alexandria, certainly the "greatest trading city of the Mediterranean" (Bowman 2010, 103) in the period, altered trading patterns throughout the eastern Mediterranean.

Internally, the development and extension of the road networks greatly facilitated trade coming from and moving through the Eastern desert. The building of the two new deep water ports at Alexandria itself played a great role in both the increased capacity of shipping moving in and out of Egypt and in security.[40] In terms of scale, compared to the Piraeus at Athens and to Roman ports, the Great Harbor (Portus Magnus)

---

[36] Sijpesteijn (1987, 2).

[37] On customs duties in Egypt in general, see Sijpesteijn (1987).

[38] *P. Cair. Zen.* 59012 (=*SB* III 6779) (May-June 259 BCE) remains an important text for Ptolemaic taxation of imports. See further Préaux (1939, 372-79); Gabrielsen (1997, 181 n. 57); Austin (2006, text 298). Bresson (2012) offers a reassessment of this important text. A new copy of the Naukratis decree has been found at Thonis (Heracleion), on which see Pfeiffer (2010). On Naukratis itself as a trading port, see Bresson (2000); Möller (2001).

[39] The papyrus, *TADAE* C.3.7 was published by Porten and Yardeni (1993); and discussed at length by Briant and Descat (1998). Cf. Briant (2002, 385-87). On the Persian shift to Thonis, see Briant and Descat (1998, 91-92); Pfeiffer (2010, 18-19).

[40] The logistics of the ports at Alexandria, and the relationships between these and the older port at Thonis (Heracleion) have now been brilliantly analyzed by Fabre and Goddio (2010) and Goddio (2011). For Ptolemaic development of eastern desert roads, see most recently Sidebotham (2011, 28-31).

at Alexandria was of average size.[41] The founding of many settlements along the Red Sea coast that supported trade as well as activities such as mining (Mueller 2006), the improved roads and the increased presence of guards, however modest, in the eastern desert, and the erection of milestones along the routes at road stations with cisterns all attest to improved conditions for long distance overland trading.[42] Other ports in the Delta, Pelousion for example, remained important (Bresson 2012). We should be careful not to overestimate the impact of all of this since the provision of internal security, guards on ships and so on, also might suggest problems with brigandage. Whatever the details, much of the early Ptolemaic activity in the desert appears to be state-directed, but nevertheless it seems clear that early Ptolemaic activity improved conditions for trade.

The demand pull of and through Alexandria, a new city of some 300,000 in the middle of the third century BCE, would have been considerable although, as with so much else, impossible to quantify.[43] Urban demand, along with state taxation from the network of tollgates on the Nile, kept prices, to the extent we know them, high in the city. Here again we are at some difficulty to assess the balance between private and state-driven mechanisms. To be sure, supply to places like Alexandria would have been driven by rent and tax demands of the Ptolemaic state, conducted largely through private ship owners (Thompson 1983). But the channels of its distribution, for example, whether by market or by the state, is not well understood. The Ptolemaic state was certainly active in other aspects of long distance trade, as the elephant hunting activities show.

The display of exotica at the procession (*pompê*) in Alexandria in the reign of Ptolemy II celebrating the dynasty (*Ptolemaiea*) also suggests that many other luxury goods were arriving and moving through Egyptian ports to points north.[44] This would come into fuller development once the monsoonal trade winds were discovered, and Egypt would become an important entrepôt for goods from India.[45] We can

---

[41] Goddio, Franck and André Bernand (2004, 153).

[42] For one milestone marker, which could not have been unique, along the Edfu-Barramiya road leading out to Marsa Nakari on the Red Sea, found at Bir 'Iayyan, (*SEG* XLVI 2120, 257 BCE), see Bagnall et al. (1996).

[43] Population estimates are notoriously difficult. I rely here on Scheidel's (2004) estimate.

[44] On the procession, see Thompson (2000) with previous literature cited therein.

[45] Raschke (1978, esp. 656-62) remains a good overview of Ptolemaic Egypt's connection to Indian trade.

begin to build a more informed picture of the historical developments of Ptolemaic trade that led to what would become the enormous volume (and value) of Indian Ocean trade in the early Roman Empire.

Fraser's overview 1972 quite rightly emphasized trade with the western Mediterranean as well. Only traces of this trade have survived, but trade with Sicily and Carthage as well as Cyrenaica, a key part of Ptolemaic territory, may have been considerable. There was trade with Italy as well, presumably one of the reasons Ptolemy II had sent an embassy to Rome, the earliest known Ptolemaic contact with Rome.[46]

It is now clear that trade was an important source of revenue for the Ptolemaic state (Préaux 1939, 353-79). How much revenue was raised by Ptolemaic control of trade remains highly problematic, and of course it is not a surprise that smuggling is documented.[47] Fraser (1972) argued that state taxation and control of long distance trade constrained development. While the degree to which the Ptolemies were able to plan and tightly control the economy has to my mind been overestimated, to some extent this must surely be correct. Yet as in the Greek world, there were institutional changes that allowed for more trade, including a greater degree of protection for shipping. Increased urban demand, and tax incentives, as the declaration of Delos as a free port after 166 BCE reveals, is suggestive of the relationship between trading and state taxation.[48] On Delos and elsewhere, there is a notable expansion in commercial building space. [49] Ptolemaic trading activity, particularly involving the grain trade, was intimately connected to its external possessions. Cyprus, Crete and above all Rhodes were the key regions for Ptolemaic trade—trading grain for, among other things, Rhodian wine. Other areas of the Ptolemaic empire were also important. Kos appears to have been a more important source of imports to Egypt than Rhodes, despite the overwhelming physical evidence for stamped Rhodian amphorae in Alexandria (and elsewhere in Egypt).

LOCATION OF TRADE—RHODES

The island of Rhodes played a dominant role in Mediterranean trade in the Hellenistic period, aided by its political neutrality. Its special

---

[46] On Roman grain imports from Egypt during the Republic, see Casson (1954, 184-87).

[47] E.g. *P. Lond.* 7 1945; *P. Cair. Zen.* 2 59240.

[48] Bresson (2008, 222-24). On the commercial structures of Delos, see Karvonis (2008a).

[49] Karvonis (2008b); Köse (2005).

connection to Egypt formed a major part of the grain trade in the Hellenistic period.[50] The island was closely connected historically with trade to Egypt through Naukratis and the Phoenician coast. Already in the time of Cleomenes in the later fourth century BCE Rhodes functioned as a clearing-house for Egyptian grain exports.[51] Rhodes' excellent location, 325 nautical miles, or 3.5 days' travel from Alexandria, its year-round access, and excellent harbors made it a natural entrepôt for the Ptolemaic grain trade.[52] Rhodes was also in a strong position politically and through its coinage to Ionia, the Cyclades islands as well as to Caria (Berthold 1984, 49). But it was Rhodes' special relationship to Egypt, generally cordial in the period, which formed a powerful trading network that linked the great port of Alexandria through Rhodes to Syria and Caria.[53] Rhodes had a strong navy and functioned as a "clearinghouse" as well as a major banking center. Rhodes certainly gained from its reputation as a fighter of pirates, known as it was as the strongest force against Mediterranean piracy, although the effectiveness of this is debatable.[54]

When Rome declared Delos to be a free port, Rhodian power, and its income from port duties, was reduced, as was its ability to suppress piracy (Polyb., 30.31.10). But its trade connection to places such as Knidos, Kos, and Chios continued, as did its increasing monopoly on trade from Alexandria at the end of second century BCE.[55] This appears to suggest that Rhodian wine trading patterns in particular adjusted to the rise of Delos by focusing on eastern Mediterranean ports in general, and on Egypt in particular.[56] Problems remain about the interpretation of amphorae, caused by the circumstances of finds. For example, many collections of amphorae were not found in a controlled archaeological context, the ratio of stamped/unstamped are difficult to discern, the function of the stamps is debated, and there is no easy way to

---

[50] On Rhodian trade, its navy, and its strong connection to Egypt, see Gabrielsen (1997).

[51] Casson (1954, 171); Gabrielsen (1997, 72-73).

[52] Distance: Gabrielsen (1997, 71-72). On the Winter trade, see e.g. Dem. 56.30; Gabrielsen (forthcoming).

[53] A letter of Demetrius to Zenon, *P. Lond.* 7 1979 (= P. Lond. Inv. 2092) (Zenon archive, from Alexandria, 252 BCE).

[54] De Souza (1999, 48-53); Gabrielsen (2003, 396); Austin (2006, 210, n.1).

[55] On Delos, see Reger (1994).

[56] Rauh (1999, 166); Gabrielsen (1997, 71). Amphorae in Egypt, see Marchand and Marangou (2007); Gates-Foster (2011, 803-07). On Rhodian amphorae at Akoris in Middle Egypt, left out of many accounts, see Kawainishi and Suto (2005).

determine the scale of amphorae trade.[57] But certain trends are visible, nonetheless.

BOUNDARIES. UNDERSTANDING THE "HELLENISTIC" ECONOMIC SPHERE

There is now a good deal more material relating to Hellenistic trade and its physical and social configurations than even twenty years ago. This is due to the intensive archaeological work throughout the Mediterranean basin. But more material has not always led to new understandings of Hellenistic trade. If the rhetoric of Finley's *The Ancient Economy* is but a soft echo now, we must also say that at least some of Rostovtzeff's thundering certainties of progress, and capitalist tendencies, have also been muffled. Moreover, the traditional temporal boundaries of "Hellenistic," i.e. the post-Alexander world, have been broadened considerably. The context of the new Hellenistic states are now set into the context of two important longer term historical trends, namely the earlier expansion of the Greek world, westward into Magna Graecia, and eastward to the Black Sea, the eastern Mediterranean basin and the Persian imperial sphere.

Yet there are indications of growth, even in the periods of political instability in the third century BCE, which was surely not due to Roman naval activity, but primarily to Hellenistic state activity in the eastern Mediterranean.[58] The increased intensity of trade—new harbors is one proxy measure—is well documented both in long distance and in internal or intra-regional trading throughout the Mediterranean. Unlike studies of Roman trade that emphasize sea-borne trade in the Mediterranean, a consideration of Hellenistic trade would emphasize the decentralized nature of much exchange, as seen in the extensive overland routes, many inherited from Achaemenid period traders.[59] The major ancient overland routes would grow into what would become the main overland silk road network. The bulk of long distance trade, in other words, from the point of view of the Ptolemies and Seleukids in particular, was differently configured from Roman trade centered on a politically unified Mediterranean. Both Hellenistic Leviathans built and extended overland routes, dotted with trading centers along the way. At the height of Seleukid political power in the early third century BCE, it

---

[57] Gibbins (2001, 291); Gabrielsen (1997, 64-71).
[58] Cf. Scheidel (2011, 34, n. 65).
[59] E.g., at the Kharga oasis in Egypt. See Marchand (2011).

straddled the major overland road from Antioch through Dura Europos and Seleukia out to central Asia. The early Ptolemies built and extended roads in the Egyptian eastern desert linked to a new port at Berenike in the Red Sea, through which came war elephants, incense, cinnamon and other spices. Sea routes were hardly ignored. Pytheas' adventures in the Atlantic at the very beginning of the period, and Ptolemaic exploration of the Red Sea and east Africa in the early third century BCE are suggestive enough, but raise serious questions about the temporal and physical boundaries of the period.[60]

TIME, SPACE AND INSTITUTIONS

First, how to take account of time? Here we encounter a serious issue, one that is not usually confronted. Should we focus on the movement of Greeks, on trading patterns and on technical improvements, or on political history, i.e. on the new states created out of the Persian Empire in the late fourth century BCE? How should we consider the impact of Alexander the Great's campaigns? Classical scholars beginning with Droysen, following a tradition that extends back to Montesquieu, had a profound influence on later writers, by emphasizing a "great man" model of Alexander's impact as military conqueror and transformer of the Asian economy. In this view, Alexander revolutionized Mediterranean trade by, among other things, opening up the stagnant Near East, in Egypt by founding Alexandria, in Mesopotamia by removing the weirs set up for irrigation, and bringing peace to the Indus river valley.[61] The Hellenistic kings, in particularly the Ptolemies in Egypt and the Seleukids in western Asia, extended Alexander's model. British India was often on the minds of French and British scholars in the early twentieth century, when they constructed this.[62] Briant cites the following passage of Wilcken that is worth considering here:

> The economic revolutions which have been described as brought about by Alexander's conquest of Asia and Egypt, and which confronted the Greek merchant and industrialist in the East, in process of time increasingly

---

[60] On Pytheas, see inter alia Roller (2006).
[61] On the historiography of Alexander and trade, emphasizing to good effect the connection between Droysen and Wilcken's view of Alexander, see Briant (2009). For a re-evaluation of Alexander's historical connections with Alexandria see Howe (2014b).
[62] Briant (2009, 183).

influenced the economic development of Greece itself;
the whole foundation indeed of Greek trade in the
Mediterranean was changed.[63]

The debate about Persian stagnation has been essentially closed by
Briant's work.[64] Neither the Near East nor Egypt was stagnant. It is clear
that focusing on Alexander, or on specific periodization in which to
understand economic change, is seriously flawed.

Confusion, or at least disagreement, on what is meant by the
term Hellenistic (does it describe political, geographic, cultural or
economic boundaries?) has caused certain things to be treated in both the
Hellenistic and the Roman literature on trade. Indian Ocean trade for
example, a phenomenon beginning in the second century BCE, has often
been treated as part of Roman trade (Bang 2009). It is of course properly
both, the vantage point, whether from India, Rome or Egypt, changes the
scholarly emphasis. But it is Ptolemaic Egypt, and the institutional and
infrastructural framework put in place by Ptolemy II and III, that led to
the exploitation of the trade route initially, and supplied the port and
harbor structure. And indeed there is a continuum from the Persian
period, when roads were built, and Greek trade expanded in Egypt.

Not the least of these is whether and how one can isolate things
as distinctively Hellenistic. There are of course sound reasons to be wary
of periodization in economic history, but few, I think, would still support
Finley's (1999, 183) dismissal of the period:

> for the study of the ancient economy it (scil. the term
> "Hellenistic") is seriously misleading because in those
> three hundred years there were two basically distinct
> "Greek" societies in existence. On the one hand, the old
> Greek world, including the "western" Greeks, underwent
> no changes in the economy that require special
> consideration despite all the political and cultural
> changes that undoubtedly did occur. On the other hand,
> in the newly incorporated eastern regions—much of Asia
> Minor, Egypt, Syria, Mesopotamia—the fundamental
> social and economic system was not changed by the

---

[63] Wilcken (1967, 293-94).
[64] See Briant (2009), with literature cited therein.

Macedonian conquerors, or by the Greek migrants who
followed behind them, or by the Romans later on...."[65]

Secondly, and far more important with respect to the role of trade in the
economies of the Mediterranean in general, is the overall character of
what we refer to as the Hellenistic period. It has been the subject of
Manichean analysis that has been the bane of economic studies of
antiquity: primitive or modern, substantive or formal, pessimistic or
optimistic, market or barter, Greek or Near Eastern. The "downbeat
position," of the Hellenistic period, to quote Paul Cartledge (1997, 4 n.
7), prominent in Peter Green's influential treatment of the period, has
emphasized a cultural and economic decline of the Greek world in the
last three centuries BCE, and a distinct lack of success in planting Greek
institutions onto places such as Egypt. This is too facile a view of the
period, in my view, and it emphasizes the wrong things. Greek culture
had a strong and vital impact in the eastern Mediterranean for nearly a
millennium. A simple narrative of decline is also insufficient for
Hellenistic economic history. What most people think of as decline is the
shift in the political economy of the Mediterranean from multiple, highly
competitive polities to a single polity, the Roman Empire.

I concur with those, including Moses Finley, who prefer a broad
time span of economic history that would cover Iron Age Mediterranean
history (ca. from the 8th century BCE through the second century CE)
and the manner in which the Sea was connected to adjoining regions.[66]
Finley was correct is seeking a broad historical view of Mediterranean
economies, but missed much in ignoring Hellenistic history, and Near
Eastern and Egyptian economic institutions. These were important
factors in the historical development of Mediterranean trade and its
expansion. Almost all studies of Hellenistic history emphasize increased
intensity and scale of human activity: larger cities in the Mediterranean
than ever before, the frequency of war, the volume of trade, the size of
public buildings, the size of ships and harbors, the mobility of people and
so on.[67]

---

[65] See Davies (2001, 17-19) for remarks on the basic problems of the term "Hellenistic"
as a distinctive phase of economic history. See also Paul Cartledge's (1997) overview of
the period.
[66] One area in which I fully agree with the approach of Horden and Purcell (2000).
[67] On mobility, see Oliver (2011).

Several recent conference volumes have attempted to delineate some of the most salient features of Hellenistic economies, if it is possible to do so.[68] There were at least two distinct phases: the third century, during which new states were formed, old states, particularly the city states of Greece, adjusted to the new realities, new institutional structures, and new culture, were created, and the second and first centuries when Rome came to play the dominant political and military role in Mediterranean economies. This second phase cannot be understood without the first. Beyond this simplified periodization looms, it must be said, Alexander himself. As elusive as he is in many ways, his campaigns, and perhaps his intentions as well, opened up a world that was, surely, already opening up. Rostovtzeff long ago emphasized not Alexander as a discoverer of some lost world of the Orient. Rather, what Alexander's campaigns did was to realign trading patterns and culture between the Greek and Persian worlds. Contact with India, the building of new cities, the formation of new "Leviathan" states in the eastern Mediterranean, the continuing effects of war, to name just a few features, shaped developments of in the period. Shipley (1993, 280), echoing Rostovtzeff (cf. Davies 1984, 270) suggests that we might look for:

> "global" *distance-related* effects attributable to the existence of a more or less homogenous, partly independent trade system stretching from southern Gaul to Afghanistan, producing—irrespective of any royal policy—a prosperous Greek "core."

Recent scholarship, clearly building on the earlier work of Rostovtzeff, Préaux, Fraser and others, has now well defined the chronological and institutional boundaries of the Hellenistic period. Beginning in the middle of the fourth century, and certainly with the added momentum brought by Alexander's campaigns, what sets out the Hellenistic period is the heterogeneity of institutional structures, the diversity of local traditions and the intensification, integration, and reorganization in socio-economic and legal structures; a new equilibrium established, once the diadochoi wars had been settled, between new state actors, principally felt in the "Leviathan" states of the Seleukids, Ptolemies and Antigonids, and private economic activity. To be sure, the new kings played a major role in state economies including trade. The small "international" elite of

---

[68] Archibald et al. (2001); (2005); (2011).

the Hellenistic world did move in the same cultural circles, distinct from the bulk of populations who continued to live in their more traditional local cultures (Davies 1984), broadly speaking, a good example of Gellner's pre-modern state social structure.[69]

It seems to me, then, that there are two basic ways to think historically about Hellenistic trade. The first is to consider what, if anything, was particular or distinctive about this phase of history. The second is to consider how the last three centuries BCE fit into the *longue durée* of Mediterranean trade. Both approaches, let's call them the medium and the long-term approaches respectively, implicate institutions as the most important aspect in the analysis of ancient trade, and temporal and spatial boundaries as the main problem.

So to the issue of geography. Do we focus on the Mediterranean, as Roman historians of trade do, or do we include western Asia and the Indian Ocean? One of the issues, surely, in Hellenistic trade has been the processes by which Mediterranean trade became integrated into Near Eastern trading patterns, including Egypt. Here the Persian Empire stands as an important nexus in our understanding of both medium and longer-term trading patterns and organization and inter-cultural exchange and its role in institutional change. Furthermore, it was Ptolemaic and Seleukid contact that opened the Indian Ocean trade to the Mediterranean. It seems reasonable, therefore, that Hellenistic trade is a two ocean framework, the Mediterranean *and* the Indian Ocean. To be sure, in the Near East and in Egypt, trading patterns in the Persian period, and indeed before, initially continued largely unchanged by Hellenistic developments. But the new cities, Alexandria and Antioch among the most important, effected demand and the administration of trade significantly. Measuring distance, "long distance" trade, local trade, segmented trade, and so on, is important if possible, since it helps understanding transportation costs, risk and trade volume among other things.

But it is difficult to produce a narrative of Hellenistic trade within the context of broader framework of economic history. That was the genius of Rostovtzeff's treatment but also its main weakness. The documentary evidence by itself is lacunose and tends in any case to be better for the second and first centuries BCE. The current study of Hellenistic trade is a series of highly specialized, often not very well connected sub-disciplines of ancient history: Epigraphy, Papyrology (for

---

[69] Gellner (1983).

Egypt), Numismatics, Amphorae studies, underwater archaeology (ship-wrecks), survey and settlement archaeology, to name just the obvious ones. Much publication of material is ongoing, and new archaeological projects in many regions promise much new information.

TRADE WITHOUT "TRADERS"?

To confront the issue of Hellenistic traders, we must get over two negatives, namely the supposed negative ancient attitude toward traders, and overcome negative evidence. These are difficult hurdles. Pro-fessional merchants and traders, those who made their living from trade, not unlike 9th century CE Carolingian merchants, do not appear in our sources as much as one would like.[70] What survives instead is lumpy, and generally comes from the second and first centuries BCE. Still, Greek sources do distinguish between risk-taking *emporoi* and the less savory profit-motivated traders called *kapeloi*.[71] Traders often seem indeed to lurk behind the scenes disguised as other kinds of persons. What comes to the fore, rather, is trade administered by kings and warlords for their own revenue and prestige. Most were, surely, like their Roman period brethren, small-scale traders of modest means, operating within a small region. Ironically perhaps, pirates and brigands appear in our sources to be more visible than do merchants. At times, as a well-known passage in Diodorus suggests, the boundary between merchants and opportunist "pirates" was a thin line, and the label "pirate" was often used of one's enemies rather than as an objective occupation category.[72]

This is true in Greek and Latin as well as in Near Eastern sources. The negative, judgmental tone of literary attitudes toward mer-chants, and toward trading in general are well known from classical sources, and it no doubt added to their seeming invisibility.[73] This dismissive stance—"don't trust a merchant, they will steal you blind"—was also very common in Hellenistic Demotic Egyptian literary

---

[70] McCormick (2001, 614): "Traders are among the least documented travelers that we have encountered."

[71] Bresson (2003). I thank Alain Bresson for the reference.

[72] E.g. "Traders and merchants" attached to Demetrius' army besieging Rhodes in 305/4 BCE: Diod. XX.82.4-83.1, discussed briefly in De Souza (1999, 44-45); Billows (1990, 358). On the subjective use of "pirate" see the remarks by Gabrielsen (2003, 398-404).

[73] Aristot., *Pol.* 1; Morley (2007, 79-89).

sources.[74] It was something "outsiders" engaged in, and the normative attitude toward them is not dissimilar to the view of pirates and brigands, and it says as much about prevailing attitudes of forces other than state regulation as it does about the merchants themselves. Their supposed absence in the historical record also says something telling about the way modern scholars are wont to categorize ancient economic actors. For example, the close association between pirates and the markets of the eastern Mediterranean, has long been noted.

Social networks and associations have been an increasingly important topic in the study of ancient trade.[75] Associations are especially important in the context of understanding historical change in the post-classical Greek polis, but they have a longer history in Athens. They also have a history outside of the structure of the Greek polis or democracy. The growth of private associations, the highest density of evidence appears from the second century BCE onward, and their variety, modeled on the polis, in the Hellenistic period are of particular interest for the study of trade. No formal trading groups as such, or "companies" were recognized, such groups only existed in the short term to undertake particular transactions. While "national" or ethnic trade associations or guilds were well known and considered an important aspect of Hellen-istic trade, the religious and social character of them (they were merely "club houses") was stressed by Rostovtzeff (1941, 1269).

State control of trade and state restriction was briefly mentioned by Rostovtzeff (1941, 1274) as one of the key problems in understanding Hellenistic trade on the macro-economic level. Such state control of trade was not absolute of course, but it does appear to be a characteristic feature.[76] Associations and how they operated show us at a local level an important aspect of private trade. Gabrielsen has argued convincingly that these social formations extended and realigned social structures within cities. In Aristotle's description, associations that had profit in mind (*chrematistikai*) were clearly involved in trade.[77] *Koina* or "national groups" of traders emerged. In Egypt, our documents only begin to

---

[74] Indeed the Egyptian tradition extends back into the New Kingdom. See further, for example, Ryholt (2005, 118-19), commenting on a new Demotic literary text, "The Avaricious Merchant."

[75] Gabrielsen (2007).

[76] Instead of premodern states, or what North, Wallis and Weingast (2009, 38-39), call "natural states."

[77] *Eth. Nic.* 8.9.4-6 (1160a); Gabrielsen (2007, 192).

appear in the later second century BCE, when trading intermediaries begin to be documented.[78] Rhodian *koina* are perhaps the best studied of the private Hellenistic associations, especially for the last two centuries BCE.[79] Certainly religion was "an indispensible framework."[80] But as Gabrielsen well emphasizes, the cult and "friendship" aspects of *koina* were just one aspect of these associations. Military (naval) functions, lending and trade were all intimately bound up in *koina* as well.

Outside of Greek urban areas it is not as easy to see economic transformation caused by the apparent expansion of similar private associations, which had written rules and were also organized around religious cults.[81] The evidence for association members and trade is indirect, but it is not difficult to think that, like their counterparts in Athens, "faith," or at least common membership in an association, fostered trust. From that followed lowered transaction costs, in particular enforcement costs, and, thus, an increase in exchange.[82] One Ptolemaic period Demotic contract, for example, states that the agreement will be enforceable except in certain specified cases. A similar clause occurs in the written rules of association from Egypt, and so it is possible that the contracting party was a member of such an association.[83] One could easily compound the examples of exchange between persons of the same occupation whether they were members of formal associations or not.

That is still often the understanding of ancient associations, but as Ogilvie has recently demonstrated for Medieval guilds, the emphasis on merely the social or religious aspects of private associations can mask economic behavior. Can we see them, as Ogilvie does in the Medieval Europe setting, as self-interested institutions of extraction that also benefitted the state elites? These associations were certainly exclusive clubs, marked off by cult practice, burial rights, as well as clubhouse activities. They also received tax breaks and state protection. Taking Ogilvie's "conflict" approach to institutions, Hellenistic associations, benefitting particular closed groups, may not have produced overall gains

---

[78] It is interesting to note that Préaux (1939, 364), suggested an evolution between the third and second centuries in the organization of the eastern trade, pointing in particular to the emergence, apparently, of "intermédiaires" in the aromatics trade.
[79] Gabrielsen (1997, 123-29); (2001b); (2011).
[80] Gabrielsen (1997, 124).
[81] On Egyptian associations, see de Cenival (1972); Muhs (2001); Monson (2010).
[82] Gabrielsen (2007, 195).
[83] On the text, see Manning (2003).

in trading efficiency. Here we may see a contrast to Roman trading institutions as more "open access," and more efficient.

Reger (2003) stressed the need of most Greek cities for imports and the dependence therefore on merchants and other state agents. Some cities developed their own funds for regular purchases of grain. Merchants, *emporoi*, and *ekdocheis*, "forwarding" or "warehouse agents," are well documented, especially at Delos, but are known from many other places.[84] Public merchants or traders, *sitonai* and *elaionai*—public expenses for oil and grain purchases were organized and facilitated. These must have taken advantage of their own networks to facilitate trade and to obtain the commodities at an advantageous price. Purchase at a good price seemed occasionally to have side benefits for the merchant.[85]

Hellenistic traders and merchants were, to be sure, generally small-scale. Kings of course, were the largest merchants, dominant in the inter-state grain trade, and so too were people like Apollonios, Ptolemy II's famous finance minister.[86] His social network and private trading activity was extensive.[87] It is enough to suggest that he was in fact a merchant albeit not a "professional" or full-time one, since other affairs, too, occupied his days. But he would not have been unique. Nekhtnebef, son of Tefnakhte, a very wealthy Egyptian merchant from Naukratis, who must have died in the early Ptolemaic period, was not shy to claim vast wealth in his biography.[88]

The second century BCE Indian merchant, and his sources of capital, provides a striking example of a private merchant and his

---

[84] A useful review of earlier Greek evidence may be found in Reed (2003).

[85] Rhodian citizenship for example: *SIG*[3] 354.

[86] His activity is documented in the largest archive from the Ptolemaic period, the Zenon archive, from Philadelphia in the northeast Fayyum where one of his large estates was located.

[87] *P. Ryl.* 4 554 (= *SB* V 7637, Philadelphia, 258 BCE) mentions, in a list of shipped goods, Abdemoun of Sidon, a merchant at Rhodes and a close associate ("his brother") of Apollonios: Gabrielsen (1997, 74).

[88] On the text, see Jansen-Winkeln (1997). Interestingly, and tellingly perhaps, the word used in the text for "merchant" (*mkr*) is a Semitic loan word. The dating is slightly tenuous, and is based on the fact that the name of the merchant, Nekhtnebef, i.e. "Nectanebo," would have been a popular personal name bestowed upon a male child in and around the reign of Nectanebo II (360-343 BCE). Jansen-Winkeln (1997, 115), concludes that the stela should probably be dated to the late Dynasty 30 therefore and not the Ptolemaic period. I personally do not see any reason, in contrast, to think that the text cannot be situated equally well in the early Ptolemaic period.

networks outside of the Mediterranean.[89] His quite remarkable funerary stela found at Kandahar, written as an acrostic poem, tells us, among other things, that he had "accumulated a vast fortune" as a merchant, the result of years of adventure:

> having received money from others to "invest," I left my country determined not to return there before having raised well high a heap of riches.

So goes his poetic monument. He had benefited from his well-connected family, from the power of the Mauryan and Greco-Indian empires and the intense trade networks that transected central Asia.[90] Such a man, who left us this superb Greek grave stela, written in highly refined Greek, may have benefitted both from Mediterranean trade as well as trade in central Asia and India itself. We will have to guess exactly how extensive his network was; it is not easy to locate the man precisely in either his home or in trading networks. But it is difficult to resist the temptation to link him to other great Hellenistic men who functioned in many spheres including the economic. Entrepreneurs like Apollonios from Egypt and Sophytos, then, stand as two rich examples, one for the middle third century BCE eastern Mediterranean, the other for second century BCE central Asia, of private traders and their networks that formed the basis of later developments. Many others, Protogenes of Olbia for example, could be listed.[91] These are only two examples, and they don't allow us to assess the role of private trader in the Hellenistic world, but these men would not have been alone.

Rhodian merchants, being very well documented, were, of course, an exception. By the last third of the fourth century BCE Rhodes was becoming a major center for merchants. If seaborne trade was of the greatest importance because of its lower relative costs, then we must consider Rhodes to be of the greatest importance in Hellenistic trade and a Republican precursor to Rome.[92] Inter-city agreements for privileged trading status with respect to duties (*ateleia*) of merchants of many ethnicities based in Rhodes were a feature of Mediterranean trade of the

---

[89] Bernard, Pinault, and Rougemont (2004); Rougemont (2005). I am grateful to my colleague Andrew Johnston for signaling to me this fascinating text.

[90] Surveys in: Thapar (2002, 174-279); Avari (2007, 105-54).

[91] *Syll.*[3] 495, *SEG* 49.1041 (= Austin 2006, text 115).

[92] On Rhodian governance and trade, see the overviews by Berthold (1984), Gabrielsen (1997) and Gabrielsen et al. (1999).

third century BCE and an important institutions by which cities attracted traders into their port.[93] For this reason the bulk of the grain trade through Rhodes was in the hands of private merchants.[94]

QUANTITY AND QUALITY

The Hellenistic period, in many spheres, was an age of large things: the first "urban giants" of the Mediterranean, the Alexandrian Lighthouse, the Colossus of Rhodes, big altars, war elephants and so on. It was also the age of large ships.[95] Those ships were both man-o-war attack vessels and merchant ships. One such war ship of Ptolemy IV was described by Plutarch in his *Life of Demetrius* 43:

> Until then nobody had ever seen a ship with fifteen or sixteen banks of oars, although it is true that at a later date Ptolemy Philopator built a vessel of forty banks of oars, which was four hundred and twenty feet long and seventy-two feet high to the top of her stern. She was manned by four hundred sailors who did not row and four thousand at the oars, and apart from these she could carry on her decks and gangways nearly three thousand soldiers. But this was only intended for show: she differed little from a stationary building, and since she was designed for exhibition rather than for use, she could only be moved with great difficulty and danger. But in the case of Demetrius' ships, their beauty did not at all detract from their fighting qualities, nor did the magnificence of their equipment make them any less operational: on the contrary their speed and their performance were even more remarkable than their size. (Trans. Scott-Kilvert 1973).

If the *Syracusia* of Hieron, coming at more than 4,000 tons displacement by some estimates, was exceptional, it indicates in any case what the Hellenistic world was capable of.[96] If that ship is only an impressive example of the capability of Hellenistic naval architecture, the increasing

---

[93] Gabrielsen (1997, 73); Bresson (1994).

[94] Gabrielsen (1997, 80).

[95] Murray (2012).

[96] Athen., *Deip.* 5.206d-209b; Casson (1971, 185-86); Wilson (2011, 39).

size of more standard ships in the fourth century and Hellenistic world is impressive enough even by later standards.[97] The fourth century, with increased inter-state competition, was an important inflection point in Mediterranean history against which the early Hellenistic period as normally conceived must be seen. Merchant ships were larger on average than before the Hellenistic period. Ships around 100 tons would have been common, but large ships, over 130 tons, would not have been unusual.[98] The average size of cargo ships increased in the third century BCE, and once again late in the first century BCE.[99]

To be sure, political developments of the period, above all in the new Leviathan states (the Ptolemaic and Seleukid states), the growth of large cities, a rise in population, the wider use of coinage, were all conducive to increase in demand and therefore of trade volume.[100] Even before the rise of the Hellenistic states in the eastern Mediterranean, very large volumes of grain entered Athens' port at the Pireaus.[101] That was not new. The Athenian population had been dependent on imported grain already by the middle of the fifth century BCE.[102]

In amphorae as in coinage production, relative quantities rather than absolute output is the cautious solution.[103] Nevertheless the circulation of coinage remains an important measurement of trade (Bresson 1993). Some states, notably the Ptolemies, attempted to carve out territorial trading space by requiring a different weight coinage within the territory they controlled. This may have added some costs to inter-state trading. While a variety of coins circulated even after Roman integration of the Mediterranean, the old Attic standard silver tetradrachm was widespread in the "monetary networks" (Von Reden 2010, 65-91) of the Hellenistic world and a key to its "monetary cohesion" (Von Reden 2010, 84).

---

[97] Casson (1971, 97-140).

[98] *IG* XII Suppl. 348 (= Austin (2006, text 126) third century BCE). See Wilson (2011b) on ship size.

[99] Wilson (2011b).

[100] On the Hellenistic state formation and the Leviathans, see Manning (forthcoming).

[101] See Kron, (forthcoming).

[102] Garnsey (1988, 107-19).

[103] Lawall (2005, 189), referring *inter alia* to de Callataÿ (2005).

POTS AND SHIPS

So far, the study of Hellenistic trade has been dominated by shipwreck and ceramic studies due to the nature of the evidence, and this will likely not change soon. Stamped amphorae have been a major component of quantitative analysis of Mediterranean trade for well more than a century. They are, as John Davies wryly comments (2001, 27), both a "dream and a nightmare." Both areas of research have profound impact on the understanding of both the volume and direction of trade and the relative influence of certain regions like Rhodes as an originating and/or an intermediary for Mediterranean trade. Greater sophistication in the study of amphorae, their sizes and circulation, their contents, and the significance of the stamps on them has been increasing since the frequently cited article by Empereur (1982). Furthermore, we now know that amphorae contained a variety of products, not just wine and oil, had different shapes and sizes for specific commodities, and at times were shipped empty.[104] All of these raise the central question of how can we assess the value of cargoes (Lawall 2005, 192), and the flow of commodities. Knowledge of ceramics has been considerably refined in recent years, but there is still some way to go in terms of sequencing, and of understanding the ranges of fabric types and so on.

For shipwrecks, it has been generally conceded that wrecks are correlated to shipping volume, and that the distribution of shipwrecks follows a Bell Curve, rising steadily from ca. 600 BCE to 200 BCE, rapidly increasing after 200 BCE and peaking in the first century BCE, and with only a slight decrease in the first century CE, after which there was a sharp decline beginning in the third century CE.[105]

---

[104] See for examples the study of fish amphorae from the Black Sea region by Opait 2007.
[105] Wilson 2011b. The data used by Wilson derives from Parker's 1992 catalogue of Mediterranean shipwrecks before CE 1500, but new data is added as well. Chart courtesy of Wilson 2011a.

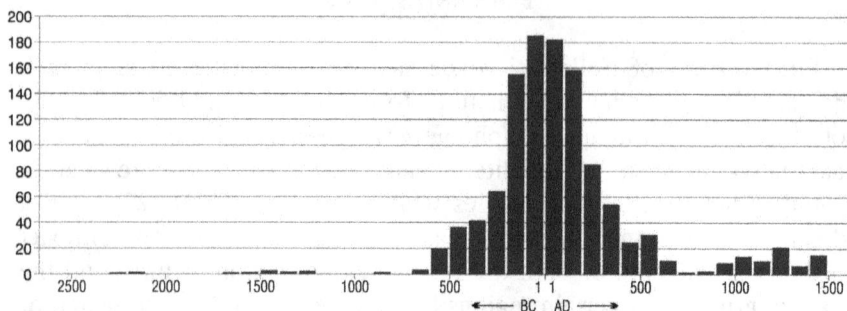

Such a picture that connects shipwreck data as a proxy measure of shipping volume has been severely criticized. As in the study of stamped amphorae, reliable statistical analysis remains a problem in the study of shipwreck data. The increase in shipwrecks in the Hellenistic period has for a long time been taken as a proxy measure for the increase in the volume and the intensity of trade (Gibbins 2001, 288). Yet beneath that broad characterization remain problems. In certain cases, debate persists about how to characterize the trade, especially in the Western Mediterranean, as "Hellenistic" or as "Graeco-Italic" (Gibbins 2001, 274). Problems with assessing exact size of cargoes, and assessment of perishable contents, particularly grain, remain and geographic holes persist in the data, especially for the eastern Mediterranean.[106]

Both shipwrecks and amphora handles present severe problems of quantification and, thus, of interpretation as well. In the case of amphorae, more publication is required, and even then, the contextualization of the stamped amphorae within the broader corpus of unstamped ones would remain a contested field. In the past it has been the stamped ones that have led to an overemphasis (Lawall 2005, 188). The drop in Rhodian amphorae numbers is usually mapped onto the political history of Rhodes, and Polybius' report (30.31.12) of the Rhodian embassy to Rome and its supposed trading decline beginning in 166 BCE after Rome had declared Delos a free port. But significant doubts about Rhodes' decline have been raised.[107] We also need consistency in quantifying sherd counts when estimating the number of vessels at a site. Methods of doing so appear to be inconsistent (Gates-Foster 2011, 804). Various theories have been propounded over the years

---

[106] Morley (2007, 5); Kron (forthcoming) here on the western Mediterranean bias.
[107] Gabrielsen (1997, 68-71).

to explain the purpose of stamping; for example, Lawall (2005, 194-95) argues that it is the product of "efficacious organization of amphora workshops and agricultural production." But more work needs to be done in order to link the managerial control over the local production, in some areas, of jars, and their distribution through an agricultural production network.[108]

WAR, PIRACY, TAXES AND TRADE

Much of the general work in building a model or a framework in which to understand ancient traders in the Mediterranean has been developed by Roman historians. Polybius is a major source, although his views especially toward Roman action against piracy, are often over-stated. The results have been increasingly more refined, but the conclusions drawn from them are generally well known only among Roman historians. In a recent paper, Walter Scheidel has suggested, on the basis of later comparative evidence largely, that the principal driver in the scale of trade volume *in the Mediterranean* (my emphasis) must have been Roman "imperial state formation (2011, 21).[109] Technical improvements were exogenous, and less important than the overall political framework of the Roman Empire and its particular ability to reduce transaction costs, principally seen in the lowering of predatory behavior that had "knock on" effects on the cost of financing. Scheidel's model also suggests that Roman state power would have reduced uncertainties in the collection of tolls. All of this lowered transportation costs, and so free trade grew under Roman monopolistic political power.

This is explicitly an institutional argument, supported by two key ideas. First, from the New Institutional framework developed in North, Thomas and Reed (1973) that suggests overall lowered transactions costs (including the costs of bargaining) was the principal determinant in "scale and productivity of international trade" (Scheidel 2011, 23) and second, that the political economic power of a state, not technological improvement, was the main driver in trade productivity (Menard 1991). In other worlds, changes in the stock of knowledge as well as technical changes in ship building and design, navigation and so on, were endogenous to the large shift in the political framework of the Mediterranean that allowed Rome to reduce predation on shipping,

---

[108] Cf. the remarks of (Stolba 2007) with particular emphasis on the wine trade.
[109] Cf. Bang (2007). Smith (2009, 74), stressed "chronic warfare" after the mid 3rd century BCE that caused a general decline in trade.

which in turn lowered transaction costs as well as the costs of financing.[110] The internal institutional logic of the argument as well as the comparative evidence deployed by Scheidel are irrefutable, and I think that the evidence is fairly clear from the viewpoint of the Mediterranean in the first two centuries CE.[111] But the model, it seems to me, is too stark and is akin, to borrow from John Davies, to viewing history "from the wrong end."[112] Scheidel's "Roman period" model argues for change beginning at the end of the First Punic War in 241 BCE when Roman naval power had become the single dominant naval power of the Mediterranean. But change in trade volume is, as he himself says (2011, 21) only "dimly perceptible." 241 BCE may mark a beginning, but it does not mark a break. In one famous moment of economic shock in Egypt, ca. 238 BCE, Ptolemy III was able to import a large amount of grain "at great expense" to rescue a starving Egypt.[113] But most of the actual evidence of Roman imperial impact comes in the later second century and first centuries BCE, and indeed in the imperial period, i.e. after 30 BCE. It hardly marks a break in trading patterns in the eastern Mediterranean, and it misses much historical development in the fourth and early third centuries.

Much of the institutional framework that Scheidel discusses, the lowering of predation and thus of risk, and the consequent reduction of transaction costs, as well as the increased aggregate demand of urban centers, are observed in third century BCE Hellenistic states. Secondly,

---

[110] Some nuanced disagreement with Scheidel's institutional argument is expressed by Wilson (2011, 231-33), in the same volume, arguing for more weight to technological improvements reducing both cost and risk. See also Bang (2007) for a powerful analytical framework of Roman trade, developed further in Bang (2008), which emphasizes market exchange within a tributary mode of production.

[111] The increased traffic is also well attested in the Red Sea at the port of Berenike and on the overland land routes in the Egyptian Eastern Desert. See Sidebotham (2011, 125-74).

[112] Davies(2001, 18).

[113] *OGIS* 56, 17-18, (the Canopus Decree = Austin (2006, text 271), 238 BCE). The text, although very well known, has not received sufficient comment with respect to the Ptolemaic economy. It is remarkable, to say the least, that such a massive grain exporter in normal times was forced to purchase and import wheat during what must have been a major shock caused (alone?) by poor Nile flooding. It is also remarkable that Ptolemy III claimed to have purchased the grain at great personal expense, which also must indicate something important about the relationships between Alexandria and its external possessions. A decade later, Ptolemy III donated to Rhodes, after its devastating earthquake, 30,000 tons (I million *artabae*) of Egyptian grain, Polyb., 5.88-90, on which see Holleaux (1938, 445-62). On timber, see Meiggs (1982); Davis (2001, 23-24); and for timber from the Black Sea, see Hannestad (2007).

piracy, as measured by slave trade volume fluctuated considerably even into the Roman imperial period, as well as the period before and after. Without question Roman dominance by the second century BCE represented a major shift in political and military power, and more gradually of economic power shifting to the west. But the connection between state power, piracy and predatory behavior is not so straightforward.[114] As Scheidel himself admits (2011, 34, n. 65), the establishment of a "Roman Mediterranean" was in fact a slow, gradual process of change, and did not alter pre-existing trading patterns especially in the eastern Mediterranean. Stamped amphorae evidence suggests that Rhodes reached the peak of its trading power between 200 and 175 BCE.[115]

Roman control of the Mediterranean was a shift, however significant it may have been, in the punctuated history of long distance shipping in the Mediterranean. War could indeed interrupt the normal trade patterns. A famous example comes from Polybius' description of a Rhodian embassy to Rome in the Summer of 169 BCE. Rhodes sought Roman permission to purchase grain from Sicily because its Egyptian supply had been temporarily cut off by Antiochus IV's invasion of Egypt.[116] Warfare and piracy were intimately connected to Hellenistic economies and, even more importantly, to their political economies. Piracy and brigandage were a part of Hellenistic trade and therefore should be considered an endogenous part of a model on Hellenistic trade.[117] Inter-state conflict certainly would have impacted long-distance traders but internal politics, war and the booty created from conflict connected to piracy, and trade networks also took account of pirates and their activity.

It is interesting to note that Strabo, in commenting on the slave market on Delos, used "pirate" and "merchant" for the same people once they had entered the harbor and desired to sell their merchandise.[118] Piracy was simply another weapon in the continuing rivalries between the states, and there are many examples of pirates placing themselves in

---

[114] Gabrielsen (2003, 395), citing Plutarch, *Pomp.* 24.

[115] Gabrielsen (1997, 66).

[116] Polyb., 28.2.17; Casson (1954, 182).

[117] Well-stressed in Gabrielsen (2003). On war and the Hellenistic economy, see Austin (1986).

[118] Gabrielsen (2003, 391).

the service of one Hellenistic king or another.[119] The lack of rivals that Rome enjoyed once it had politically united the Mediterranean made a substantial difference. State protection of trade was a major force behind Rhodes' success and to some extent, at least as an excuse, for Roman expansion into the Hellenistic world during the First Illyrian War in 229 BCE. Political solutions to long-distance trade by treaties—*isopoliteia* treaties and *asylia* decrees—often involved institutions to better protect exchange between Greek cities.[120]

Archaeological survey work in Cilicia, for example, suggests that both the Ptolemies and the Seleukids built up defenses and monitoring stations there.[121] Rhodes spent considerable effort fighting pirates, and even after Rome and Roman merchants had begun to dominate trade in the western Mediterranean, Rhodes still controlled the eastern Mediterranean and its important trade flows, particularly to Alexandria.

What is less clear, and this has implications for other aspects of Hellenistic history as well, is what the impact of Roman state formation and protection was in the expansion of Indian Ocean and Red Sea trade. For Scheidel (2011, 26), these regions are configured as "outer trade," with higher risk but also higher reward. The early Hellenistic period was a time of linking Indian Ocean and Mediterranean traffic for the first time. The Red Sea coast and the western Arabian coast both received a good deal of attention by the Ptolemies and Seleukids. The *Periplus*, of course is well known in the context of Roman trade in the Indian Ocean but it, as with the roads and ports, built upon Hellenistic development. Archaeological work in the Egyptian eastern desert confirms that the volume of trade coming from Red Sea ports as well as state mining activity (gold, porphyry marble) substantially increased with the Roman annexation of Egypt after 30 BCE.[122] Activities in the eastern desert at Mons Claudianus map well onto the shipwreck data on large shipments of porphyry to Rome.

The Kingdom of Hagar, in north-east Arabia, befitted from both Ptolemaic and Seleukid demand.[123] The use of coinage was an important medium between these states and the Hagar kingdom. The aromatic trade

---

[119] Rostovtzeff (1941/1, 196-97); Gabrielsen (2003, 395).
[120] De Souza (1999, 69).
[121] Rauh (2013). For the archaeological survey of this region, see Rauh et al. (2009).
[122] Schörle (2010); Sidebotham (2011).
[123] See briefly Kitchen (2001, 166-70).

was important in both kingdoms, coming from Dhofar and shipped through Sumhuram (mod. Khor Rori), via a series of intermediaries and consequent toll collection points, to Gaza and Indian trade. Bahrain served as an important way station between India and the Mediterranean. If the Muziris papyrus is any guide here, ships leaving southern India must have attracted pirates like bears to honey.[124] But how are we to understand protection in these waters? We know of a Roman fort at the Farasan Islands from the second century CE—did the Roman navy patrol the Indian Ocean, or were merchants responsible for protecting their cargoes?[125]

Scheidel's model should be usefully extended to Hellenistic trade, and it would offer some contrast to Roman imperial history once the Mediterranean had been integrated into a single imperial space. The processes that Scheidel has outlined—state formation, political and economic integration, and the resulting political stability and reduction of war, the lowering of predation and the costs of transactions and of finance— can all be traced in the Hellenistic evidence. War, and local crop failure, certainly affected demand and supply on strategic commodities such as grain. The situation in early Hellenistic Athens as described in the detailed study by Oliver (2007) illustrates the effects of war but also the extensive shipment of grain into Attic ports. Disruption caused by war and competing generals, and problems of distributing grain even to cavalry are clear. Athens and its territory was dependent both on gifts from external benefactors and on the Athenian *sitonai*.[126]

To be sure, there were attempts by states to lower transaction costs. Rhodes and its control of piracy reduced predatory behavior. Tax exemptions were given to certain merchant groups.[127] Such exemptions, however rare they were, are also documented in Egypt.[128] Tolls were generally also low, as in the Roman imperial period, but they were perhaps more unpredictable, while private trade may have been taxed at high rates. We have less data from the Hellenistic period to be certain.

---

[124] On the Muziris text, see the important study by Morelli (2011) with previous literature cited therein.

[125] On the Farasan Island evidence, see Villeneuve (2004); Sidebotham (2011, 188).

[126] See Oliver (2007, 228-59) for an excellent review of the evidence.

[127] Gabrielsen (2011).

[128] In Egypt: *P. Hib.* 2 198 (= Bagnall and Derow (2004, text 122), 242 BCE). Bagnall and Derow (2004, 204), suggest that internal trade was heavily taxed and such exemptions "were few in number." I see no way of being certain one way or the other on the basis of current evidence.

Evidence from shipwrecks suggests a different picture, one of small mixed cargoes, and cargoes that were split up over several ships to reduce risk (Gibbins 2001, 293). This picture of small cargoes would accord with Scheidel's model (2011, 30) that posits an increase in the size of ships and a higher trade volume resulting from lowered transaction costs and increased organizational efficiencies in shipping. The highly problematic shipwreck data forbids certainty on this point.

CONCLUSIONS

Hellenistic trade, or more broadly, exchange in the Mediterranean between ca. 400 BCE and 200 BCE, can and should be analyzed in its own terms. The legacy of Near Eastern trade, the movement and settlement of people, and the increasing interconnectedness of the Mediterranean with western Asia all shaped the period. Polybius' *symploke* was, importantly, an accelerating trend in the Mediterranean from the 8th century onward. The nature and characteristics of Roman trade was a continuation and an extension of Hellenistic trade in the eastern Mediterranean. The Hellenistic period may well have been a time of higher risk, and therefore of higher transportation costs compared to the first two centuries CE, but it was also, compared to later Roman developments, a time of smaller, diverse cargoes. Equally important are the new trends of the period, an expansion of trade volume that came though the new cities in the eastern Mediterranean, facilitated by new roads and new entrepôts built on the Red Sea coast and elsewhere, and the new political structures of the Hellenistic monarchies. The lowered transaction cost environment stressed by Scheidel for Roman trade was the direct result of Hellenistic state building in the Third Century BCE. These features, new urban centers, new or newly extended trade routes, new ports, and the new political relationships established especially by the Hellenistic "Leviathans," e.g., the Ptolemaic-Rhodian network, also shaped the behavior of traders and merchants of the period. And yet, the role of private traders and merchants has often been underestimated. They are best documented in the private associations of Rhodes, but this is probably merely a vestige of the survival of a particular type of document. In Egypt, and in places as far as Afghanistan, the image of the well-to-do merchant was probably just the tip of an iceberg of an underlying beehive of small scale private trading throughout the Mediterranean and western Asia, fostered by the new political frameworks of the period, and by the increased circulation of coinage, among other things.

V

RISKY BUSINESS: TRADERS IN THE ROMAN WORLD[1]
David Hollander
Iowa State University

There has been tremendous growth in the study of the Roman economy since M. I. Finley penned his rather gloomy "Further Thoughts" on the topic in 1984. The sheer amount of material now available is both impressive and intimidating. Generally speaking, the New Institutional Economics approach, which views institutions as the primary determinants of economic performance because of their effect on transaction costs, has come to dominate Roman economic history. This is a positive development, but attempts to answer macroeconomic questions, such as the nature and extent of growth in the Roman economy, sometimes obscure the role of the individual economic actor: much has been published recently on trade and markets, not enough on traders and merchants.[2] This chapter approaches the Roman economy from the perspective of the trader. I begin by asking who traders were, where, with whom, and under what conditions they worked, what they traded, as well as the environmental, social, and technological factors constraining their behavior. Then I turn to two narrower questions. First, to what extent did Roman traders compete with one another? Second, what can Roman discourse about "business ethics" tell us about the market context in which traders operated? Because substantial changes took place in the late antique economy,[3] this chapter focuses on the late Republican and early Imperial periods. In addition to illustrating the world inhabited by the Roman trader, I hope to demonstrate that modern

---

[1] Encyclopedias have considerably facilitated the writing of this chapter, in particular Pliny the Elder's *Natural History* and Wiley-Blackwell's *Encyclopedia of Ancient History* (on which I have been fortunate to work as the economy editor). The section on competition began as a presentation at a conference of the Classical Association of the Canadian West on Competition in the Ancient World in March of 2004, while I first presented the section on "business ethics" at the annual meeting of the Society of Biblical Literature in November of 2011. I would like to thank those who commented on these papers at conferences, the anonymous readers of the manuscript, the many authors of entries for the encyclopedia, as well as Gary Reger and Walter Scheidel for sharing forthcoming work.

[2] But see Holleran (2012), a notable exception to this tendency.

[3] For a discussion of "The Transition to Late Antiquity" see Giardina (2007).

economic approaches *do* help us understand the Roman economy, in part because modern traders continue to grapple with many of the same challenges faced by their ancient colleagues.

MERCHANTS, PRODUCTS, AND THE INFRASTRUCTURE OF ROMAN TRADE

When Braudel sought to understand early modern traders, he could blithely consult their papers.[4] The Roman historian is not so fortunate but still has access to some texts emanating directly from traders and those who worked closely with them. These documents include loan agreements such as those appearing in the *Tabulae Pompeianae Sulpiciorum*,[5] descriptions of routes, harbors, and markets such as, most notably, the *Periplus Maris Erythraei*,[6] and numerous inscriptions such as that of A. Herennuleius Cestus who described himself as a *mercator omnis generis mercium transmarinarum*.[7] Other documents, somewhat further removed from the trader's day-to-day existence, nevertheless provide extremely valuable information. Legal texts like the *Digest* describe the rights and obligations of traders with respect to, for example, shipwrecked merchandise (47.9) and maritime loans (22.2). Pliny the Elder's *Natural History* lists the many goods traded within and beyond the Empire and often gives prices, notes changes in consumer demand, and comments on the behavior of traders, such as how they sometimes adulterated their products. The agricultural writers provide considerable insight into short and medium distance trade. Cato the Elder recommends the best places to buy farm equipment (*Ag.* 22.3) while Varro talks about the importance to a villa of access to transportation in order to bring goods to market (*Rust.* 1.16.2-6). Even Cicero, notoriously hostile to the trader (*Off.* 1.150), gives us some important clues about their working conditions (*Ver.* II 5.157) and influence (*Leg. Man.* 11). Tantalizing references to traders appear throughout Roman literature, though it is true that the passages often leave much to be desired. This is no doubt why we still devote so much attention to the fictional ex-trader Trimalchio.[8]

---

[4] Braudel (1982, 138).
[5] Camodeca (1999).
[6] Casson (1989).
[7] *ILS* 7484 = *CIL* IX 4680.
[8] D'Arms (1981, 97ff.).

Archaeological excavation continues to expand our understanding of the conditions and contexts in which Roman traders operated. Shipwrecks, for example, are an invaluable source since they help us reconstruct trade routes, provide insight into ship design, naval technology, navigation, and storage strategies, as well as indicate some of the products traded over long distances.[9] DNA analysis of amphorae contents from shipwrecks can yield unexpected results.[10] The distribution of wrecks across time and space may reflect changes in the nature and intensity of trade,[11] but it is increasingly clear that shipwrecks do not constitute a straightforward sample of the ships traversing the Roman Mediterranean. Indeed, Bang notes that the "shipping operation of the Alexandrian grain fleet goes virtually undetected in the wreck statistics."[12] Excavations of harbors and port facilities contribute to debates about the likely sizes of ships,[13] as well as the scale of commerce.[14] Remains of markets and warehouses indicate the onshore environment in which traders worked.[15] Even remote sites can yield surprising results. Marzano argues that finds of Italian snails at Mons Claudianus suggest that private traders exported this "luxury food" from Italy to Egypt during the winter.[16] Mosaics, reliefs, and frescoes provide a host of scenes from the daily life of the trader. Perhaps most famously, the mosaics in the Piazzale delle Corporazioni at Ostia depict ships, lighthouses, and cargo. A relief now in the Metropolitan Museum of Art shows a porter delivering amphorae, perhaps to a merchant,[17] while a fresco from the Praedia of Julia Felix, now in the National Archaeological Museum at Naples, depicts traders interacting with customers in a market.[18] Coins also contribute to our picture of Roman traders, although, here too, the evidence must be treated with caution. The geographical distribution of coins may suggest patterns of trade, and

---

[9] See, e.g., Wilson (2009, 219ff.).

[10] E.g., Foley et al. (2009, 294).

[11] Hopkins (1980, 105).

[12] Bang (2007, 15 n. 28).

[13] Houston (1988).

[14] Castagnoli (1980).

[15] E.g., Köse (2005) and Rickman (1971).

[16] Marzano (2011).

[17] Accession number 25.78.63.

[18] Inventory number 9062.

the range of denominations in circulation, while their level of wear may indicate the nature and intensity of market transactions.[19]

In an economy in which the "modal form of economic integration was market exchange,"[20] nearly everyone was, to a certain extent, a trader. While I will concentrate here mainly on professional traders (whom our sources often refer to as *mercatores* and *negotiatores*), i.e., those who earned their living primarily by buying from producers and selling to retailers or consumers, it is important to emphasize that trade happened everywhere, even without the presence of middlemen. Farmers traded produce for coinage and other goods; workers of all kinds exchanged their labor for various forms of money. Even reciprocity involves a kind of trading. Traders were merely specialists. Short-distance trade between farm households or within a small community no doubt involved few such specialists but the longer the distance traveled by goods between producer and consumer or the larger the community in which the goods circulated, the more professional traders are likely to appear.

Mercator and *negotiator* can both mean "trader" but their precise meanings are hard to pin down. Cicero (e.g., *Verr.* 2.2.188, *Planc.* 64) implies that they are distinct groups engaged in different kinds of activities. During the Republic, *negotiatores* appear to have been Italians working in the Roman provinces or client kingdoms and involved in banking, finance, the exploitation of real estate, and perhaps trade while *mercatores* were traders proper or in some cases shopkeepers.[21] Under the Empire, as Rougé argues, the *negotiator* became "un grand commerçant, un marchand en gros."[22] *Mercatores* were likely of lesser wealth and stature. Of an even lower stature were the *caupones* who could be smalltime traders or innkeepers and shopkeepers. While scholars frequently emphasize the need for traders to deal in a variety of goods in order to manage the risks inherent in long-distance commerce, there seem to have been plenty of specialists. The *mercator bovarius* traded cattle while the *mercator suarius* bought and sold pigs.[23] For wine,

---

[19] E.g., Crawford (1977) and Duncan-Jones (1987).
[20] Temin (2001, 181).
[21] Feuvrier-Prévotat (1981). See also Rougé (1966, 275-9), who considers the Republican *negotiator* to generally not be a trader but possibly a financier of commerce.
[22] Rougé (1966, 282).
[23] *Mercatores bovarii: AE* 1902, 85 = *AE* 1903, 50; *CIL* VI 37806 = *ILLRP* 802; *AE* 1991, 682c. A *mercator suarius: CIL* IX 2128.

there were *mercatores vinarii*, for grain, *mercatores frumentarii*, and for olive oil, we find *olearii*.[24] The freedman L. Arlenus Artemidorus was a *mercator sagarius*, dealing in *saga* (mantles),[25] while L. Nerusius Mithres had great success, judging from his lengthy funerary inscription, selling goat skins.[26] The freedman P. Murrius Zetus, a *mercator purpurarius* (dealer in purple dye), apparently did very well for himself prior to his untimely death while traveling in Campania.[27] We find the same kinds of specialization in inscriptions mentioning *negotiatores*. In addition to *negotiatores vinarii*,[28] *frumentarii*,[29] *olearii*,[30] *sagarii*,[31] and *purpurarii*,[32] there were *negotiatores ferrarii* (iron-mongers),[33] *materiarii* (timber dealers),[34] *cretarii* (pottery dealers),[35] *vestiarii* (clothes dealers),[36] *lanarii* (wool dealers),[37] *marmorarii* (marble dealers),[38] *gladiarii* (sword-dealers),[39] *sericarii* (silk dealers),[40] *salarii* (salt fish dealers),[41] *allecarii* (fish sauce dealers),[42] and *margaritarii* (pearl dealers)[43] to mention some of the specialties appearing in inscriptions. The epigraphic evidence reinforces the conclusion that there was an important distinction between a *negotiator* and a *mercator*. A. Herennuleius Cestus described himself as a *mercator omnis generis mercium transmarinarum* but a *negotiator vinarius*.[44] The *mercator sagarius* L. Arlenus Artemidorus shared his

---

[24] *Mercatores vinarii: CIL* X 545 and 6493. *Mercatores frumentarii: CIL* XIV 4234. *Mercatores frumentarii et olearii: CIL* VI 1620.

[25] *CIL* VI 9675 = *ILS* 7577.

[26] *CIL* IX 4796.

[27] *AE* 1972, 74.

[28] *CIL* III 2131, IX 4680, XII 1896, XIII 1954.

[29] *CIL* VI 814, 9668, XIII 1972.

[30] *CIL* III 2936, XIV 4458.

[31] *CIL* V 5925, 5928, 5929, X 1872.

[32] *AE* 1982, 709.

[33] *AE* 1922, 82; *CIL* VI 9666.

[34] *AE* 1960, 29.

[35] *AE* 192, 1374; 1994, 1350.

[36] *CIL* III 5800 and 5816, VI 33889, XIII 4564.

[37] *CIL* VI 9669.

[38] *CIL* VI 33886.

[39] *CIL* XIII 6677.

[40] *CIL* XIV 2793, 2812.

[41] *AE* 1973, 362, 364, and 378; 2003, 1228.

[42] *AE* 2003, 1228; 1973, 365 and 375.

[43] Lettich (2003, 290).

[44] *CIL* IX 4680.

epitaph with L. Arlenus Demetrius, also a *negotiator sagarius*.[45] Some chose to mention multiple areas of expertise such as C. Clodius Euphemus, who was a *negotiator penoris et vinorum* on the Velabrum in Rome,[46] while many inscriptions referring to someone as a *negotiator* or *mercator* make no mention of a specialty. Although Erdkamp claims that the "grain trade was seldom a specialized business,"[47] it is not clear how much confidence we can place in such generalizing claims and, of course, funerary inscriptions represent only a tiny fraction of traders. It is possible that many traders simply neglected to have their specialties listed on their tombs. Given the great variety of goods circulating in and beyond the Empire, it is also likely that many specialists occasionally dabbled in other types of merchandise when the right opportunity arose.

Although traders could become quite wealthy, there is general agreement that the average trader's net worth was quite modest. Friesen's Poverty Scale places most traders and merchants in PS6, designated as "at subsistence level."[48] His model locates many traders in PS5, "stable near subsistence level," but only a few achieved PS4, "moderate surplus resources," or PS3, the municipal elites.[49] Given the capital necessary to pay for merchandise, storage, and transportation, traders are likely to have relied heavily on credit. Ships could be quite expensive and long-distance traders did not necessarily own their own ships nor were the owners and operators of merchant vessels necessarily traders themselves. The *Lex Claudia* of 218 BCE, apparently intended to limit senatorial involvement in commerce, shows that, as early as the third century BCE, senators might own ships (Livy 21.63) but it would be well beneath their dignity to personally engage in commerce. Consequently, trading was not a high status occupation. Cicero calls small-scale trade sordid and is only willing to praise large-scale traders if they abandon the profession for agriculture (*Off.* 1.150). Nevertheless, it seems clear that senators and equestrians financed trade. Plutarch (*Cat. Mai.* 21.5-6) reports that Cato the Elder developed an elaborate scheme to profit safely from loans made to those engaged in maritime commerce.

---

[45] *CIL* VI 9675.

[46] *CIL* VI 9671.

[47] Erdkamp (2005, 106).

[48] Friesen (2004, 341).

[49] See also Longenecker (2010). It should be cautioned that both Friesen and Longenecker are primarily concerned with poverty rather than the economic status of merchants and traders. However, Bang (2010, 95) agrees that traders were typically "men of modest substance." See also: Rauh (2003, 135-6) and Morley (2007, 88).

Other direct evidence for senatorial and equestrian investment is scarce but the elite certainly made use of their slaves, freedmen, and clients to profit from trade.[50]

If short-distance trade might occur without specialist intermediaries between producers and consumers, long-distance trade was considerably more complicated. A trader moving goods from one region to another could require a wide variety of services. He might need the help of financiers or bankers to purchase the goods he intended to sell elsewhere; he might have to hire mule drivers, porters, or other kinds of land transport to get the merchandise to a port, the services of other porters there to transfer the goods onto a river boat, and later others to transfer them again onto a seagoing vessel. The same process might be necessary in reverse to get the merchandise to its final destination, e.g., up a river like the Tiber that was not navigable by large ships. Along the way, the trader might have to deal with *praecones* (auctioneers), *navicularii* (shipowners), *magistri navium* (ship captains), *gubernatores* (pilots), *saburrarii* (people who supplied ballast to ships), *naupegi* (shipwrights or carpenters), operators of tugboats and barges, *urinatores* (divers, if goods were lost due to shipwreck or jettisoned during a storm), *custodes* (guards), *publicani* (toll collectors) and their *scrutatores* (examiners),[51] *interpretes* (translators or negotiators), and magistrates overseeing local markets as well as the personnel of storehouses, inns, taverns, and probably brothels too from time to time.[52] Money was essential if such voyages were to take place, and traders probably tended not to carry much coinage with them,[53] so bankers and credit had to be available. Rathbone and Temin estimate there were at least a thousand banks in Italy in the first century CE although most of them would have been quite small.[54] Bang argues that Cicero (*Verr. II* 5.167) "implies a general need for merchants to have people who could vouch for them in

---

[50] Andreau (1995, 309) suggests that the government and aristocrats supported Roman traders financially while, slightly more cautiously, Rauh (1993, 244-5) notes that, "Roman senators possibly engaged in business through their slaves, freedmen, friends, or relatives." However, Morley (2007, 5) claims there is an "absence of clear evidence for the involvement of any senatorial families in commerce." See also: D'Arms (1977), (1980), and (1981); Gabba (1980).

[51] van Tilburg (2012).

[52] See, e.g., Rauh et al. (2008).

[53] Parker (1992, 30).

[54] Rathbone and Temin (2008, 406-7).

foreign harbours," no doubt in order to secure credit.[55] Verboven draws attention to the *proxenetae* who were available in large cities to help traders facilitate transactions and contracts.[56] Maritime loans, whose interest rates were unregulated, provided a kind of insurance for the trader since the loan need not be paid back in the event the cargo was lost due to shipwreck. However, the terms of such a loan might diminish the trader's autonomy. Scaevola (*Dig.* 45.1.122.1) describes the following hypothetical situation involving a maritime loan for trade. Stichus, a slave of Seius, lends money to Callimachus at Berytus in Syria. The security for the loan, by *pignus* and *hypotheca*, is the cargo purchased in Berytus to be shipped to Brundisium as well as the goods purchased at Brundisium to be shipped back to Berytus. Callimachus was required either to set sail from Brundisium back to Berytus by a particular date or to repay the entire loan at that point as well as the expense involved in transferring that money to Rome. The same passage indicates that the creditor could send a slave to accompany the trader and his merchandise and that this slave might have authorization to amend the terms of the original loan agreement. While traders probably relied on local bankers for cash and credit, the bankers may well have made use of the traders to arrange long-distance transfers of funds (*permutationes*) since banks tended to be local in character, lacking branches in other cities.[57] If traders did carry money, they might have to make use of *nummularii* (moneychangers) to convert foreign coins into locally acceptable specie, gold coins into silver and bronze or vice versa.

To help traders navigate (both literally and figuratively) the expensive, complicated, and frequently dangerous tasks of buying, transporting, and selling goods, there existed physical as well as public and private institutional infrastructure. The physical infrastructure, not necessarily designed and built with traders in mind, included at least a hundred thousand miles of road,[58] bridges, warehouses,[59] marketplaces, ports, and associated structures. Their quantity and quality varied around the Empire. The port facilities at Caesarea Maritima, for example,

---

[55] Bang (2007, 29 n. 68).

[56] Verboven (2008, 226).

[57] Verboven (2002, 138). On *permutationes* see Hollander (2007, 40-44). On the local nature of banks, see Andreau (1999, 43). For financial intermediation in general, see Rathbone and Temin (2008).

[58] Bekker-Nielsen (2012, 5852).

[59] Sometimes *mercatores* stored their goods at home (*Dig.* 33.7.12.43, 33.9.4.2).

included breakwaters, inner and outer basins, quays, warehouses, and a lighthouse while others might simply consist of a sandy beach.[60] Ports could feature *stationes* ("offices") for merchants and shippers, although their precise functions remain unclear.[61] Markets had specialized structures in which to conduct business, such as *basilicae* or *chrematisteria*,[62] and shrines "where the gods witnessed the oaths used to bind contractual agreements."[63] The public institutional infrastructure consisted of Roman and local law, the officials who implemented that law, and the forces who (ideally) protected traders and their property from thieves, bandits, and pirates. The spread of Roman legal institutions undoubtedly facilitated trade but local legal systems persisted under the Empire, no doubt making a trader's rights and responsibilities ambiguous or at least complicated in some regions.[64]

Our sources do not inspire much confidence in the competence or benevolence of Roman officials with respect to merchants and markets. Pythias, the admittedly fictional *aedile* in Apuleius' *Metamorphoses,* is utterly ineffectual when he discovers that a fishmonger has overcharged Lucius for his dinner: he has the fish destroyed and neglects to get even a refund for his friend (*Met.* 1.24-25). Less amusing is the behavior of Verres who, according to Cicero (*Verr.* II 5.146-7), executed Roman merchants in Sicily in order to steal their goods. It is not especially surprising that most of the three hundred Roman merchants and moneylenders in Utica, whom Cato the Younger tried to rally to the Republican cause in 46 BCE, instead plotted to seize the senators based there (Plutarch, *Cat. Min.* 59-61). Some officials must have treated merchants fairly—Cicero (*Planc.* 64) boasts that during his Sicilian quaestorship he was just to the *mercatores* and courteous to the *negotiators*—but, as we shall see later, the Romans were consumer oriented and the interests of traders were seldom at the forefront of the minds of their officials.

What of the protective services provided by the Roman government? The Romans occasionally attempted to suppress piracy, as the campaigns of Cn. Fulvius Centumalus and A. Postumius Albinus against the Illyrians in 229 BCE, of M. Antonius against Cilician pirates

---

[60] Hohlfelder (1988) on Caesarea Maritima; Houston (1988) on ports in general.
[61] Peacock and Williams (1986, 66). But see Terpstra (2011).
[62] Köse (2005, 155).
[63] Rauh (1993, 339).
[64] Johnston (1999, 11); Bang (2009, 183-190); Riggsby (2010, 221).

in 102 BCE, and the broader anti-piracy mandates of M. Antonius Creticus in the late 70s BCE and Pompey the Great in 67 BCE show. Creticus' campaign ended in disaster and De Souza argues that even Pompey's monumental efforts "did little to reduce piracy."[65] Under the empire, the situation may have improved somewhat.[66] On land, brigandage was frequently a threat though, again, the state occasionally attempted to suppress it.[67]

Aside from the banks, the most important institutions facilitating trade (i.e., lowering transaction costs) were probably the private organizations and networks to which traders could belong. These included *collegia, corpora, sodalicia,* and *societates* as well as *familiae,* and *amici.* Many types of professionals formed *collegia* and some of them were involved in trade. In the late Republic, we have evidence for a *collegium mercatorum* at Capua and a *collegium mercatorum pecuariorum* at Praeneste.[68] Under the Empire we find the *collegium vinariorum* and the *corpus splendidissimum importantium et negotiantium vinariorum* at Ostia.[69] Influenced by Finley,[70] scholars have frequently stressed the social and religious purposes of these associations but recent work has pointed out that *collegia* could provide their members with valuable information, contacts, and probably access to capital.[71] The same considerations hold true for *sodalicia* ("fellowships"). Rauh has convincingly argued that religious associations, such as the *sodalicia* he studied on Delos, may have used "joint voluntary fund-raising efforts, as a means to raise 'start up' capital for commercial ventures."[72] Access to *eranos* loans perhaps gave members of these

---

[65] De Souza (2012b, 5330).

[66] De Souza (2012b, 5330) argues that the early emperors "effectively restricted piracy to the margins of the Roman Empire" but Morley (2007, 18) suggests it "remained a problem throughout antiquity."

[67] For example, Plutarch reports (*Marius* 6) that Marius while governor of Further Spain rid the territory of bandits.

[68] *ILS* 7274 = *CIL* I² 672 = X 3773; *CIL* XIV 2878 = *ILLRP* 106.

[69] *AE* 1940, 66; and *AE* 1955, 165. There was also a *corpus negotiatorum fori vinari* (*AE* 1974, 123a) and *corpus mercatorum frumentariorum* (*CIL* XIV 161) at Ostia. *Corpus* is apparently just another term for *collegium* (Liu 2009, 135). See also: de Salvo (1992, 237-40).

[70] Finley 1985, 138 declared that the "*collegia* played an important part in the social and religious life of the lower classes... [but] never became regulatory or protective agencies in their respective trades."

[71] Gibbs (2012, 1650-1). See also Morley (2007, 76).

[72] Rauh (1993, 287).

organizations "considerable financial advantages." [73] Although the members of many professions formed *collegia*, it is unclear how common *merchant* associations were and it is possible that only the more affluent traders were able to join them.[74]

Societates were partnerships that might be explicitly for the purpose of trade. The partnership created by Cato the Elder (Plutarch, *Cat. Mai.* 21) suggests that they could be both large and profitable, but Malmendier cautions that *societas* "never evolved into a general framework suitable for business entities that require more permanence and stability."[75] Morley suggests that these kinds of partnerships were "relatively uncommon"[76] and Bang argues that Roman businesses were usually "organized on the basis of the household."[77] Certainly, *familiae* and ties of *amicitia* created networks that Romans could exploit in the interest of trading. Kirschenbaum shows how, particularly by means of the institution of *peculium*, "in overseas commerce and inland trade, freedmen, slaves and, to a lesser degree, sons acted as agents of their patrons, masters and fathers, respectively."[78] With respect to *amicitia*, Verboven has explored its role in late Republican trade, showing how wealthy Romans "organized their patrimonies... by means of their extensive personal networks and their 'friendships' with important *negotiatores* and *faeneratores*."[79] Traders themselves could, of course, take advantage of ties of friendship and patronage relationships to gain protection, financing, or advantageous commercial information.

In addition to the financial and organizational parameters of Roman trade, we must also consider the technological and environmental constraints. Transportation is the crucial issue here. A wide range of merchant vessels plied the Mediterranean and, while some were quite large, occasionally more than six hundred tons in capacity, most were relatively small, under a hundred tons.[80] Usually powered by sails, these ships were capable of 4 to 6 knots, depending on conditions,[81] and could

---

[73] Rauh (1993, 269).
[74] Morley (2007, 42-3).
[75] Malmendier (2012, 6305).
[76] Morley (2007, 75).
[77] Bang (2010, 95).
[78] Kirschenbaum (1987, 152).
[79] Verboven (2002, 32).
[80] Houston (1988); McGrail (2008, 623); Wilson (2009, 229); Bang (2010, 94); Wilson (2011, 214-5).
[81] Davis (2012, 4714).

travel abeam or even against the wind.[82] High-sided merchant ships could handle rougher seas than a warship.[83] The introduction of chain pumps in the first century BCE (one of many innovations in shipbuilding of the Roman period) may have improved overall safety, lowering the frequency of shipwreck, or merely prompted sailors to take even greater risks.[84] Sailing was always dangerous. Pliny warns of ships colliding in the night (*HN* 2.128) and pirates remained a threat even under the Empire.[85] Furthermore, the lack of nautical charts and the inability to determine longitude could make navigation quite a challenge.[86] The volume of shipping slowed down during the stormier winter months (November to March) but certainly did not stop altogether.[87] Shipping on rivers and canals might have been somewhat safer but posed its own set of challenges and constraints.[88] Although land transport was more expensive than shipping by sea, many goods nevertheless moved along the roads at least short and medium distances.[89] With respect to harnessed transport, Raepsaet has shown that ancient yoke technology was well suited to the morphology of donkeys, mules, and oxen (the main non-human sources of motive power), and even argues that the efficiency of land transportation "reached a very exceptional peak during the Roman Empire, in terms of both public administration and private use."[90] As Strabo (5.3.8) famously remarked, Roman roads carried boatloads. However, by land or sea, travel was not especially fast and so information also moved slowly, making it difficult for traders to respond quickly to changing market conditions.[91]

A catalogue of the goods traded in the Empire would be vast, requiring at least several large volumes to enumerate and analyze everything Pliny the Elder mentions in his *Natural History*. Instead, I will briefly consider the major items of trade (grain, wine, and olive oil)

---

[82] Arnaud (2011, 147ff.).

[83] Davis (2012, 4714).

[84] Harris (2009, 260); (2011, 13).

[85] In the early third century CE Paul (*Digest* 14.2.2.3) relayed from earlier jurists the (apparently still pertinent) information that all passengers had to contribute if it became necessary to ransom a ship from pirates.

[86] Davis (2012, 4714).

[87] Bang (2010, 94); Marzano (2011); Pliny *HN* 2.47.125.

[88] Cooper (2011, 206).

[89] Laurence (1999, 108).

[90] Raepsaet (2008, 590-592).

[91] Bang (2010, 94).

and then a selection of other products of differing value and importance in order to provide a general sense of the nature of the Roman market.

As they were the staples of the Mediterranean diet, it is fairly certain that grain, wine, and olive oil formed the bulk of the goods transported over long distances. Through the collection of in-kind taxes and the provision of armies and the city of Rome, the state was heavily involved (as a buyer and seller) in the trade of these commodities, especially grain, by the late Republic. Under the Empire, the state's role grew even larger, especially once the *annona* expanded to include wine, olive oil, and pork in the third century CE. With respect to grain, Erdkamp estimates that "public channels may have supplied the city with two thirds or more of its requirements," with the state selling the excess grain, not distributed in the *frumentationes*, to traders and bakers.[92] Trade in some goods, like tableware, probably piggybacked on state grain shipments and other bulk cargoes.[93]

Changes in the containers used to transport wine prevent us from forming a complete picture of its trade, but Italy clearly exported a considerable quantity of wine to Gaul in the late Republic. Tchernia notes that this seems to be "the only important trade movement exporting food products over large distances where the principal destination was not Rome or the armies."[94] A vigorous wine trade seems to have continued under the empire, judging from Domitian's abortive attempt to suppress wine production, but "our knowledge of the Roman wine trade disintegrates once clay amphorae began to be superseded by barrels as the main means of conveyance."[95] As for olive oil, Monte Testaccio attests to Rome's considerable demand for it in the late Republic and early Empire while the distribution of amphorae as well as the remains of kilns and presses in Iberia and North Africa suggest trade on a massive scale.[96]

Beyond the Mediterranean triad a great variety of foodstuffs circulated within the Empire. Pliny the Elder reports that Vitellius imported Syrian figs to his Alban estate during the reign of Tiberius, and the Romans brought considerable numbers of figs and other produce into

---

[92] Erdkamp (2005, 257).
[93] Greene (1992, 58-60).
[94] Tchernia (1983, 91-2).
[95] Greene (2000, 48).
[96] Mattingly (1996); Hitchner (2002).

Central Europe.[97] Dates may not have been traded extensively over long distances since Pliny notes that those grown in Africa, Syria, and Cyprus did not keep well (*HN* 13.6.26 and 13.9.49). The almonds of Thasos and Alba were famous (*HN* 15.90), as were the chestnuts of Tarentum and Naples (*HN* 5.94). Given its use as a sweetener, preservative for food and dead bodies,[98] and component of drugs (*HN* 21.79), there must have been a sizeable trade in honey. Varro (*Rust.* 3.16.10) records the story of the Veiani brothers of Falerii who earned at least HS 10,000 a year from the honey produced on their small estate. *Garum* clearly served Umbricius Scaurus well judging from his mosaics,[99] and salted fish and fish sauces were traded throughout the Empire.[100] Pliny even reports that oysters from Brundisium were fattened in Lake Avernus (*HN* 32.61). Some cheeses traveled *trans maria* to reach their consumers according to Columella (7.8) who advised owners of livestock, living too far away from markets to sell their milk in them, to make their own cheese. This could imply that it was common practice, even for those with milk-producing livestock, to purchase cheese from other producers.

Since pork was the most common meat in the Roman diet,[101] there must have been a considerable trade in pigs. Pliny claims that some pigs, the *duces*, were smart enough to lead their herds between home and the market (Pliny *HN* 8.208). Both Varro (*Rust.* 3.9.2) and Columella (*Rust.* 8.2.4) call attention to the profits earned by Delian poultry farmers, while Varro also notes that the popularity of African hens in his own day had driven up their prices (*Rust.* 3.9.19). Geese traveled by foot from Gaul to Rome and German goose feathers, for bedding, were the most highly praised (*HN* 10.27.53). There was even trade in pigeons (as pets); the Roman *eques* L. Axius was asking 400 *denarii* for a pair in the late Republic (*HN* 10.53.110). Even more impressively, in the same period M. Aufidius Lurco reportedly earned HS 60,000 profit from the sale of fattened peacocks (Pliny *HN* 10.23.45).

Textiles and associated products probably contributed substantially to the volume of trade.[102] Roman clothes may have been

---

[97] Bakels and Jacomet (2003).

[98] Lindsay (2000, 158).

[99] Curtis (1988), (1991).

[100] Bekker-Nielsen (2005, 14).

[101] MacKinnon (2012, 4372).

[102] As Jongman (2000, 188) points out, "A look at pre-industrial consumer budgets shows that, after food (by far the most important) and housing, clothing is the third large item of expenditure." See also: Hopkins (1988, 764).

relatively simple,[103] but there was still demand for high quality fabrics as well as dyes and the chemicals necessary to clean them. Wool was always available in Italy but silk, by the late Republic or reign of Augustus, was arriving all the way from China.[104] The island of Cos also produced a kind of silk fabric and Pliny disapprovingly notes that even men were willing to wear this light material (*HN* 11.26.77-8). Linen, used for ropes, sails, and tents in addition to clothing, came from Spain, the Po Valley, and the eastern Mediterranean. However, Wild points out that "flax was a regular component of mixed farming regimes," so many rural areas could have supplied their own needs and perhaps even met local urban demand.[105] Urine for fulling was, of course, always available locally, but substances like *Sarda*, used to brighten white cloth, had to be imported to Rome from Sardinia or Umbria (Pliny *HN* 35.196-7). Sulfur, from Campania and various islands, also had a role in fulling in addition to its medicinal and religious uses (*HN* 35.50.175). The purple dye extracted from shellfish in Phoenicia and Crete was only the most famous of the substances used to color textiles. The Gauls, for example, used whortleberry to dye the clothes of slaves (*HN* 16.31.77). Other dyes included woad, indigo, madder, kermes, weld, and saffron. Goat skins and cattle hides would, in most places, have been available locally but there is evidence for the long distance trade in leather. There was a *corpus pellionum ostiensium et portensium* and, according to Pliny the Elder, a shipwrecked cargo of hides from Gaul once attracted a killer whale to the port at Ostia during the reign of Claudius (*HN* 9.5.14). The demand for leather goods must have been enormous. The army used it for boots, tents, bags, harnesses, and other equipment while the desire for fashionable footwear, van Driel-Murray suggests, even "drew rural communities into marketing networks."[106]

The trade in aromatics was also quite substantial, even if, as Pliny claims (*HN* 12.41.84), it accounted for only a fraction of the HS 100 million which Arabia, along with India and China, took from the Empire every year.[107] Frankincense traveled from south Arabia, by camel and ship, to Alexandria, where it was processed under heavy guard before being distributed for sale throughout the Empire (*HN* 12.32.59).

---

[103] Cleland (2012, 1589).

[104] Wild (2008, 469).

[105] Wild (2008, 468).

[106] Van Driel-Murray (2008, 492).

[107] Pliny *HN* 6.26.101 states India alone took at least HS 50 million per year.

Pliny the Elder gives transport costs of 688 *denarii* per camel to get to the Mediterranean, not including Roman customs payments (*HN* 12.32.63-65). Under the Empire, Capua became a major center for the sale and processing of aromatics and the production of perfumes.[108] Many regions both within and outside the Empire contributed to the aromatics trade. *Rhodinum*, once a popular ingredient in perfumes, came from Phaselis (*HN* 13.5), while Egypt provided *aspalathus*, a plant whose roots were used in unguents (*HN* 12.52.110). Galbanum, burnt to drive away snakes, came from Syria while Gaul, Crete, Syria, and India all produced varieties of nard (*HN* 12.26.43-6). For some of these commodities Pliny provides a single price. Galbanum, for example, went for 5 *denarii* a pound. For others we get a set of prices for various grades. The third best kind of frankincense cost 3 *denarii* per pound. The implication seems to be that these prices were quite stable. By contrast, myrrh prices varied considerably, from 3 to 50 *denarii* per pound, depending on demand.[109] Consumer tastes changed over time, with different perfumes coming into and out of fashion (Pliny *HN* 13.4), as also happened with dyes (*HN* 9.137). Creative merchants were able to talk up the price of their merchandise with, in the case of cassia, tales of menacing bats and flying snakes guarding the plants (*HN* 12.42.85). Given the important role of incense in Roman funeral rites, it is likely that merchants took advantage of inexperienced and distracted customers in much the same way that Jessica Mitford described twentieth century American funeral directors manipulating grief-stricken relatives into paying for goods and services they did not really need.[110] Pliny seems to indicate that product adulteration was widespread in the aromatics trade (e.g., *HN* 12.35.71).[111]

Wood, essential for buildings, ships, furniture, tools, and also used for fuel, was another major item of trade. By the early second century BCE the area outside the *Porta Trigemina* seems to have been associated with the timber trade (Livy 35.40). Much of this trade was probably short distance, but there was long-distance commerce, for

---

[108] Young (2001, 23).

[109] Pliny, *HN* 12.35.70: *ex occasione ementium*.

[110] Mitford (1963, 18): "choice doesn't enter into the picture for the average individual, faced, generally for the first time, with the necessity of buying a product of which he is totally ignorant, at a moment when he is least in a position to quibble."

[111] For further discussion of adulteration as well as the production and distribution of perfume more generally, see Reger (2005) and (2011).

example, in the expensive citrus wood that the Romans imported from Mauretania (*HN* 13.95). [112] Wood samples from Pompeii and Herculaneum suggest that the inhabitants imported timber from western Austria as well as the Apennines.[113] Wherever there were kilns, baths, and furnaces for metalworking, there would be demand for charcoal (e.g., *HN* 16.23). Charcoal made from different types of trees had useful properties or annoying deficiencies. For example, *haliphloeos*, or "seabark" (a kind of oak), was deemed unsuitable for sacrifices (*HN* 16.8.24). There was probably long distance trade in "specialty" charcoal.

Even if the major commodities thus far mentioned (grain, wine, and oil) constitute the largest share, at least by weight, of the goods traded over any distance, a thousand other products moved between and beyond the provinces and cities of the Empire. Amber came from the Baltic coast while ebony came from India. Varro reports that the farmers of Latium grew flowers to sell at Rome (*Rust.* 1.16.3) while Cato recommended purchasing millstones at Pompeii (*Ag.* 22.3). Many regions exported paints and pigments (e.g., *HN* 35.18.36, 27.46). Papyrus, primarily from Egypt, provided a writing medium but also wrapping paper and a kind of rope among other products (*HN* 13.23.76-7). A shortage of *charta* under Tiberius led the Senate to appoint *arbitri* to handle the distribution of remaining supplies.[114] Wherever people kept bees, there would be commerce in wax since it served several important functions: coating for writing tablets as well as general waterproofing, medium for seal impressions and metal casting, and ingredient in cosmetics and medicines (*HN* 21.49.83-5).[115] While scholars will no doubt continue to debate the degree of market integration within the Empire, there can be no question that Roman trade linked together, at least loosely, communities, cities and their hinterlands, as well as Rome and the other major metropolises with the provinces and the broader world.

Given the complex and expensive trading environment, how could traders be successful? There was no one grand strategy. Instead, available capital, market conditions, and specialized knowledge (of particular products or markets) would dictate the trader's approach. It

---

[112] Harris (2011, 187).

[113] Kuniholm (2002, 235).

[114] Pliny, *HN* 13.27.89.

[115] In addition to goods, slaves were similarly traded although there were also local supplies. Harris (1980) and (1999); Bradley (1987); and Scheidel (1997).

certainly made sense to cultivate friendships as they could yield valuable information and ease credit.[116] Investing in a variety of merchandise and, if possible, transporting that merchandise on a variety of vessels, were good ways to manage risk.[117] Adequate storage would allow traders to hoard and speculate in goods.[118] Scholars frequently suggest that many merchants engaged in *cabotage*,[119] small-scale, coastal trade in a variety of goods, but even this form of commerce required considerable advanced planning to take account of seasonal winds, harvest times and important festivals.[120] To sell goods, traders would gravitate toward the bigger markets, such as Rome, free ports like Delos, *nundinae* and festivals, where they could count on plenty of buyers, high prices, or even the temporary suspension of tolls (e.g., *Mon. Eph.* 128-33). The state provided many opportunities: to deliver grain to Rome in exchange for exemptions, supply various goods to armies, buy booty cheaply from soldiers, or sell them necessities.[121] To what extent, though, did traders need to consider the strategies of rival merchants?

COMPETITION?

Economic competition has rarely received the attention it deserves among ancient historians.[122] As long as the ideas of primitivists and substantivists held sway, this situation was hardly surprising. As Andreau noted, "Finley was convinced" that the ancient economy was not a market economy "and therefore denied that ancient commerce and its evolution could be studied according to ideas such as competition or the law of supply and demand."[123] If, however, the Romans possessed a market economy, competition becomes by definition a pivotal issue.[124] In a market economy scarce resources are rationed by means of prices as buyers and sellers compete for wealth. Supply and demand, along with the cost of production, determine these prices. Competition *is* the

---

[116] Bang (2012).

[117] Bang (2010, 95-6).

[118] Garnsey (1988, 176).

[119] E.g., Horden and Purcell (2000, 140).

[120] Marzano (2011, 186).

[121] For army supply, see Roth (1999).

[122] Archaeologists have shown much more interest. See, for example, Bradley (1971, 347-352), Greene (1986, 162-3), and Peacock and Williams (1986, 25-26).

[123] Andreau (2002, 36).

[124] Temin (2001, 181). See also Harris (1993, 14-18).

"invisible hand." Buyers compete with each other for goods, bidding up the price of products. The winners are those able to purchase the products they need. Sellers compete with other sellers to produce or deliver goods and services to consumers. The winners make a profit and the losers go out of business. What evidence, then, exists for competition among Roman traders?

The two basic forms of economic competition are consumer competition and entrepreneurial rivalry. Consumer competition or rivalry among buyers is most evident at auctions, a typical feature of Roman economic life, where everything from real estate to olives on the tree was sold.[125] Entrepreneurial rivalry, on the other hand, occurs when producers, merchants or firms compete with each other for buyers. Such competition often hinges on the price of the goods being sold but can also entail such issues as "product quality, producer reliability, convenience, location or service."[126] In the modern world, where cell phone, car, and soft-drink manufacturers regularly compete for market share, advertising tends to emphasize these factors as much as price. It is difficult, however, to detect this kind of competition in the Roman world. When different versions of the same product are compared, it is usually the point of origin rather than the producer that gets emphasized. So, for example, when Cato the Elder discusses farm equipment (*Agr.* 135), he notes the best city in which to buy particular items but only once singles out particular producers, the rope makers L. Tunnius and C. Mennius.

The papyrus trade provides a partial exception to this tendency. *Amphitheatrica*, named after its place of production, was the fourth best type of paper (*charta*) on the market while *Saitica*, from the town of Sais, was fifth. At some point the Roman workshop of a certain Fannius developed a process that greatly improved *amphitheatrica* such that the resulting *Fanniana* rivaled the best quality *chartae* (*Augusta, Liviana*, and *hieratica*).[127] Later on, the emperor Claudius had *Augusta* adapted, making it stronger and less transparent, as well as changing its dimensions, with the result that once again it became the clear favorite for most purposes (*HN* 13.24.79-80). *Garum* may be another example of a product entailing significant differences between producers: the *tituli picti* on fish sauce containers could indicate that *garum* "brands"

---

[125] See, e.g., Cato, *Agr.* 146; Cic., *Caecina* 15, *Att.* 13.45.3; and Rauh (1989, 451-71).
[126] Gwartney and Stroup (1995, 551).
[127] Pliny, *HN* 13.24.74-5.

mattered to Roman consumers.[128] Other signs of Roman entrepreneurial competition are surprisingly hard to come by. Cicero (*Att.* 1.17) reports that in the late 60s BCE the *publicani* who purchased the right to collect taxes in Asia found that they had overbid and asked the senate for relief. This implies competition between tax farming companies but it is essentially consumer competition for the right to purchase a monopoly. Did any other kinds of entrepreneurial competition occur in the marketplace? In the absence of any clear and compelling examples of this type of behavior, it is necessary to ask how Roman authors conceive of commercial activity in general. Three anecdotes about Roman entrepreneurialism suggest that rivalry among traders did not form a substantial part of the Roman view of commercial life. In each case, one would expect to find some reference to economic rivalry but none appears.[129]

One of the most well known anecdotes about Roman entrepreneurialism concerns Cato the Elder. According to Plutarch (*Cat. Mai.* 21.6), not only did Cato make high-interest maritime loans but he formed his many borrowers into a company (κοινωνία) in which he held a share. By sending his freedman, Quintio, along on the trading voyages, Cato seems to have maintained a high degree of oversight as well. Cato made money by reducing his financial risk, also spreading his investment among a large group of ship-owners. If Cato was trying to achieve economies of scale or dominate the shipping industry, we do not hear about it. There is no mention of rivals. Profit came through being able to reduce the impact of natural disaster, i.e., shipwreck. Plutarch (*Cat. Mai.* 21.5) makes Cato's strategy abundantly clear:

> Engaging in business very intensely, he considered agriculture to be a pastime rather than a source of profit and invested his resources in safe and reliable enterprises. He acquired ponds, hot springs, fulleries, pitch works, land with natural pastures and woods, places which earned him lots of money but were, as he himself says, strong enough not to be damaged by Zeus.

---

[128] See Curtis (1991, 159ff.).

[129] Note that I do not mean to suggest that Roman markets were *peaceful* places. There are other forms of rivalry aside from that between traders such as haggling (i.e., competition between vendor and buyer to determine price).

Cato was not worried about the competition; he was worried about bad luck.

A story about goats in Varro (*Rust.* 2.3.10) reveals a similar understanding of Roman commerce. The *eques* Gaberius had learned that a goatherd earned ten *denarii* a day by bringing his ten nanny goats into the city. Hoping to earn a thousand *denarii* a day from his large estate near Rome, Gaberius assembled a herd of a thousand goats. Gaberius' scheme failed but what went wrong? Several possible explanations would no doubt occur to an economist. He or she might speculate that there was insufficient demand for goat milk and the increased supply created by Gaberius' giant herd caused milk prices to drop dramatically. Or perhaps more established goat milk merchants, threatened by Gaberius' large enterprise, drove him out of business by undercutting his prices. Someone who had recently read Finley's *The Ancient Economy* would no doubt suppose that goat milk transactions were embedded in Roman social relations and so customers stayed with Gaberius' rivals because of their pre-existing relationships. But, of course, what actually happened was that disease wiped out Gaberius' entire herd. Again, the lesson is that profit comes to those who reduce risk. If Gaberius had 20 herds of 50 goats (the recommended maximum herd size), Varro seems to suggest, he could have made his 1000 *denarii* a day. As long as you can deliver your product to market, you will make money.

Delivery is also the central problem in the third entrepreneurial anecdote. Petronius (*Sat.* 76) has Trimalchio describe his rise to great wealth as follows:

> I built five ships and loaded them with wine – at that time it was worth its weight in gold – and sent them to Rome. You'd think I'd ordered it: all the ships sunk. True story! In one day Neptune swallowed up thirty million *sestertii*. Do you think I lost my nerve? No, by Hercules, this mishap was nothing to me. I built other ships, bigger, better, and luckier ones so nobody could say I wasn't a brave man... I loaded them with more wine, bacon, beans, Seplasian unguents, and slaves. What the gods will soon happens. In one trip I made back ten million *sestertii*.

Initially Trimalchio fails because of bad luck. Neptune drank all his wine. A number of reasons are given for his ultimate success: persistence, bravery and self-sacrifice (his wife sells her jewelry and clothes to help finance the second trip). Trimalchio's new ships are bigger, better but most importantly *feliciores*. There is no mention of competitors bested. Trimalchio succeeds because Mercury, god of merchants, watches over him.[130]

Why is it that Plutarch, Varro and Petronius never discuss economic competition? The obvious explanation is that while competition did take place between Roman entrepreneurs, our upper-class sources were reluctant to discuss such disreputable behavior. Since such competition must have entailed trickery and deception, it would be decidedly vulgar.[131] Indeed, this might explain Varro's behavior. In book 1 of the *Rerum Rusticarum*, a murder conveniently interrupts the dialogue just as it turned to the question of marketing the produce of the villa. But Plutarch and Petronius both clearly disapprove of their subjects so there would be no reason for them to hold back on this point. Perhaps, then, these authors did not discuss entrepreneurial rivalry because there was little such behavior for them to observe. But how can a market economy lack entrepreneurial rivalry? There are three possible explanations. First, the government might suppress such competition through market regulations, the creation of artificial monopolies, the oversight of magistrates, and similar measures. Secondly, *collegia* could stifle competition by creating entrance barriers, restricting access to the market and regulating the behavior of their members. Thirdly, the nature of the market itself may have limited entrepreneurial rivalry. All three factors probably played a role in the Roman economy.

As far as government suppression of competition is concerned, laws regulating prices are attested, though there are few examples from the late Republic or early Empire.[132] Magistrates such as the *aediles* at Rome and *agoranomoi* in Greek cities were responsible for the care of the market, but what did such officials actually do to suppress

---

[130] Trimalchio's close relationship with Mercury is mentioned three times: *Sat.* 29, 67 & 77.

[131] Cic., *Off.* 1.150-1. See D'Arms (1981, 20-47) for a discussion of Roman attitudes towards commerce.

[132] Diocletian's Price Edict is the most famous example. Laws occasionally attempted to limit interest rates, and we know of some local attempts to regulate prices. See, e.g., Liebeschuetz (1972, 130-2); Harl (1996, 277); Aubert (2004, 165 and 169); Zanda (2011, 126).

entrepreneurial rivalry? They certainly played a role in preventing fraud through, for example, making sure there were accurate weights and measures. They might require a merchant to declare a price and abide by it in the market but they rarely mandated prices.[133] In acting against grain-dealers who were hoarding grain, the *aediles* seem to have acted like trustbusters, forcing such dealers to compete rather than cooperate.[134] The *lex Iulia de annona* (*Dig.* 48.12) penalized those who attempted to form *societates* in order to raise the price of grain. Roman law adapted only gradually to the needs of businessmen and thus, it might be argued, promoted competition by hampering the formation of large and complex firms capable of dominating markets.[135] The use of auctions also must have encouraged competition. Sumptuary laws, by suppressing (or at least trying to suppress) consumer demand for luxuries, would presumably increase competition among the suppliers of such goods.[136]

Only in one instance does a Roman law seem specifically designed to stifle a kind of entrepreneurial competition. Cicero (*Rep.* 3.16) reports that the Romans forbade the Gauls to grow olives and grapes in order to increase the value of their own olive groves and vineyards.[137] An edict of Domitian, which sought to halt the growth of viticulture in Italy and halve the amount of provincial land devoted to vineyards, would also have limited competition had it been implemented.[138] According to Suetonius (*Dom.* 7.2), the high price of grain, rather than any desire to suppress competition, prompted the measure. Imperial ownership (and regulation) of many mines and quarries[139] may have limited rivalry in the private metal and building stone trade by confining competition to the auctions at which the right to exploit these resources were sold. State-managed monopolies would

---

[133] See Descat (2000, 16-24).

[134] Livy, 38.35.5.

[135] See Nicolas (1962, 185); Garnsey and Saller (1987, 54-55); and Aubert (2001, 94).

[136] Sulla's sumptuary laws regulated market prices, but most apparently sought to limit social competition e.g., by capping expenditure or the number of guests permitted at banquets. See Macrob., *Sat.* 3.17; Daube (1969, 124); Zanda (2011).

[137] For a discussion of Cicero's claim see Patterson 1978.

[138] Suet., *Dom.* 7.2 and 14.2. Garnsey and Saller (1987, 60) point out that the edict's context was "a shortfall in cereals that coincided with a bumper wine harvest" and that the "edict represents the impulsive reaction of an emperor who knew... the political dangers involved in permitting his subjects, in particular the plebs of Rome, to go hungry." It is possible but not evident that Italian producers were suffering due to provincial competition (see Launaro 2011, 180).

[139] Hirt (2010).

have had the same effect on the salt trade.[140] Roman law governing patron-client relations also prevented competition. Scaevola (*Dig.* 38.1.45) implies that a freedman merchant could only engage in the same business as his patron if the latter was unharmed by it. Although the evidence is meager, *collegia* could act to limit competition too by keeping out unwanted rivals, limiting supplies or setting minimum prices. The salt-dealers in Tebtunis in the first century CE and ferrymen at Smyrna in the early Empire both set minimum prices and acted to keep out potential rivals.[141] It remains unclear how common this type of behavior was.

While government and *collegia* had a role in suppressing competition in some sectors of the economy or for certain goods and services, the nature of the market itself can limit entrepreneurial rivalry when the conditions of "perfect competition" apply.[142] Although in Classical economics competition simply meant rivalry between individuals, economists have come to recognize many different kinds of competition such as "monopolistic competition" and competition without rivalry, i.e., "perfect competition." Though perfect competition is usually considered a hypothetical situation, economists have long held that "its conditions are approximated in a few important industries, most notably in many parts of agriculture."[143] Perfect competition precludes rivalry between buyers and sellers in the market in the sense that no individual buyer or seller can influence the "market outcome."[144] Gwartney and Stroup describe the necessary conditions of perfect competition as follows:

1. All firms in the market are producing a homogeneous product;
2. A large number of independent firms produce the product;

---

[140] For regulation of the salt trade in the late 3rd century BCE, see Livy, 29.37. For salt and gypsum monopolies around Tebtynis in the 1st century CE, see *P. Mich.* V 245.

[141] *P. Mich* V 245 and *IK* 24.1 712. See also *OGIS* 572 (2nd or 3rd century CE) for a ferry monopoly at Myra, Lycia. See *P.Oxy.* XLIV 3192 for a group of donkey dealers in 4th century CE Oxyrhynchus.

[142] The phrases "pure competition," "absolute competition," and even simply "competition" are sometimes used in the same sense. See Hunt (2000, 7-8); Gwartney and Stroup (1995, 530); Dillingham (1992, 101); and Ekelund (1997, 484).

[143] Gwartney and Stroup (1995, 531).

[144] Dillingham (1992, 101).

3. Each buyer and seller is small relative to the total market; and
4. There are no artificial barriers to entry into or exit from the market.[145]

Under these conditions entrepreneurial rivalry makes no sense since an individual firm cannot affect prices. If you sell for less than the equilibrium market price, you lose money but are unable to lower the market price or force competitors either to lower their prices or to leave the market. If you raise your prices above the market price, no one will buy your product since there are plenty of other sellers. There would still, no doubt, be haggling in the marketplace—such negotiations were the "process of price formation"[146]—but that is competition between buyer and seller rather than entrepreneurial rivalry.

With respect to the major agricultural goods traded in the Roman Empire, all of the conditions of perfect competition apply fairly well. Grain, wine and olive oil were all rather homogeneous products. There were as many "firms" as there were farmers and estate owners, and the size of both buyers and sellers relative to the market was small (in most cases). This does not apply to the state, of course, which had the resources to gather and transport large quantities of grain and was, at least in times of food crisis, willing to sell at artificially low prices. It is unclear, however, to what extent the Roman state participated in commodity markets. Finally, there is no indication that artificial barriers prevented new producers from entering these markets.

Perfect competition is by no means a new idea but only a handful of historians seem to have considered applying the concept to the ancient world. Whittaker briefly mentions perfect competition but seems to regard it a purely hypothetical situation.[147] De Ligt employs the theory to good effect, suggesting that peasant markets produce a situation akin to perfect competition and so "depress[ed] market prices to the... benefit of the urban consumer."[148] Kudlien, who devoted an article to the topic of ancient economic competition, notes de Ligt's reference to perfect

---

[145] Gwartney and Stroup (1995, 530).
[146] Uchendu (1967, 37).
[147] Whittaker (1986, 131).
[148] De Ligt (1993, 213-214).

competition but comments only that he found it "ohne Erläuterung nicht sehr klar."[149]

There are several reasons why perfect competition is a good fit for some sectors of the Roman economy in the late Republic and early Empire. Perfect competition may explain why *collegia* did not (apparently) become guilds; since lack of demand or excess supply were seldom problems, the *collegia* would rarely need to limit competition. As Plutarch, Varro and Petronius imply, there was plenty of profit to go around, if only you could deliver your goods to market. Perfect competition may also help explain why the Romans apparently never developed a more sophisticated understanding of economic phenomena. They could not be expected to know about things they could not observe. Marketing may have seemed like the easiest part of managing a farm or estate.

Ex silentio arguments are, of course, rarely definitive. That Varro, Petronius and Plutarch failed to mention entrepreneurial competition does not prove its absence. It is, however, a suggestive omission. As Hopkins and others have pointed out, models are the most important tool ancient economic historians have at their disposal.[150] Perfect competition provides an attractive model for some sectors of the Roman economy in the late Republic and early Empire. Entrepreneurial rivalry is more likely to have been a factor in the trade of processed and manufactured goods where there would be fewer producers and less homogeneous merchandise such as shoes, pottery, *charta*, metal tools, and furniture. But, if entrepreneurial rivalry was rare, the relationship between merchant and customer assumes even greater importance.

BUSINESS ETHICS: YEARNING FOR THE EMBEDDED ECONOMY?

Midway through book three of the *De Officiis*, in an extended discussion of "expediency" (*utilitas*) versus "moral rectitude" (*honestas*), Cicero introduces the following hypothetical situation: a good man has imported a large quantity of grain from Alexandria to Rhodes at a time when Rhodes was experiencing a famine and food prices were very high. However, this merchant knows that many other ships full of grain are on the way from Alexandria. If the Rhodians knew about the other ships, the

---

[149] Kudlien (1994, 38).
[150] Hopkins (1995/6, 41).

price of grain would drop and the merchant's profit would be considerably less. Cicero asks whether the merchant should tell the Rhodians about the other ships (*Off.* 3.50). While the outcome of the ensuing discussion is fairly predictable (Cicero believes the merchant *should* reveal his information about the other ships), the discussion itself contains much of interest to economic historians since it entails several other scenarios involving transactions and "business ethics." Cicero stages a debate about the merchant between the Stoic philosopher Diogenes the Babylonian and Antipater, his student (*Off.* 3.51). Antipater, standing in for Cicero himself, argues that the merchant should inform the Rhodian customers of the other ships while Diogenes argues that the merchant is only obligated to reveal his product's defects to whatever extent that the law requires. As long as the merchant does not engage in trickery, he can sell his grain for the going market price without wronging anyone. Antipater responds that the merchant has an obligation to humanity that should compel him to mention the other ships. Diogenes counters by pointing out that there is a difference between concealing information and not revealing information. There is all sorts of useful information that Diogenes is not revealing at that very moment, such as the nature of the gods, and that information is much more important than the price of grain. He says he is not under any obligation to tell Antipater these things either (*Off.* 3.52). Antipater insists that he *is* obliged to reveal such information because of the joint fellowship among men. Diogenes then asks, if this fellowship is so important, why should there be any private property whatsoever (*Off.* 3.53)?

Just how far was a Roman's obligation to fellow human beings supposed to go? At this point in his life Cicero had made his commitment to private property very clear in both his writings and actions.[151] It would be nice to see how he reconciled private property with the strong obligation to help one's fellow humans he asserts in this text. Unfortunately, Cicero does not attempt this. Instead, we get more hypothetical scenarios. While these scenarios are also supposed to illustrate the seller's obligations, they are not truly analogous to the grain merchant's dilemma. For example, Cicero asks if a man trying to sell his house should tell the buyer if the house is unsanitary or poorly built and *ruinosa* (*Off.* 3.54). Antipater once again says that the seller should

---

[151] Wood (1983).

inform the buyer of the defects. Diogenes argues against any obligation to report. Diogenes, who has already conceded that defects in a trade good should be declared to the extent that the law requires, says that the *buyer* is responsible for checking the merchandise himself. Essentially, this is the *caveat emptor* position. Diogenes adds that no one really expects advertisements to be truthful and then imagines the absurdity of an auctioneer announcing "dangerous house for sale!" Once again, Cicero sides with Antipater but does not really address Diogenes' points which essentially ask how any of Anitpater's principles are supposed to function in the real world.

At this point Cicero largely abandons Diogenes and Antipater and switches from hypothetical situations to apparently real transactions. First, we hear about C. Canius who wanted to buy "some little gardens" in Sicily where he could relax (*Off.* 3.58-60). Pythius, a Syracusan banker, tricks Canius into buying one of his properties at an inflated price. The banker got all the local fishermen to fish along the shore by the estate while Canius was over for a banquet. Although you could not own the rights to offshore fishing (*Dig.* 1.8.4-5), the estate was apparently worth much more simply by virtue of its easy access to fresh seafood. Canius eagerly buys the place but, once the trick was discovered, he had no legal recourse because, Cicero tells us, C. Aquilius had yet to create the legal formulas for criminal fraud.

In the ensuing discussion of fraud, Cicero mentions another kind of sharp practice: a seller enlisting accomplices to bid up the prices of goods for sale and buyers using fake bidders to keep prices low. It is not clear how the latter scheme would work as he does not elaborate on these practices. Ideally, according to Cicero, each party to a potential transaction should simply state the price they think is fair. To illustrate this, Cicero next mentions the exemplary honesty of a certain Q. Scaevola who once paid more for a farm than the seller's asking price because he thought the farm was actually *worth* more (*Off.* 3.62). However, Cicero acknowledges that people would not generally regard Scaevola's action as wise.

At this point, Cicero brings up Hecaton of Rhodes who also attempts to justify something less than full honest disclosure of *everything* relating to a transaction (*Off.* 3.63). Cicero quotes Hecaton to the effect that the wise man will take his economic interests into account while not acting against the law, morals, or customs, because people seek wealth not just for themselves but to benefit their children, relatives, and friends as well as the Republic. Once again we have here an allusion to the possibility that traders might conduct business with the interests of others in mind. Cicero dismisses Hecaton as unworthy of praise but, as though channeling Diogenes for a moment, he concedes that, by the standard he is setting out, most transactions do involve criminal fraud (*Off.* 3.64).

Cicero next turns to a discussion of Roman real estate law which held that one had to declare defects in property for sale and that the seller had to make restitution if he knew of, but failed to disclose, a defect (*Off.* 3.65). We get another illustration: the augurs had ordered T. Claudius Centumalus to tear down part of an *insula* he owned on the Caelian Hill so that the augurs' view was unobstructed. Instead of complying, Claudius quickly sold the *insula* to one P. Calpunius Lanarius. The augurs then told Calpurnius that *he* needed to tear down parts of the building. Calpurnius did as directed but then successfully sued Claudius for damages because he knew parts of the building had to be torn down but did not inform Calpurnius (*Off.* 3.66). Cicero claims that this ruling established that good faith (*bona fides*) required the seller to tell the buyer about any defect (*vitium*) of which he was aware (*Off.* 3.67). This brings Cicero finally back to the grain merchant at Rhodes. Cicero claims that, if you apply this ruling to that case, the Rhodians should be informed of the other approaching ships carrying grain. This conclusion is hardly compelling since all Cicero's other examples involved real defects in a thing being sold: the house is unsanitary or about to fall down, the fishing is not really as good as it appears, parts of the building need to be torn down. But there is nothing actually *wrong* with the merchant's grain and he is not actively deceiving his customers. Diogenes' questions continue to go unanswered. Just how far do one's obligations to the other party in a transaction go?

Cicero consistently veers away from addressing the possibility that the grain dealer might have obligations to others that would compel him to seek the greatest legal profit. He briefly mentions, but dismisses, obligations to children, family, and friends and he does not raise the possibility that the merchant has business partners to whom he might owe something. Modern companies, for example, are obliged to act in the interest of their shareholders. Cicero certainly knew about *societates* given his dealings with *publicani*[152]—indeed, it is precisely in Cicero's

---

[152] See Malmendier (2005, 38), for *societates publicanorum*, admittedly a special case.

time that Roman law is developing to accommodate traders by establishing clearer rules for partnerships and agency[153] — so why are they absent from his discussion?

In other works, Cicero acknowledges the dangers inherent in the trader's life: there are pirates, storms, and rapacious governors; *luck* is a major factor.[154] These uncertainties and dangers are reflected in the high interest rates lenders could charge for maritime loans.[155] Cicero, however, does not examine the obligations of a merchant who might have financed his grain shipment by means of such high interest loans.

What conclusions, then, can we draw from this discussion of business ethics? Cicero strongly advocates for the interests of the buyer. Although he knows about merchant partnerships and the financing of trade, Cicero is unwilling to use this information to justify (or even attempt to justify) the grain merchant not telling the Rhodians about the other ships. Cicero comes across as a relentless "consumer advocate" and his perspective largely won out in later Roman law. For example, Ulpian, in the *Digest* (4.3.1), states that the praetor's edict "provides help against untrustworthy and deceitful people who injure others by means of some guile" and quotes the *Edict* to the effect that "a trial will be granted for things done by fraud if there is no other action concerning those things and the cause seems to be just." In other words, the Roman jurists were quite willing to punish bad faith actors beyond the explicitly enumerated cases of real property transactions and slave sales.[156] Ulpian also mentions the charge of trickery (*stellionatus*) as a possibility for fraud cases not otherwise addressed in Roman law (*Dig.* 47.20.3). There was no set penalty for *stellionatus* and in fact Ulpian says that the punishment was limited: for the lower orders you could do nothing more than condemn the guilty to the mines. In cases where something is sold but only later transferred to the purchaser, the *Digest* again sides strongly with the consumer. Paul (*Dig.* 18.6.3) notes that, "the seller must provide the kind of care that those who borrow things do, such that he provides better care than he would employ in the case of his own possessions."

---

[153] Aubert (2001, 94).

[154] Cic., *Verr.* II 5.157: *Parumne multa mercatoribus sunt necessario pericula subeunda fortunae.*

[155] Hollander (forthcoming).

[156] In book 21 of the *Digest* there is an extensive discussion of the *Aedile's Edict* with respect to the obligations of those who sell slaves to reveal their defects and what constitutes a defect.

Ulpian does make one concession to the position of Diogenes, however, when he states that "what the seller says in order to recommend [his products] must be regarded as neither affirmed nor promised" (*Dig.* 4.3.37). Not even Roman jurists expected advertising to be honest.

In an essay on slave dealers Bodel has suggested that "Roman animosity toward slave-dealers centered on their reputation for deceiving buyers."[157] He points out that the derivation of the Latin word *mango* (a term for slave-dealers) derives from the Greek verb *manganeuein* which essentially means "to enchant or trick." Slave dealers are notorious for tricking their customers but Cicero's *De Officiis* suggests a much broader anxiety concerning dealers in all sorts of goods. Bodel describes Roman culture as "focused on the interests of the consumer,"[158] and Cicero certainly bears this out. It is not too much to say that Cicero yearns for an embedded economy—a good sign that the Romans did not have one.

Roman elites almost certainly financed Roman trade and, through their slaves, freedmen, and friends, may well have run it. They would not have done this if there were not profits to be had since they regarded merchants as particularly vile and liars by nature. Furthermore, if agriculture were not as lucrative as was once supposed,[159] long-distance trade may have formed a rather important part of elite investment portfolios. Nonetheless, elite authors are unwilling to give traders any moral cover despite the fact that they stood to benefit from the profits.

Why does Cicero want to hold traders to such an incredibly high standard for the disclosure of information? And why is he unwilling to entertain the idea that a trader could have valid reasons, other than simple greed, for withholding certain information? This blind spot may be further indication that business partnerships were rare in trade, that competition among traders was unusual, and that interest rates were not especially high.[160] If luck was indeed a major factor in determining success or failure, few opportunities existed to increase "market share" by besting one's competitors, and it was hard to manipulate the market, perhaps one of the best ways to earn extra profit *was* to cheat the customer.

---

[157] Bodel (2005, 193).

[158] Bodel (2005, 195).

[159] Rosenstein (2008, 23-4) argues that "money-lending and urban enterprises offered much more enticing business opportunities" for senators in the mid to late Republic.

[160] Hollander (forthcoming).

CONCLUSION

The picture developed here of the world of Roman traders invites a number of conclusions. First of all, the scale of the trade, while difficult in most cases to quantify satisfactorily, involved so many producers and consumers of such a wide array of goods that it should caution us against trusting (at least without heavy qualification) the claims of domestic and regional self-sufficiency occasionally put forth by our sources and some scholars.[161] Secondly, modern economics *can* help us understand the Roman economy. Cicero's Rhodian merchant story presupposes a grain market governed by supply and demand. Economics has moved well beyond its own classical roots and has much to offer the ancient historian. Thirdly, while the Romans certainly did not have a command economy, the role of the state, despite the small size of the bureaucracy, was substantial in creating markets (through public contracts and imperialism in general), suppressing or managing competition (through law and state monopolies), and lowering transaction costs (through, for example, road building and the production of a reliable coinage).[162] Finally, the considerable influence of the state, the importance of networks of family and friends, and the role of luck in Roman trade do not mean that we can only make useful comparisons with other pre-modern economies. Friends and family remain crucial in many modern businesses,[163] government regulations, spending, and incentives still drive the economy,[164] and, given the fickle nature of taste and fashion, luck remains a factor.

---

[161] E.g., Bang (2007, 29).

[162] Although, as Bang (2007, 44) would insist, "The imperial interest was in tribute first" rather than fostering commerce.

[163] For example, the family-owned South Korean *chaebol* or the Murdoch media empire.

[164] E.g., Eisenhower's "Military-Industrial Complex" or the American Recovery and Reinvestment Act of 2009.

LIST OF ABBREVIATIONS

Abbreviations of journals and works employed in this book are those from *L'Année Philologique* and the *Oxford Classical Dictionary* 4th ed., in addition to the following:

DULAT   Del Olmo Lete, G. and J. Sanmartin. 2003. *A Dictionary of the Ugaritic Language in the Alphabetic Tradition*. I-II. Leiden and Boston: Brill.

EAH   Bagnall, R. et al., ed. 2012. *The Encyclopedia of Ancient History*. Malden, MA: Blackwell.

Emar 6.3   Arnaud, D. 1986. *Recherches au pays d'Aštata-Emar VI.3 Textes sumériens et accadiens. Transcriptions et traductions*. Paris: ÉRC.

KAJ   Ebeling, E. 1927 *Keilschrifttexte aus Assur. Juristischen Inhalts*. Leipzig [reprint, Osnabrück 1968].

KTU   Dietrich, M. et al. 1995. *The Cuneiform Alphabetic Texts from Ugarit, Ras Ibn Hani and Other Places* (KTU). 2nd Engl. ed. Munster: Ugarit Verlag.

PRU 3   Nougayrol, J. 1955. *Le palais royal d' Ugarit 3*: *Textes accadiens et hourrites des archives est, ouest et centrales. Mission de Ras Shamra 6*. Paris: Klincksieck.

PRU 4   Nougayrol, J. 1956 *Le palais royal d' Ugarit 4*: *Textes accadiens des archives sud (archives internationales)*, 2 vols. *Mission de Ras Shamra 9*. Paris: Klincksieck.

RSO 7   Bordreuil, P. ed. 1991. *Une bibliothèque au sud de la ville. Ras Shamra-Ougarit 7*. Paris: ÉRC.

Ug. 5   Nougayrol, J. et al. 1968. *Ugaritica V*: *Nouveaux textes accadiens, hourrites et ugaritiques des archives et bibliotheques privees d' Ugarit*. Paris: Geuthner.

BIBLIOGRAPHY

Abraham, K. 2004. *Business and Politics under the Persian Empire: The Financial Dealings of Marduk-nāṣir-apli of the House of Egibi (521-487 B.C.E.).* Bethesda: CDL Press.

Abulafia, D. 2011. *The Great Sea: A Human History of the Mediterranean.* Oxford: Oxford University Press.

Alberti, M.E. and N. Parise. 2005. "Towards a Unification of Mass-units between the Aegean and the Levant." In Laffineur and Greco, 2005, 381-91, pls. 83-86.

Alston, R. and O.M. van Nijf, eds. 2008. *Feeding the Ancient Greek City. Groningen-Royal Holloway Studies on the Greek City after the Classical Age vol. 1.* Leuven: Peeters.

Ampolo, C. and E. Bresciani. 1988. "Psammetico re d'Egitto e il mercenario Pedon." *Egitto e Vicino Oriente* 11: 237-53.

Anderson, B.L. and A.J.H. Latham, eds. 1986. *The Market in History.* London: Croon Helm.

Andreau, J. 1995. "Italy, Europe and the Mediterranean: Relations in Banking and Business during the Last Centuries B.C." In Swaddling et al., 1995, 305-12.

———. 1999. *Banking and Business in the Roman World.* Cambridge: Cambridge University Press.

———. 2002. "Twenty years after Moses I. Finley's *The Ancient Economy.*" In Scheidel and von Reden, 2002, 33-49.

Andreau, J. et al., eds. 1994. *Les échanges dans l'Antiquité: le role de l'État.* Saint-Bertrand de Comminges: Musée archéologique départemental.

Antonaccio, C. 2002. "Warriors, Traders, and Ancestors: The 'Heroes' of Lefkandi." In Hotje, 2002, 13-42.

Archibald, Z. 2007. "Contacts between the Ptolemaic Kingdom and the Black Sea in the early Hellenistic Age." In Gabrielsen and Lund, 2007, 253-71.

———. 2011. "Mobility and Innovation in Hellenistic Economies: the Causes and Consequences of Human Traffic." In Archibald et al., 2011, 42-65.

Archibald, Z. et al., eds. 2001. *Hellenistic Economies.* London: Routledge.

———. 2005. *Making, Moving, and Managing: The New World of Ancient Economies, 323-31 BC.* Oxford: Oxbow.

————. 2011. *The Economies of Hellenistic Societies, Third to First Centuries BC*. Oxford: Oxford University Press.

Arnaud, D. 1991. *Textes syriens de l'âge du Bronze recent (AuOr* Suppl 1). Barcelona: Sabadell.

Arnaud, P. 2011. "Sailing 90° from the Wind: Norm or Exception?" In Harris and Iara, 2011, 147-60.

Aro, S. and R.M. Whiting, eds. 2000. *The Heirs of Assyria: Proceedings of the Opening Symposium of the Assyrian and Babylonian Intellectual Heritage Project. Held in Tvärminne, Finland, October 8-11, 1998*. Helsinki: The Neo-Assyrian Text Corpus Project.

Artzy, M. 1995. "Nami: A Second Millennium International Maritime Trading Center in the Mediterranean." In Gitin, 1995, 17-40.

Aruz, J. et al., eds. 2008. *Beyond Babylon: Art, Trade, and Diplomacy in the Second Millennium B.C*. New York, Metropolitan Museum of Art.

Asheri, D. et al. 2007. *A Commentary on Herodotus Books I-IV*. Oxford: Oxford University Press.

Astour, M. 1972. "The Merchant Class of Ugarit." In *Gesellschaftsklassen im Alten Zweistromland und in den angrenzenden Gebieten (XVIIIth Rencontre assyriologique internationale, München, 29. Juni bis 3. Juli 1970)*, ed. D.O. Edzard, 12–26. München: Verlag der Bayerischen Akademie der Wissenschaften.

Aubet, M.E. 2001. *The Phoenicians and the West. Politics, Colonies and Trade*, 2nd ed. Cambridge: Cambridge University Press.

————. 2013. *Commerce and Colonization in the Ancient Near East*. Cambridge: Cambridge University Press.

Aubert, J.-J. 2001. "The Fourth Factor: Managing Non-Agricultural Production in the Roman World." In Mattingly and Salmon, 2001, 90-111.

————. 2004. "The Republican Economy and Roman Law: Regulation, Promotion, or Reflection?" In Flower, 2004, 160-78.

Austin, M.M. 1986. "Hellenistic Kings, War, and the Economy." *CQ* 36.2: 450-66.

————1994. "Society and Economy." *CAH* 6: 524-64.

————. 2006. *The Hellenistic World from Alexander to the Roman Conquest: A Selection of Ancient Sources in Translation*, 2nd ed. Cambridge: Cambridge University Press.

Avram, A. 2007. "Some Thoughts about the Black Sea and the Slave Trade before the Roman Domination (6th – 1st centuries BC)." In Gabrielsen and Lund, 2007, 239-51.

Bächle, A.E., ed. 2007. *Keimelion: Elitenbildung und elitörer Konsum von der Mykenischen Palastzeit bis zur Homerischen Epoche*. Wien: Verlag der Österreichischen Akademie der Wissenschaften.

Bagnall, R. et al. 1996. "A Ptolemaic Inscription from Bir 'Iayyan." *CE* 71: 317-30.

Bairoch, P. 1988. *Cities and Economic Development: From the Dawn of History to the Present*. Chicago: University of Chicago Press.

Bakels, C. and S. Jacomet. 2003. "Access to Luxury Foods in Central Europe during the Roman Period: the Archaeobotanical Evidence." *World Archaeology* 34 (3): 542-57.

Baker, H. 2008. "Babylon in 484 BC: the Excavated Archival Tablets as a Source for Urban History." *Zeitschrift für Assyriologie* 98: 100-16.

Banaji, J. 2001. *Agrarian Change in Late Antiquity: Gold, Labour, and Aristocratic Dominance*. Oxford Classical Monographs. Oxford: Oxford University Press.

Bang, P.F. 2004. "The Mediterranean: A Corrupting Sea? A Review Essay on Ecology and History, Anthropology and Synthesis." *Ancient West & East* 3.2: 385-99.

———. 2006. "Imperial Bazaar: Towards a Comparative Understanding of Markets in the Roman Empire." In Bang et al., 2006, 51-88.

———. 2007. "Trade and Empire: In search of Organizing Concepts for the Roman Economy." *P&P* 195: 3-54.

———. 2008. *The Roman Bazaar: A Comparative Study of Trade and Markets in a Tributary Empire*. Cambridge: Cambridge University Press.

———. 2009. "Commanding and Consuming the World: Empire, Tribute, and Trade in Roman and Chinese History." In Scheidel, 2009, 100-20.

———. 2010. *Oxford Encyclopedia of Ancient Greece and Rome*, ed. M. Gargarin and E. Fantham. Oxford: Oxford University Press. s.v. "Roman Trade and Commerce."

———. 2012. s.v. "Markets, Roman." In *EAH*.

Bang, P.F. et al., eds. 2006. *Ancient Economies, Modern Methodologies: Archaeology, Comparative History, Models and Institutions.* Bari: Edipuglia.

Bass, G. 1995. "Sea and River Craft in the Ancient Near East." In Sasson, 1995, 1421-31.

Baumol, W. and J. Mokyr, eds. 2010. *The Invention of Enterprise: Entrepreneurship from Ancient Mesopotamia to Modern Times.* Princeton: Princeton University Press.

Baynham, E.J. 2014. "Cleomenes of Naucratis, Villian or Victim?" In Howe et al., 2015, 127-34.

Beaulieu, P.-A. 2000. "A Finger in Every Pie: The Institutional Connections of a Family of Entrepreneurs in Neo-Babylonian Larsa." In Bongenaar, 2000, 43-72.

———. 2003. *The Pantheon of Uruk during the Neo-Babylonian Period.* Leiden: Brill.

———. 2006. "Official and Vernacular Languages: The Shifting Sands of Imperial and Cultural Identies in First Millennium B.C. Mesopotamia." In Sanders, 2006, 187-216.

Bedford, P. R. 2005. "The Economy of the Near East in the First Millennium." In Manning and Morris, 2005, 58-83.

Bekker-Nielsen, T., ed. 2005. *Ancient Fishing and Fish Processing in the Black Sea Region.* Aarhus: Aarhus University Press.

———. 2012. s.v. "Roads, Roman Empire." In *EAH.*

Bernard, P., et al. 2004. "Deux nouvelles inscriptions grecques de l'Asie central." *JS* 2004/2: 227-356.

Berthold, R.M. 1984. *Rhodes in the Hellenistic Age.* Ithaca: Cornell University Press.

Bikai, P.M. 2000. "The Iron Age Potter from Kommos." In Shaw and Shaw, 2000, 302-21.

Bilde, P. et al., eds. 1993. *Centre and Periphery in the Hellenistic World.* Aarhus: Aarhus University Press.

Billows, R.A. 1990. *Antigonos the One-Eyed and the Creation of the Hellenistic State.* Berkeley: University of California Press.

Boardman, J. 1987. "Silver is White." *RA* 2: 279-95.

———. 1988. "Trade in Greek Decorated Pottery." *OJA* 7: 27-33.

———. 1999. "Greek Colonization: The Eastern Contribution." In Vallet et al., 1999, 39-50.

———. 2002. "Greeks and Syria: Pots and People." In Tsetskhladze and Snodgrass, 2002, 1-16.

Bodel, J. 2005. "*Caveat Emptor:* Towards a Study of Roman Slave-Traders." *JRA* 18: 181-95.

Bongenaar, A.C.V.M. 2000. *Interdependency of Institutions and Private Entrepreneurs: Proceedings of the Second MOS Symposium (Leiden 1998).* Istanbul: Nederlands Historisch-Archaeologisch Instituut.

Bopearachchi, O. and M.-F. Boussac, eds. 2005. *Afghanistan, ancien carrefour entre l'Est et l'Ouest.* Turnhout: Brepols.

Bordreuil P. and D. Pardee. 2010. "Textes alphabétiques inédits du Musée du Louvre." In van Soldt, 2010, 1-15.

Bosman, P.R, ed. 2014. *Alexander in Africa. AClass Supplementum* V. Pretoria: V&R Printing Works.

Bowden, H. 1996. "The Greek Settlement and Sanctuaries at Naukratis." In Hansen and Raaflaub, 1996, 17-37.

Bowman, A. 2010. 'Trade and the flag: Alexandria, Egypt and the Imperial House." In Robinson and Wilson, 2010, 103-109.

Bowman, A. and A. Wilson. 2009. *Quantifying the Roman Economy: Methods and Problems.* Oxford: Oxford University Press.

Bradley, K.R. 1987. "On the Roman Slave Supply and Slavebreeding." *Slavery and Abolition* 8: 42-64.

Bradley, R. 1971. "Trade Competition and Artefact Distribution." *World Archaeology* 2.3: 347-52.

Braudel, F. 1982. *The Wheels of Commerce. Civilization and Capitalism 15th-18th Century*, vol. 2, trans. S. Reynolds. New York: Harper and Row.

———. 1984. *The Perspective of the World. Civilization and Capitalism 15th-18th Century*, vol. 3, trans. S. Reynolds. New York: Harper and Row.

Bravo, B. 1977. "Remarques sur les assises sociales, les formes d'organisation et la terminologie du commerce maritime grec à l'époque archaique." *DHA* 10: 99-160.

Bresson, A. 1993. "La circulation des monnaies rhodiennes jusqu'en 166." *DHA* 19: 119-69.

———. 1994. "L'attendat d'Hieron et le commerce grec." In J. Andreau, et al., 1994, 47-68.

———. 2000. *La cité marchande.* Bordeaux: Ausonius.

———. 2002. "Quatre *emporia* antiques: Abul, La Picola, Elizavetovskoie, Naucratis." *REA* 104: 475-505.

———. 2003. "Merchants and Politics in Ancient Greece: Economic Aspects." In Zaccagnini, 2003, 139-63.

———. 2005. "Ecology and Beyond: The Mediterranean Paradigm." In Harris, 2005, 94-114.

———. 2007. *L'économie de la Grèce des cités (fin VIe-Ier siècle a. C.). Vol. I. Les structures et la production.* Paris: A. Colin.

———. 2008. *L'économie de la Grèce des cités (fin VIe-Ier siècle a. C.). Vol. II. Les espaces de l'échange.* Paris: A. Colin.

———. 2011. "Grain from Cyrene." In Archibald, et al., 2011, 66-95.

———. 2012. "Wine, Oil and Delicacies at the Pelousion Customs." In Günther and Grieb, 2012.

Bresson, A., ed. 2006. *Approches de l'économie hellénistique.* Saint-Bertrand-de-Comminges: Musée Archéologique.

Briant, P. 2002. *From Cyrus to Alexander. A History of the Persian Empire.* Winona Lake, IN: Eisenbrauns.

———. 2009. "Alexander and the Persian Empire, Between 'Decline' and 'Renovation.' History and historiography." In Heckel and Tritle, 2009, 171-88.

Briant, P. and R. Descat. 1998. "Un registre douanier de la satrapie d'Égypte à l'époque achéménide." In Grimal and Menu, 1998, 59-104.

Briant, P. and F. Joannès, eds. 2006. *La transition entre l'empire achéménide et les royaumes hellénistiques.* Paris: De Boccard.

Bringmann, K. 2001. "Grain, Timber, and Money: Hellenistic Kings, Finance, Buildings and Foundations in Greek Cities." In Archibald et al., 2001, 205-14.

Bron, F. and A. Lemaire. 1989. "Les inscriptions araméennes de Hazael." *RA* 83: 35-43.

Buraselis, K. and M. Stephanou, eds. (Forthcoming). *The Ptolemies, the Sea and the Nile.* Cambridge: Cambridge University Press.

Burford, A. 1994. "Greek Agriculture in the Classical Period."*CAH* 6: 661-67.

Burkert, W. 1992. *The Orientalizing Revolution; Near Eastern Influence on Greek Culture in the Early Archaic Age.* Cambridge, MA: Harvard University Press.

de Callataÿ, F. 2005. "A Quantitative Survey of Hellenistic Coinages: Recent Achievements," In Archibald et al., 2005, 73-91.

Caminos, R. A. 1954. *Late Egyptian Miscellanies*. Oxford: Oxford University Press.

Camodeca, G. 1999. *Tabulae Pompeianae Sulpiciorum (TPSulp): edizione critica dell'archivio puteolano dei Sulpicii*. Rome: Edizioni Quasar.

Campbell, G. ed., 2014. *The Oxford Handbook of Animals in Classical Thought and Life*. Oxford: Oxford University Press.

Carter, J.B. and S.P. Morris, eds. 1995. *The Ages of Homer*. Austin: University of Texas.

Cartledge, P. 1983. "'Trade and Politics' Revisited: Archaic Greece." In Garnsey et al., 1983, 1-15.

———. 1998. "The Economy (Economies) of Ancient Greece." *Dialogos* 5: 4-24.

———. 1997. "Introduction." In Cartledge et al., 1997, 1-19.

Cartledge, P. et al., eds. 1997. *Hellenistic Constructs. Essays in Culture, History, and Historiography*. Berkeley: University of California Press.

Carruba, O. et al., eds. 1983. *Studi F. Pintore*. Pavia: GJES.

Casson, L. 1954. "The Grain Trade of the Hellenistic world." *TAPA* 85: 168-87.

———. 1989. *The Periplus Maris Erythraei: Text with Introduction, Translation, and Commentary*. Princeton: Princeton University Press.

Casson, L. 1995/1971. *Ships and Seamanship in the Ancient World*. Princeton: Princeton University Press.

Castagnoli, F. 1980. "Installazioni portuali a Roma." *MAAR* 36: 35-42.

Castle, E. W. 1992. "Shipping and Trade in Ramesside Egypt." *JESHO* 35.3: 239-77.

Chase-Dunn, C. and T. Hall. 1997. *Rise and Demise: Comparing World-Systems*. Boulder, CO: Westview Press.

Clancier, Ph. et al. 2005. *Autour de Polanyi, vocabulaires, théories et modalités des échanges*. Paris: De Boccard.

Cleland, L. 2012. s.v. "Clothing, Greece and Rome." In *EAH*.

Cobet, J. et al., eds. 2007. *Frühes Ionien: Eine Bestandsaufnahme*. Mainz am Rhein: Von Zabern.

Cogan, M. and I. Eph'al, eds. 1991. *Ah, Assyria: Studies in Assyrian History and Ancient Near Eastern Historiography Presented to Hayim Tadmor*. Jerusalem: Magnes Press, Hebrew University.

Cohen, E.E. 1973. *Ancient Athenian Maritime Courts*. Princeton: Princeton University Press.

———. 2005. "Commercial Law." In Gagarin and Cohen, 2005, 290-302.

Cohen, R. and R. Westbrook, eds. 2008. *Isaiah's Vision of Peace in Biblical and Modern Internationa Relations: Swords into Plowshares*. New York: Palgrave Macmillan.

Cole, S. 1996. *Nippur in Late Assyrian Times, c. 755-612 B.C.* Helsinki: Neo-Assyrian Text Corpus Project.

Collon, D. 1987. *First Impressions: Cylinder Seals in the Ancient Near East*. London: British Museum.

Courtois, J.-C. 1990. "Poids, prix, taxes et salaires à Ougarit (Syrie) au IIe millénaire." In Gyselen, 1990, 119-27.

Crawford, M.H. 1977. "Republican denarii in Romania: The Suppression of Piracy and the Slave-Trade." *JRS* 67: 117-24.

Cueva, E.P., ed. 2009. *Jesuit Education and the Classics*. Cambridge: Cambridge Scholars Press.

Curtis, R.I. 1988. "A. Umbricius Scaurus of Pompeii." In *Studia Pompeiana & Classica in Honor of Wilhelmina F. Jashemski*, ed. R. I. Curtis, 19-50. New York: Aristide D. Caratzas.

———. 1991. *Garum and Salsamenta: Production and Commerce in Materia Medica, Studies in Ancient Medicine*. Leiden: Brill.

D'Arms, J.H. 1977. "M. I. Rostovtzeff and M. I. Finley: The Status of Traders in the Roman World." In D'Arms and Eadie, 1977, 159-79.

———. 1980. "Republican Senators' Involvement in Commerce in the Late Republic: Some Ciceronian Evidence." *MAAR* 36: 77-90.

———. 1981. *Commerce and Social Standing in Ancient Rome*. Cambridge, MA: Harvard University Press.

D'Arms, J.H. and J.W. Eadie, eds. 1977. *Ancient and Modern: Essays in Honor of Gerald F. Else*. Ann Arbor: University of Michigan Press.

Daube, D. 1969. "The Protection of the Non-Tipper." In *Roman Law: Linguistic, Social and Philosophical Aspects*, ed. D. Daube, 117-28. Edinburgh: Edinburgh University Press.

Davies, J.K. 1984. "Cultural, Social and Economic Features of the Hellenistic World." *CAH* 7.1: 257-320.

———. 2001. "Hellenistic Economies in the Post-Finley Era." In Archibald et al., 2001, 11-62.

Davis, D.L. 2012. s.v. "Navigation (economy)." In *EAH*.

Deger-Jalkotzy, S. and I. S. Lemos, eds. 2006. *Ancient Greece: From the Mycenaean Palaces to the Age of Homer*. Edinburgh: University of Edinburgh Press.

Demetriou, D. 2012. *Negotiating Identity in the Ancient Mediterranean: The Archaic and Classical Greek Multi-ethnic Emporia*. Cambridge: Cambridge University Press.

Depeyrot, G. et al., eds. 1987. *Rythmes de la production monétaire, de l'antiquité à nos jours: actes du colloque international organisé à Paris du 10 au 12 Janvier 1986*. Louvain-la-Neuve: Seminaire de numismatique Marcel Hoc College Erasme.

Dercksen, J.G., ed. 1999. *Trade and Finance in Ancient Mesopotamia: Proceedings of the First MOS Symposium (Leiden 1997)*. Leiden: Nederlands Instituut voor het Nabije Oosten.

Desborough, V.R.d'A. 1972. *The Greek Dark Ages*. London: Benn.

Descat, R. 2000. "L'etat et les marchés dans le monde grec." In Lo Cascio, 2000, 13-29.

Descoeudres, J.-P., ed. 1990. *Greek Colonists and Native Populations*. Oxford: Oxford University Press.

Dever, W. et al., eds. 2006. *Confronting the Past: Archaeological and Historical Essays on Ancient Israel in Honor of William G. Dever*. Winona Lake, IN: Eisenbrauns.

Diakonoff, I.M. 1968. "Main Features of the Economy in the Monarchies of Ancient Western Asia." In Eversley, 1968, 13-32.

———. 1973. *Ancient Mesopotamia: Socio-Economic History, a Collection of Studies by Soviet Scholars*. Moscow: Nauka Pub. House, Central Dept. of Oriental Literature.

Dietrich, M. and O. Loretz, eds. 1995. *Ugarit. Ein ostmediterranean Kulturzentren im Alten Orient. Band 1*. Münster: Ugarit Verlag.

———. 2009. "Die keilalphabetischen Briefe aus Ugarit (I) KTU 2.72, 2.76, 2.86, 2.87, 2.88, 2.89 und 2.90." *Ugarit-Forschungen* 41: 109-65.

Dillingham, A.E., et al. 1992. *Economics: Individual Choice and its Consequences*. Boston: Allyn and Bacon.

Domingo Gygax, M. 2003. "Euergetismus und Gabentausch." *Métis* n.s. 1: 181-200.

Drake, B.L. 2012. "The Influence of Climatic Change on the Late Bronze Age Collapse and the Greek Dark Ages." *JAS* 39.6: 1862-70.

Drews, R. 1993. *The End of the Dark Age: Changes in Warfare and the Catastrophe ca. 1200 B.C.* Princeton: Princeton University Press.

Duncan-Jones, R.P. 1987. "Weight-Loss as an Index of Coin-Wear in Currency of the Roman Principate." In Depeyrot et al., 1987, 237-56.

Edey, H. and B.S. Yamey, eds. 1974. *Debts, Credits, Finance, and Profits.* London: Sweet and Maxwell.

Edzard, D.O., ed. 1972. *Gesellschaftsklassen im Alten Zweistromland und in den angrenzenden Gebieten (XVIIIth Rencontre assyriologique internationale, München, 29. Juni bis 3. Juli 1970).* München: Bayerischen Akademie der Wissenschaften.

Ekelund, R.B., Jr. and R.F. Hébert. 1997. *A History of Economic Theory and Method.* New York: McGraw-Hill.

Elat, M. 1978. "The Economic Relations of the Neo-Assyrian Empire with Egypt." *JAOS* 98: 20-34.

―――. 1987. "Der *tamkaru* im neuassyrischen Reich." *JESHO* 30: 233-54.

―――. 1991. "Phoenician Overland Trade within the Mesopotamian Empires." In Cogan and Eph'al, 1991, 21-35.

―――. 1998. "Die Wirtschaftlichen Beziehungen der Assyrer mit den Araben." In Maul, 1998, 39-57.

Eliade, M. 1987 [1959]. *The Sacred and the Profane.* Trans. W. Trask. New York: Harcourt.

Empereur, J.-Y. 1982. "Les anses d'amphores timbrées et les amphores: aspects quantitatifs." *BCH* 106: 219-33.

Empereur, J.-Y. and Y. Garlan, eds. 1986. *Recherches sur les amphores grecques.* Paris: de Boccard.

Engen, D.T. 2010. *Honor and Profit. Athenian Trade Policy and the Economy and Society of Greece, 415-307 B.C.E.* Ann Arbor: University of Michigan Press.

―――. 2011. "Democracy, Knowledge, and the Hidden Economy of Athens." *Journal of Economic Asymmetries* 8.1: 93-106.

Eph'al, I., and J. Naveh. 1989. "Hazael's Booty Inscription." *IEJ* 39: 192-200.

―――. 1993. "Jar of the Gate." *BASOR* 289: 60-65.

Erdkamp, P. 2005. *The Grain Market in the Roman Empire. A Social, Political and Economic Study.* Cambridge: Cambridge University Press.

Eriksen, T.H. 1993. *Ethnicity and Nationalism: Anthropological Perspectives*. Boulder, CO: Pluto.

Evers, H.-D. 1994. "The Trader's Dilemma: A Theory of the Social Transformation of Markets and Society." In Evers and Schrader, 1994, 7-14.

Evers, H.-D. and H. Schrader, eds. 1994. *The Moral Economy of Trade: Ethnicity and Developing Markets*. New York: Routledge.

Eversley, D.E.C., ed. 1968. *Troisième conférence internationale d'histoire économique = Third International Conference of Economic History: Munich, 1965*, vol. 4. The Hague: Mouton.

Fabre, D. and F. Goddio. 2010. "The Development and Operation of the Portus Magnus in Alexandria: An Overview." In Robinson and Wilson, 2010, 53-74.

Fales, F.M. 2008. "On *Pax Assyriaca* in the Eighth-Seventh Centuries BCE and its Implications." In Cohen and Westbrook, 2008, 17-35.

Farber, H. 1978. "A Price and Wage Study for Northern Babylonia during the Old Babylonian Period." *JESHO* 21: 1-51.

Feuvrier Prévotat, C. 1981. "Negotiator et mercator dans le discours cicéronien: essai dedéfinition." *DHA* 7: 367-405.

Finkielsztejn, G. 2001. *Chronologie détaillée et révisée des eponyms amphorique rhodiens, de 270 à 108 av. J-C. environ: Premier bilan*. Oxford: Archaeopress.

Finley, M.I., ed. 1968. *Troisième conférence internationale d'histoire économique = Third International Conference of Economic History: Munich, 1965*, vol. 3. Paris: Mouton.

———. 1970. "Aristotle and Economic Analysis." *P&P* 47: 3-25.

———. 1973. *The Ancient Economy*. Berkeley: University of California Press.

———. 1985. *The Ancient Economy*, rev ed. Berkeley: University of California Press.

———. 1999. *The Ancient Economy*. 2nd ed. Updated with new foreword by I. Morris. Berkeley: University of California Press.

Flower, H.I., ed. 2004. *Cambridge Companion to the Roman Republic*. Cambridge: Cambridge University Press.

Foley, B.P., et al. 2009. "The 2005 Chios Ancient Shipwreck Survey: New Methods for Underwater Archaeology." *Hesperia* 78.2: 269-305.

Foster, B.R. 1993. *Before the Muses: An Anthology of Akkadian Literature*. Bethesda: CDL Press.

Foxhall, L. et al., eds. 2010. *Intentional History: Spinning Time in Ancient Greece*. Stuttgart: Franz Steiner.

Fraser, P.M. 1972. *Ptolemaic Alexandria*. 3 vols. Oxford: Clarendon Press.

Frayn, J.M. 1984. *Sheep-Rearing and the Wool Trade in Italy during the Roman Period*. Liverpool: F. Cairns.

—————. 1993. *Markets and Fairs in Roman Italy: Their Social and Economic Importance from the Second Century B.C. to the Third Century A.D.* Oxford: Clarendon Press.

Freydank, H. 1976. *Mittelassyrische Rechtsurkenden und Verwaltungstexte (MARV)*. Berlin: Akademie Verlag.

Friesen, S.J. 2004. "Poverty in Pauline studies: Beyond the So-called New Consensus." *Journal for the Study of the New Testament* 26: 323-61.

Gabba, E. 1980. "Riflessioni antiche e moderne sulle attività commerciali a Roma nei secoli II e I a.C." *MAAR* 36: 91-102.

Gabrielsen, V. 1997. *The Naval Aristocracy of Hellenistic Rhodes*. Aarhus: Aarhus University Press.

—————. 2001a. "Economic Activity, Maritime Trade, and Piracy in the Hellenistic Aegean." *REA* 103: 219-40.

—————. 2001b. "The Rhodian Associations and Economic Activity." In Archibald et al., 2001, 215-44.

—————. 2003. "Piracy and the Slave-Trade." In *A Companion to the Hellenistic World*, ed. A. Erskine, 389-404. Malden, MA: Blackwell.

—————. 2005. "Banking and Credit Operations in Hellenistic Times." In Archibald et al., 2005, 136-64.

—————. 2007. "Brotherhoods of Faith and Provident Planning: The Non-Public Associations of the Greek World." *MHR* 22.2: 183-210.

—————. 2011. "Profitable Partnerships: Monopolies, Traders, Kings and Cities." In Archibald et al., 2011, 216-50.

—————. (Forthcoming). "Rhodes 6and the Ptolemaic Kingdom: Commercial Infrastructure." In Buraselis and Stephanou, (forthcoming).

Gabrielsen, V. et al, eds. 1999. *Hellenistic Rhodes: Politics, Culture, and Society*. Aarhus: Aarhus University Press.

Gabrielsen, V. and J. Lund, eds. 2007. *The Black Sea in Antiquity: Regional and Interregional Economic Exchanges*. Aarhus: Aarhus University Press.

Gagarin M. and D. Cohen, eds. 2005. *The Cambridge Companion to Ancient Greek Law*. Cambridge: Cambridge University Press.

Gale, N. ed. 1991. *Bronze Age Trade in the Mediterranean*. Jonsered: P. Åströms Förlag.

Garelli, P. 1984. "Importance et rôle des araméens dans l'administration de l'empire assyrien." In Kühne, Nissen, and Renger, 1984, 437-47.

Garland, R. 1987. *The Piraeus*. London: Duckworth.

Garnsey, P. 1988. *Famine and Food Supply in the Graeco-Roman World*. Cambridge: Cambridge University Press.

Garnsey, P. et al. 1983. *Trade in the Ancient Economy*. Berkeley: University of California Press.

Garnsey, P. and C.R. Whittaker, eds. 1983. *Trade and Famine in Classical Antiquity*. Cambridge: The Cambridge Philological Society.

Garnsey, P., and R.P. Saller. 1987. *The Roman Empire: Economy, Society and Culture*. Berkeley: University of California Press.

Gellner, E. 1983. *Nations and Nationalism*. Ithaca: Cornell University Press.

Giardina, A. 2007. "The Transition to Late Antiquity." In Scheidel et al., 2007, 743-68.

Gibbins, D. 2001. "Shipwrecks and Hellenistic Trade." In Archibald et al., 2001, 273-312.

Gibbs, M. 2012. s.v. "Collegia." In *EAH*.

Gibson, M. 1991. "Duplicate Systems of Trade: A Key Element in Mesopotamian History." In Haellquist, 1991, 27-37.

Gill, D.W.J. 1988. "'Trade in Greek Decorated Pottery': Some Corrections." *OJA* 7: 369-70.

———. 1991. "Pots and Trade: Spacefillers or Objets d'art?" *JHS* 111: 29-47.

———. 1994. "Positivism, Pots, and Long-Distance Trade." In Morris, 1994, 99-107.

Gitin, S., ed. 1995. *Recent Excavations in Israel. A View to the West* (Archaeological Institute of America Colloquia and Conference Papers No. 1). Dubuque, IA: Kendall Hunt.

Goddio, F. 2011. "Heracleion-Thonis and Alexandria, Two Ancient Egyptian Emporia." In Robinson and Wilson, 2011, 121-37.

Goddio, F. and A. Bernand. 2004. *Sunken Egypt. Alexandria*. London: Periplus.

Goedicke, H. and J.J.M. Roberts, eds. 1975. *Unity and Diversity: Essays in the History, Literature, and Religion of the Ancient Near East*. Baltimore, MD: Johns Hopkins University Press.

Goetzmann, W. and G. Rouwenhorst, eds. 2005. *The Origins of Value. The Financial Innovations that Created Modern Capital Markets*. Oxford: Oxford University Press.

Goldberg, J.L. 2012. *Trade and Institutions in the Medieval Mediterranean. The Geniza Merchants and their Business World*. Cambridge: Cambridge University Press.

Graeber, D. 2011. *Debt: The First 5,000 Years*. Brooklyn: Melville House.

Graham, A. J. 1983 [1964]. *Colony and Mother City in Ancient Greece*. 2nd ed. Chicago: Ares.

———. 2001. *Collected Papers on Greek Colonization*. Leiden: Brill.

Grant, M. and R. Kitzinger, eds. 1988. *Civilization of the Ancient Mediterranean*. New York: Charles Scribner's Sons.

Graslin-Thomé, L. 2009. *Les échanges à longue distance en Mésopotamie au Ier millénaire: une approche économique*. Paris: De Boccard.

Grayson, A.K. 1976. "Studies in Neo-Assyrian History in the Ninth Century B.C." *BO* 33: 134-45.

Greene, E.S. and M.L. Lawall. 2005/06. "Amphora Capacities in Early Monetary Asia Minor: The Pabuç Burnu Shipwreck." *Skyllis* 7: 17-23.

Greene E.S. et al., eds. 2008. "Inconspicuous Consumption: The Sixth-Century B.C.E. Shipwreck at Pabuç Burnu." *AJA* 112: 685-711.

Greene, K. 1986. *The Archaeology of the Roman Economy*. London: B. T. Batsford Ltd.

———. 1992. *Roman Pottery*. Berkeley and Los Angeles: University of California Press.

———. 2000. "Technological Innovation and Economic Progress in the Ancient World: M. I. Finley reconsidered." *EHR* 53: 29-59.

Grieb, V. et al., eds. 2012. *Piraterie von der Antike bis zur Gegenwart*. Stuttgart: Franz Steiner Verlag.

Grimal, N. and B. Menu, eds. 1998. *Le commerce en Égypte ancienne*. Cairo: Institut Français d'Archéologie Orientale.

Günther, L.-M. and V. Grieb, eds. 2012. *Das imperial Rom und der hellenistische Osten. Festschrift für Jürgen Deininger zum 75. Geburtstag*. Stuttgart: Franz Steiner Verlag.

Gwartney, J.D. and R.L. Stroup, eds. 1995. *Economics: Private and Public Choice*. Orlando: The Dryden Press.

Gyselen, R., ed. 1990. *Res Orientales II. Prix, salaires, poids et mesures*. Leuven: Peeters.

Habicht, C. 2003. "Rhodian Amphora Stamps and Rhodian Eponyms." *REA* 105: 541-78.

Haellquist, K.R., ed. 1991. *Asian Trade Routes*. London: Curzon.

Hall, J.M. 2004. "How 'Greek' were the Early Western Greeks?" In Lomas, 2004, 35-54.

———. 2007. *A History of the Archaic Greek World ca. 1200-479*. Malden, MA: Wiley-Blackwell.

Hallager, B.P. 1983. "A New Social Class in Late Bronze Age Crete: Foreign Traders in Khania." In Nixon and Krzyszkowska, 1983, 111–19.

Hallo, W. and K.L. Younger, eds. 2002. *The Context of Scripture. Vol. 3: Archival Documents from the Biblical World*. Leiden: Brill.

Hallo, W. and W. K. Simpson. 1997. *The Ancient Near East: A History*. New York: Harcourt Brace Jovanovich.

Hannestad, L. 2007. "Timber as a Trade Resource of the Black Sea." In Gabrielsen and Lund, 2007, 85-99.

Hansen, M.H. and T.H. Nielsen, eds. 2004. *An Inventory of Archaic and Greek Poleis*. Oxford: Oxford University Press.

Hansen, M.H. and K. Raaflaub, eds. 1996. *More Studies in the Ancient Greek Polis*. Stuttgart: Franz Steiner.

Harl, K.W. 1996. *Coinage in the Roman Economy, 300 B.C. to A.D. 700, Ancient Society and History*. Baltimore: The Johns Hopkins University Press.

Harris, E.M. 2013. "Were there Business Agents in Classical Greece? The Evidence of Some Lead Letters." In Yiftach-Firanko, 2013, 105-24.

Harris, W.V. 1980. "Towards a Study of the Roman Slave Trade." *MAAR* 36: 117-40.

———. 1993. "Between Archaic and Modern: Problems in Roman Economic History." In *The Inscribed Economy: Production and*

Distribution in the Roman Empire in the Light of Instrumentum Domesticum: The Proceedings of a Conference Held at the American Academy in Rome on 10-11 January, 1992, ed. W. V. Harris, 11-29. Ann Arbor: University of Michigan.

———. 1999. "Demography, Geography and the Sources of Roman Slaves." *JRS* 98: 62-75.

———. 2000. "Trade (70-192 AD)." *CAH* 9: 710-39.

———. 2005. *Rethinking the Mediterranean*. Oxford: Oxford University Press.

———. 2009. "A Comment on Andrew Wilson: 'Approaches to Quantifying Roman Trade'." In Bowman and Wilson, 2009, 259-65.

———. 2011a. "Trade [70-192 AD]." In *Rome's Imperial Economy: Twelve Essays*, ed. W.V. Harris, 155-87. Oxford: Oxford University Press.

———. 2011b. "Introduction." In Harris and Iara, 2011, 9-20.

Harris, W.V. and G. Ruffini, eds. 2004. *Ancient Alexandria between Egypt and Greece*. Leiden: Brill.

Harris, W.V. and K. Iara, eds. 2011. *Maritime Technology in the Ancient Economy: Ship-Design and Navigation*. Portsmouth, RI: Journal of Roman Archaeology.

Harvey, F.D. 1976. "The Maritime Loan in Eupolis' 'Marikas' (*P.Oxy* 2741)." *ZPE* 23: 231-33.

Hasebroek, J. 1928. *Staat und Handel im alten Griechenland*. Tübingen: J.C.B. Mohr.

———. 1933. *Trade and Politics in Ancient Greece*. Tr. L.M. Fraser and D.C. Macgregor. London: G. Bell and Sons.

Hatzfeld, J. 1919. *Les trafiquants italiens dans l'Orient hellénique*. Paris: Boccard.

Heckel W. and L. Tritle, eds. 2009. *Alexander the Great: A New History*. Malden, MA: Wiley-Blackwell.

Hekster, O. et al., eds. 2007. *Crises and the Roman Empire: Proceedings of the Seventh Workshop of the International Network Impact of Empire (Nijmegen, June 20-24, 2006)*. Leiden: Brill.

Heichelheim, F.M. 1958. *An Ancient Economic History. From the Paleolithic Age to the Migrations of the Germanic, Slavic, and Arabic Nations*. Revised and Complete English Edition. Leiden: A.W. Sijthoff's Uitgeversmaatschappij.

Helms, M. 1988. *Ulysses' Sail: An Ethnographic Odyssey of Power, Knowledge, and Geographical Distance*. Princeton: Princeton University Press.

————. 1998. *Access to Origins: Affines, Ancestors and Aristocrats*. Austin: University of Texas Press.

Heltzer, M. 1978. *Goods, Prices and the Organization of Trade in Ugarit*. Wiesbaden: Reichert.

————. 1999. "The Economy of Ugarit." In Watson and Wyatt, 1999, 423-54.

Henkelman, W. et al., eds. 2001. "Herodotus and Babylon reconsidered." In Rollinger et al., 2001, 449-70.

Heubeck, A. and A. Hoekstra. 1989. *A Commentary on Homer's Odyssey. Volume II: Books IX-XVI*. Oxford: Oxford University Press.

Hirt, A.M. 2010. *Imperial Mines and Quarries in the Roman World: Organizational Aspects 27 BC-AD 235*. Oxford: Oxford University Press.

Hitchner, R.B. 2002. "Olive Production and the Roman Economy: The Case for Intensive Growth in the Roman Empire." In Scheidel and Von Reden, 2002, 71-83.

Hodder, I. 2012. *Entangled. An Archaeology of the Relationships between Humans and Things*. Malden, MA: Wiley-Blackwell.

Hoff, M. and R. Townsend, eds. 2013. *Rough Cilicia: New Historical and Archaeological Approaches*. Oxford: Oxbow Books.

Hoffner, H. 1997. *The Laws of the Hittites: A Critical Edition. Documenta et Monumenta Orientis Antiqui* 23. Leiden: Brill.

Hoftijzer, J., and W.H. Van Soldt. 1998. "Texts from Ugarit Pertaining to Seafaring." In Wachsmann, 1998, 333-44.

Hohlfelder, R.L. 1988. "The 1984 Explorations of the Ancient Harbors of Caesarea Maritima, Israel." *BASOR* 25: 1-12.

————. 2008. *The Maritime World of Ancient Rome: Proceedings of "The Maritime World of Ancient Rome" Conference Held at the American Academy in Rome, 27-29 March 2003*. Ann Arbor, Michigan: University of Michigan Press.

Holladay, J.S. 2006. "Hezekiah's Tribute, Long-Distance Trade, and the Wealth of Nations ca. 1000-600 BC: A New Perspective." In Dever et al., 2006, 309-31.

Hollander, D.B. 2007. *Money in the Late Roman Republic*. Leiden: Brill.

―――. (Forthcoming). "Roman Interest Rates." In *Oxford Handbook of Economies in the Classical World*, ed. A. Bresson, et al. Oxford: Oxford University Press.

Holleaux, M. 1938. *Études d'épigraphie et d'histoire grecques*. ed. L. Robert. Vol. 1. Paris: Boccard.

Holleran, C. 2012. *Shopping in Ancient Rome: The Retail Trade in the Late Republic and the Principate*. Oxford: Oxford University Press.

Hope, V.M. and E. Marshall, eds. 2000. *Death and Disease in the Ancient City*. New York: Routledge.

Hopkins, K. 1980. "Taxes and Trade in the Roman Empire (200 B.C. - A.D. 400)." *JRS* 70: 101-25.

―――. 1983. "Introduction." In Garnsey et al., 1983, ix-xxv.

―――. 1988. "Roman Trade, Industry, and Labor." In Grant and Kitzinger, 1988, 753-77.

―――. 1995/1996. "Rome, Taxes, Rents and Trade." *Kodai* 6/7: 41-75.

Hopper, R.J. 1961. "'Plain,' 'Shore,' and 'Hill' in Early Athens." *ABSA* 56: 189-219.

Horden, P. and N. Purcell. 2000. *The Corrupting Sea: A Study of Mediterranean History*. Oxford: Blackwell.

Hotje, J.M., ed. 2002. *Images of Ancestors*. Aarhus: Aarhus Studies in Mediterranean Antiquity 5.

Houston, G.W. 1988. "Ports in Perspective: Some Comparative Materials on Roman Merchant Ships and Ports." *AJA* 92 (4): 553-64.

Howe, T. 2008. *Pastoral Politics. Animals, Agriculture and Society in Ancient Greece. Publications of the Association of Ancient Historians 9*. Claremont, CA: Regina Books.

―――. 2013. "Athens, Alexander and the Politics of Resistance." *AncW* 44.1: 55-65.

―――. 2014a. "Value Economics: Animals, Wealth and the Market." In Campbell, 2014, 136-55.

―――. 2014b. "Founding Alexandria: Alexander the Great and the Politics of Memory." In Bosman, 2014, 72-91.

Howe, T. et al., eds. 2015. *Greece, Macedon and Persia: Studies in Social, Political and Military History in Honour of Waldemar Heckel*. Oxford: Oxbow.

Hudson, M. and M. van de Meiroop, eds. 2002. *Debt and Economic Renewal in the Ancient Near East*. Bethesda: CDL Press.

Hudson, M. and C. Wunsch, eds. 2004. *Creating Economic Order: Record-keeping, Standardization, and Development of Accounting in the Ancient Near East*. Bethesda: CDL Press.

Humphreys, S.C. 1978. "Homo Politicus and Homo Economicus." In *Anthropology and the Greeks*, 136-74. London: Routledge and Kegan Paul.

Hunt, S.D. 2000. *A General Theory of Competition: Resources, Competences, Productivity, Economic Growth*. London: Sage Publications, Inc.

Hurst, H. and S. Owen, eds. 2005. *Ancient Colonizations: Analogy, Similarity and Difference*. London, Duckworth.

Huxley, G.L. 1965. "A War between Astyages and Alyattes." *GRBS* 6: 201-206.

Hyde, J. K. 1993. *Literacy and Its Uses: Studies on Late Medieval Italy*. Manchester: Manchester University Press.

Ingham, G. 2004. *The Nature of Money*. Malden, MA: Polity Press.

Irwin, D.A. and K.H. O'Rourke. 2011. "Coping with Shocks and Shifts: The Multilateral Trading System in Historical Perspective." *Discussion Papers in Economic and Social History* 92. Oxford: Oxford University Press. http://www.economics.ox.ac.uk/materials/papers/5469/irwinorourke92.pdf

Jacobs, B. and R. Rollinger, eds. 2010. *Der Achämenidenhof / The Achaemenid Court: Akten des 2. Internationalen Kolloquiums zum Thema "Vorderasien im Spannungsfeld klassischer und altorientalischer Überlieferungen," Landgut Castelen bei Basel, 23.-25. Mai 2007*. Wiesbaden: Harrassowitz Verlag.

Jankowska, N.B. 1973. "Some Problems of the Economy of the Assyrian Empire." In Diakonov, 1973, 253-76.

Jansen-Winkeln, K. 1997. "Ein Kaufmann aus Naukratis." ZÄS 124: 105-15.

Jardé, A. 1925. *Les cereales dans l'antiquité grecque*. Paris: de Boccard.

Jashemski, W.F. and F.G. Meyer, eds. 2002. *The Natural History of Pompeii*. Cambridge: Cambridge University Press.

Joannès, F. 2000. "Relations entre intérêts privés et biens des sanctuaires à l'époque néobabylonienne." In Bongenaar, 2000, 25-41.

Johnson, M. 1996. *An Archaeology of Capitalism*. Malden, MA: Wiley-Blackwell.

Johnston, A.W. 1972. "The Rehabilitation of Sostratus." *PdP* 27: 416-23.

————. 1979. *Trademarks on Greek Vases*. Warminster: Aris and Phillips.

Johnston, A.W. and R.E. Jones. 1978. "The 'SOS Amphora." *ABSA* 73: 103-41.

Johnston, D. 1999. *Roman Law in Context*. Cambridge: Cambridge University Press.

Jones, E.L. 1988. *Growth Recurring: Economic Change in World History*. Ann Arbor: Michigan University Press.

Jongman, W. 2000. "Wool and the Textile Industry of Roman Italy: A Working Hypothesis." In Lo Cascio, 2000, 187-97.

————. 2007. "Gibbon was Right: The Decline and Fall of the Roman Economy." In Hekster et al., 2007, 183-99.

Jursa, M. 2002. "Debts and Indebtedness in the Neo-Babylonian Period: Evidence from the Institutional Archives." In Hudson and van de Meiroop, 197-220.

————. 2004. "Accounting in Neo-Babylonian Institutional Archives: Structure, Usage, and Implications." In Hudson and Wunsch, 2004, 145-98.

————. 2005. "Money-Based Exchange and Redistribution: The Transformation of the Institutional Economy in First Millennium Babylonia." In Clancier et al., 2005, 171-86.

————. 2005. *Neo-Babylonian Legal and Administrative Documents: Typology, Contents, and Archives*. Münster: Ugarit Verlag.

————. 2010. *Aspects of the Economic History of Babylonia in the First Millennium BC: Economic Geography, Economic Mentalities, Agriculture, The Use of Money, and the Problem of Economic Growth*. Munster: Ugarit Verlag.

————. 2013. "Epistolographic evidence for trips to Susa by Borsippean priests and for the crisis in Borsippa at the beginning of Xerxes' reign." *ARTA* 2013: 003 (www.achemenet.com)

Kallet, L. 2007. "The Athenian Economy." In Samons, 2007, 70-95.

Kaniewski D. et al. 2013. "Environmental Roots of the Late Bronze Age Crisis." *PLoS ONE* 8(8): 1-10. (doi:10.1371/journal.pone.0071004).

Kaniewski, D. et al. 2010. "Late Second-Early First Millennium BC Abrupt Climate Changes in Coastal Syria and Their Possible Significance for the History of the Eastern Mediterranean." *Quaternary Research* 74: 207-15.

Karvonis, P. 2008a. "Les installations commerciales dans la ville de Délos à l'époque hellénistique." *BCH* 132.1: 153-219.

————. 2008b. "Typologie et evolution des installations commerciales dans les villes grecques du IVe siècle av. J.-C. et de l'époque hellénistique." *REG* 110: 57-81.

Kawanishi, H. and Y. Suto. 2005. *Akoris I: Amphora Stamps*. Kyoto: Akoris Archaeological Project.

Kemp, B. J. 2006. *Ancient Egypt: Anatomy of a Civilization*. 2nd ed. New York: Routledge.

Kessler, K. 1997. "'Royal Roads' and other Questions of the Neo-Assyrian Communication System." In Parpola and Whiting, 1997, 129-36.

————. 2004. "Urukäische Familien versus babylonische Familien: Die Namengebung von Uruk, die Degradierung der Kulte von Eanna und der Aufstieg des Gottes Anu." *Altorientalische Forschungen* 31: 237–62.

Kitchen, K. 2001. "Economics in Ancient Arabia. From Alexander to the Augustans." In Archibald et al., 2001, 157-73.

Kirschenbaum, A. 1987. *Sons, Slaves and Freedmen in Roman Commerce*. Washington, D.C.: The Catholic University of America Press.

Kleber, K. 2008. *Tempel und Palast: die Beziehungen zwischen dem König und dem Eanna-Tempel im spätbabylonischen Uruk*. Münster: Ugarit Verlag.

Klengel, H. 1979. "Handel und Kaufleute im hethitischen Reich." *AF* 6: 69–80.

Klengel, H. and J. Renger, eds. 1999. *Landwirtschaft im Alten Orient (CRRAI 41, 1994)*. Berlin.

Knorringa, H. 1926. *Emporos*. Amsterdam: H. J. Paris.

Knuf, H. et al., 2010. *Honi soit qui mal y pense. Studien zum pharaonischen, griechisch-römischen und spätantiken Ägypten zu Ehren von Heinz-Josef Thissen*. *Orientalia Lovaniensia Analecta 194*. Leuven: Peeters.

Köse, V. 2005. "The Origin and Development of Market-Buildings in Hellenistic and Roman Asia Minor." In Mitchell and Katsari, 2005, 139-66.

Kozuh, M. 2014. *The Sacrificial Economy: Assessors, Contractors, and Thieves in the Management of Sacrificial Sheep at the Eanna Temple of Uruk (ca. 625-520 BC)*. Winona Lake: Eisenbrauns.

Kroll, J. H. 2008. "Early Iron Age Balance Weights at Lefkandi, Euboea." *OJA* 27: 37-48.

Kron, G. (Forthcoming). "Classical Greek Trade in Comparative Perspective: Literary and Archaeological Evidence." In *Beyond Self-Sufficiency: Households, City-States and Markets in the Ancient Greek World,* ed. E.M. Harris. Cambridge: Cambridge University Press.

Kristiansen, K. and T.B. Larsson, eds. 2005. *The Rise of Bronze Age Society: Travels, Transmissions and Transformations.* Cambridge: Cambridge University Press.

Kudlien, F. 1994. "Die Rolle der Konkurrenz im antiken Geschäftsleben." *MBAH* 13: 1-39.

Kühne, H. H. Nissen and J. Renger, eds. 1984. *Mesopotamien und seine Nachbarn: Politische und Kulturelle Wechselbeziehungen im alten Vorderasien vom 4. bis 1. Jahrtausend v. Chr (Proceedings of 25th Rencontre Assyriologique Internationale).* Berlin: Reimer.

Kuhrt, A. 1995. *The Ancient Near East, c. 3000–330 B.C.,* 2 vols. London: Routledge.

Kuhrt, A. and S. Sherwin-White. 1987. "Xerxes' Destruction of Babylonian Temples." In Sancisi-Weerdenburg and Kuhrt, 1987, 69–78.

Kuniholm, P.I. 2002. "Dendrochronological Investigations at Herculaneum and Pompeii." In Jashemski and Meyer, 2002, 235-39.

Kyrieleis, H. 1993. "The Heraion at Samos." In *Greek Sanctuaries: New Approaches,* ed. N. Marinatos and R. Hägg, 125-53. London: Routledge.

Lanfranchi, G.B. 2000. "The Ideological and Political Impact of the Assyrian Imperial Expansion on the Greek World in the 8th and 7th Centuries BC." In Aro and Whiting, 2000, 7-34.

———. 2003. "The Assyrian Expansion in the Zagros and the Local Ruling Elites." In Lanfranchi et al., 2003, 79-118.

Lanfranchi, G.B. et al., eds. 2003. *Continuity of Empire (?): Assyria, Media, and Persia.* Padua: SARGON.

Larsen, M.T., ed. 1979. *Power and Propaganda: A Symposium on Ancient Empires.* Copenhagen: Akademisk Forlag.

Larson, S. 2000. "Boeotia, Athens, the Peisistratids, and the *Odyssey*'s Catalogue of Heroines." *GRBS* 41: 193-222.

Laffineur, R. and E. Greco, eds. 2005. *EMPORIA: Aegeans in the Central and Eastern Mediterranean (Aegaeum 25)*. Liège: Universite de Liège

Launaro, A. 2011. *Peasants and Slaves: The Rural Population of Roman Italy (200 BC to AD 100)*. Cambridge: Cambridge University Press.

Laurence, R. 1999. *The Roads of Roman Italy: Mobility and Cultural Change*. London: Routledge.

Lavelle, B.M. 2009. "Egypt, Ionia and the *Epikouroi*." In Cueva et al., 2009, 193-219.

Lawall, M. 2005. "Amphoras and Hellenistic Economies: Addressing the (over)-emphasis on Stamped Amphora Handles." In Archibald et al., 2005, 188-232.

Legon, R.P. 1981. *Megara: The Political History of a Greek City-State to 336 B.C.* Ithaca: Cornell University Press.

Leick, G., ed. 2003. *The Babylonians: An Introduction*. New York: Routledge.

Lemos, I.S. 2002a. *The Protogeometric Aegean: The Archaeology of the Late Eleventh and Tenth Centuries BC*. Oxford: Oxford University Press.

———. 2002b. "Craftsmen, Traders, and Some Wives in Early Iron Age Greece." In Stampolidis and Karageorghis, 2002, 187-93.

———. 2007a. "... ἐπεὶ πόρε μύρια ἔδνα..." (*Iliad* 22,472): Homeric Reflections in Early Iron Age Elite Burials." In Bächle, 2007, 275-83.

———. 2007b. "The Migrations to the West Coast of Asia Minor: Tradition and Archaeology." In Cobet et al., 2007, 713-27.

Lettich, G. 2003. *Itinerari epigrafici aquileiesi*. Triest: Editreg.

Lichtheim, M. 2006. *Ancient Egyptian Literature. Volume II. The New Kingdom*. Berkeley: University of California Press.

Lidov, J.B. 2002. "Sappho, Herodotus, and the Hetaira." *CP* 97: 203-37.

Liebeschuetz, J.H.W.G. 1972. *Antioch: City and Imperial Administration in the Later Roman Empire*. Oxford: Oxford University Press.

de Ligt, L. 1993. *Fairs and Markets in the Roman Empire: Economic and Social Aspects of Periodic Trade in a Pre-Industrial Society*. Amsterdam: J. C. Gieben.

Lindsay, H. 2000. "Death-pollution and funerals in the city of Rome." In Hope and Marshall, 2000, 152-73.

Liu, J. 2009. *Collegia centonariorum: The Guilds of Textile Dealers in*

BIBLIOGRAPHY

the Roman West. Leiden: Brill.
Liverani, M. 1962. *Storia di Ugarit nell'eta' degli archivi politici*. Roma: Centro di studi semitici, Universita.
———. 1979. "The Ideology of the Assyrian Empire." In Larsen, 1979, 297-317.
———. 1988. "The Growth of the Assyrian Empire in the Habur/Middle Euphrates Area: A New Paradigm." *State Archives of Assyria Bulletin* II/2: 81-98.
———. 1990. *Prestige and Interest. International Relations in the Near East ca. 1600-1100 B.C.* Padova: Sargon.
Lo Cascio, E., ed. 2000. *Mercati permanenti e mercati periodici nel mondo romano: atti degli Incontri capresi di storia dell'economia antica (Capri 13-15 ottobre 1997)*. Bari: Edipuglia.
Lomas, K., ed. 2004. *Greek Identity in the Western Mediterranean. Papers in Honour of Brian Shefton*. Leiden: Brill.
Longenecker, B.W. 2010. *Remember the Poor: Paul, Poverty, and the Greco-Roman World*. Grand Rapids, MI: Eerdmans.
Lorimer, H. L. 1950. *Homer and the Monuments*. London: MacMillan.
Lund, J. 1999. "Rhodian Amphorae in Rhodes and Alexandria as Evidence of Trade." In Gabrielsen et al., 1999, 187-204.
Luraghi, N. 2006. "Traders, Pirates, Warriors: The Proto-history of Greek Mercenary Soldiers in the Eastern Mediterranean." *Phoenix* 60: 21-47.
———. 2010. "The Demos as Narrator: Public Honors and the Construction of Future and Past." In Foxhall et al., 2010, 246-63.
Ma, J. 2003. "Peer Polity Interaction in the Hellenistic age." *P&P* 180: 9-39.
MacGinnis, J. 1994. "The Royal Establishment at Sippar in the 6th Century BC." *Zeitschrift für Assyriologie und vorderasiatische Archäologie* 84: 198–219.
Machinist, P. 1993. "Assyrians on Assyria in the First Millennium B.C." In Raaflaub, 1993, 135-44.
MacKinnon, M. 2012. s.v. "Meat, Consumption of." In *EAH*.
Maddison, A. 2007. *Contours of the World Economy, 1-2030 AD. Essays in Macro-Economic History*. Oxford: Oxford University Press.
Malkin, I. 1998. *The Returns of Odysseus: Colonization and Ethnicity*. Berkeley: University of California Press.

————. 2011. *A Small Greek World. Networks in the Ancient Mediterranean.* Oxford: Oxford University Press.

Malkin, I. et al., eds. 2007. *Networks in the Ancient Mediterranean. Special issue of the MHR* 22.1-2.

Malmendier, U. 2005. "Roman Shares." In Goetzmann and Rouwenhorst, 2005, 31-42, 361-65.

————. 2012. s.v. "Societas." In *EAH.*

Mann, M. 1986. *The Sources of Social Power*, Vol. 1. Cambridge: Cambridge University Press.

Manning, J.G. 2003. "A Ptolemaic Agreement Concerning a Donkey with an Unusual Warranty Clause. The Strange Case of P. dem. Princ. 1 (inv. 7524)." *Enchoria* 28 (2003): 46-61.

————. 2011. "Networks, Hierarchies and Markets in the Ptolemaic Economy." In Archibald et al., 2011, 296-323.

————. (Forthcoming). *The Economy of the Ancient Mediterranean World.* Princeton: Princeton University Press.

Manning, J.G. and I. Morris, eds. 2005. *The Ancient Economy: Evidence and Models.* Stanford: Stanford University Press.

Maran, J. and P.W. Stockhammer, eds. 2012. *Materiality and Social Practice. Transformative Capacities of Intercultural Encounters.* Oxford: Oxbow.

Marasco, G. 1988. *Economia, commerci e politica nel Mediterraneo fra il III e il II secolo a. C.* Florence: Dipartimento di Storia.

Marchand, S. and A. Marangou, eds. 2007. *Amphores d'Égypte de la Basse Époque à l'époque arabe.* Cairo: Institut français d'archéologie orientale.

Marinatos, N. and R. Hägg, eds. 1993. *Greek Sanctuaries: New Approaches.* London: Routledge.

Markoe, G.E. 2000. *Phoenicians.* Berkeley: University of California Press.

Marx, K. 1976 [1867]. *Capital: Vol 1. A Critique of Political Economy.* New York: Penguin.

Marx, K. and M. Engels. 1988 [1848]. *The Communist Manifesto.* New York: Penguin.

Marzano, A. 2011. "Snails, Wine and Winter Navigation." In Harris and Iara, 2011, 179-87.

Mazar, E. 2004. *The Phoenician Family Tomb n.1 at the Northern Cemetery of Achziv (10th-6th Centuries BCE).* Cuadernos de Arqueología Mediterránea 10. Barcelona: Edicions Bellaterra.

Mattingly, D.J. 1996. "First Fruit? The Olive in the Roman World." In Salmon and Shipley, 1996, 213-53.

Mattingly, D.J. and J. Salmon, eds. 2001. *Economies Beyond Agriculture in the Classical World*. London: Routledge.

Maul, S., ed. 1998. *Festschrift für Rykle Borger zu seinem 65. Geburtstag am 24. Mai 1994: tikip santakki mala bašmu*. Groningen: Styx.

Mauss, M. 1990 [1925]. *The Gift. The Form and Reason for Exchange in Archaic Societies*. Trans. W.D. Halls; foreword by Mary Douglas. London: Routledge.

McCormick, M. 2001. *Origins of the European Economy. Communications and Commerce AD 300-900*. Cambridge: Cambridge University Press.

McGeough, K. 2007. *Exchange Relationships at Ugarit. Ancient Near Eastern Studies, Supplement 26*. Leuven: Peeters.

McGrail, S. 2008. "Sea Transport, Part 1: Ships and Navigation." In Oleson, 2008, 606-37.

McKechnie, P. 1989. *Outsiders in the Greek Cities in the Fourth Century BC*. London: Routledge.

Meiggs, R. 1982. *Trees and Timber in the Ancient Mediterranean World*. Oxford: Oxford University Press.

Meiggs, R., and D.M. Lewis. 1969. *A Selection of Greek Historical Inscriptions to the End of the Fifth Century B.C.* Oxford: Oxford University Press.

Meikle, S. 1995. *Aristotle's Economic Thought*. Cambridge: Cambridge University Press.

Mele, A. 1979. *Il commercio greco arcaico: prexis ed emporie*. Naples: Institut Français de Naples.

Menu, B. and A. Gasse. 2001. *The Oxford Encyclopedia of Ancient Egypt*, ed. D.B. Redford, 422-36. Oxford: Oxford University Press. s.v. "Economy."

Michel, C. 1996. "Propriétés immobilieres dans les tablettes paléo-assyriennes." In Veenhof, 1996, 285–300.

Mikasa no Miya, T. et al., eds. 1991. *Near Eastern Studies Dedicated to H. I. H. Prince Takahito Mikasa on the Occasion of His Seventy-Fifth Birthday*. Wiesbaden: Harrassowitz.

Millett, P. 1983. "Maritime Loans and the Structure of Credit in Fourth-Century Athens." In Garnsey, et al., 1983, 36-52.

Mills, D.H. 2002. *The Hero and the Sea: Patterns of Chaos in Ancient Myth*. Wauconda, IL: Bolchazy-Carducci.

Mitchell, S. and C. Katsari, eds. 2005. *Patterns in the Economy of Roman Asia Minor*. Swansea: The Classical Press of Wales.

Mitford, J. 1963. *The American Way of Death*. New York: Simon and Schuster.

Mokyr, J. 1990. *The Lever of Riches: Technological Creativity and Economic Progress*. Oxford: Oxford University Press.

Möller, A. 2000. *Naukratis. Trade in Archaic Greece*. Oxford: Oxford University Press.

———. 2007. "Classical Greece: Distribution." In Scheidel et al., 2007, 362-84.

Monroe, C. 2005. "Money and Trade." In Snell, 2005, 155-68.

———. 2007. "Vessel Volumetrics and the Myth of the Cyclopean Bronze Age Ship." *JESHO* 50.1: 1-18.

———. 2009. *Scales of Fate. Trade, Tradition, and Transformation in the Eastern Mediterranean, ca. 1350–1175 BCE. Alter Orient und Altes Testament 357*. Münster: Ugarit Verlag.

———. 2010. "Sunk Costs at Late Bronze Age Uluburun." *BASOR* 357: 15-29.

———. 2011. "From Luxuries to Anxieties: A Liminal View of the Late Bronze Age World-system." In Wilkinson et al., 2011, 87-99.

Monson, A. 2010. "Rules of an Egyptian Religious Association from the Early Second Century BCE." In Knuf et al., 2010, 113-22.

Mooren, L. 2000. *Politics, Administration and Society in the Hellenistic and Roman World. Proceedings of the International Colloquium, Bertinoro 19-24 July 1997. Studia Hellenistica 36*. Leuven: Peeters.

Moran, W.L. 1992. *The Amarna Letters*. Baltimore: Johns Hopkins University Press.

Morelli, F. 2011. "Dal Mar Rosso ad Alessandria. Il *verso* (ma anche il *recto*) del 'papiro di Muziris' (SB XVIII 13167)." *Tyche* 26: 199-233.

Moreno, A. 2007a. "Athenian Wheat-Tsars: Black Sea Grain and Elite Culture." In Gabrielsen and Lund, 2007, 69-84.

Moreno, A. 2007b. *Feeding the Democracy*. Oxford: Oxford University Press.

Morley, N. 2007. *Trade in Classical Antiquity*. Cambridge: Cambridge University Press.

Morris, I., ed. 1994. *Classical Greece. Ancient Histories and Modern Ideologies*. Cambridge: Cambridge University Press.

———. 2003. "Mediterraneanization." *MHR* 18: 30-55.

Müller, C. and C. Hasenohr, eds. 2002. *Les Italiens dans le monde grec: IIe siècle av. J.-C.-Ier siècle ap. J.-C. Circulation, activités, integration*. Paris: École Française d'Athènes.

Müller, G. 1997. "Gedanken zur neuassyrischen Geldwirtschaft." In Waetzoldt and Hauptman, 1997, 115–21.

Mueller, K. 2006. *Settlements of the Ptolemies: City Foundations and New Settlement in the Hellenistic World*. Leuven: Peeters.

Muhs, B.P. 2001. "Membership in Private Associations in Ptolemaic Tebtunis." *JESHO* 44.1: 1-21.

Murray, O. 1980. *Early Greece*. Stanford: Stanford University Press.

———. 1993. *Early Greece*. 2nd ed. London: Fontana.

Murray, O. and S. Price, eds. 1990. *The Greek City from Homer to Alexander*. Oxford: Oxford University Press.

Murray, W.M. 2012. *The Age of Titans. The Rise and Fall of the Great Hellenistic Navies*. Oxford: Oxford University Press.

Na'aman, N. 2005. *Ancient Israel and its Neighbors: Interaction and Counteraction*. Winona Lake, IN: Eisenbrauns.

Na'aman, N. and R. Zadok. 1988. "Sargon II's Deportations to Israel and Philistia (716-708 B.C.)." *JCS* 40: 36-46.

Nicholas, B. 1962. *An Introduction to Roman Law*. Oxford: Clarendon Press.

Niemeyer, W.-D. 2001. "Archaic Greeks in the Orient: Textual and Archaeological Evidence." *BASOR* 322: 11-32.

Nijboer, A.J. 2008. "A Phoenician Family Tomb, Lefkandi, Huelva, and the Tenth Century BC in the Mediterranean." In Sagona, 2008, 365-77.

Nixon, L. and O. Krzyszkowska, eds. 1983. *Minoan Society*. Bristol: Bristol Classical Press.

Noonan, T.S. 1973. "The Grain Trade of the Northern Black Sea in Antiquity." *AJP* 94: 231-242.

North, D.C. et al. 2009. *Violence and Social Orders. A Conceptual Framework for Interpreting Recorded Human History*. Cambridge: Cambridge University Press.

Obbink, D. 2014. "Two New Poems by Sappho." *ZPE* 189: 32-49.

Ober, J. 2008. *Democracy and Knowledge: Learning and Innovation in Classical Athens*. Princeton: Princeton University Press.

Oded, B. 1979. *Mass Deportations and Deportees in the Neo-Assyrian Empire*. Wiesbaden: Reichert.

Ogilvie, S. 2011. *Institutions and European trade. Merchant guilds, 1000-1800*. Cambridge: Cambridge University Press.

Oleson, J.P., ed. 2008. *The Oxford Handbook of Engineering and Technology in the Classical World*. Oxford: Oxford University Press.

Oliver, G.J. 2011. "Mobility, Society, and Economy in the Hellenistic Period." In Archibald et al., 2011, 345-67.

———. 2007. *War, Food, and Politics in Early Hellenistic Athens*. Oxford: Oxford University Press.

Opiat, A. 2007. "A Weighty Matter: Pontic Fish Amphorae." In Gabrielsen and Lund, 2005, 101-21.

Oppenheim, A.L. 1968. "Comment on the Intervention of Diakonoff, Main Features of the Economy in the Monarchies of Ancient Western Asia." In Finley, 1968, 32-40.

Oren, E.D., ed. 2000. *The Sea Peoples and Their World: A Reassessment. University Museum Monograph 108*. Philadelphia: The University Museum.

Orrieux, C. 1983. *Les Papyrus de Zenon. L'horizon d'un grec en Égypte au IIIe siècle avant J.C.* Paris: Éditions Macula.

Osborne, R. 1987. *Classical Landscape with Figures: The Ancient Greek City and its Countryside*. London: George Philip.

———. 1996. "Pots, Trade, and the Archaic Greek Economy." *Antiquity* 70: 31-44.

———. 2004. *Greek History*. London: Routledge.

———. 2007. "Archaic Greece." In Scheidel et al., 2007, 277-301.

Palaima, T.G. 1991 "Maritime Matters in the Linear B Tablets." *Aegaeum* 7: 273–310.

Papadopoulos, J.K. 1993. "To Kill a Cemetery: The Athenian Kerameikos and the Early Iron Age in the Aegean." *JMA* 6: 175-206.

———. 1997. "Phantom Euboeans." *JMA* 10: 191-219.

Pardee, D. 2002. "Ugaritic Letters." In Hallo and Younger, 2002, 87-115.

Pardee, D. and P. Bordreuil. 2009 *A Manual of Ugaritic*. Winona Lake, IN: Eisenbrauns.

Pare, C., ed. 2000. *Metals Make the World Go Round: Supply and Circulation of Metals in Bronze Age Europe*. Oxford: Oxbow.

Parker, A. J. 1992. *Ancient Shipwrecks of the Mediterranean and the Roman Provinces*. Oxford: British Archaeological Reports.

Parker, H. 2008. "The Linguistic Case for the Aiolian Migration Reconsidered." *Hesperia* 77: 431-64.

Parkins, H. and C. Smith, eds. 1998. *Trade, Traders and the Ancient City*. New York: Routledge.

Parkinson, W., D. Nakassis, and M. Galaty. 2013. "Crafts, Specialists, and Markets in Mycenaean Greece: Introduction." *AJA* 117: 413-22.

Parpola, S. and K. Watanabe. 1988. *Neo-Assyrian Treaties and Loyalty Oaths*. Helsinki: Helsinki University Press.

Parpola, S. and R.M. Whiting, eds. 1997. *Assyria 1995: Proceedings of the 10th Anniversary Symposium of the Neo-Assyrian Text Corpus Project, Helsinki, September 7-11, 1995*. Helsinki: Neo-Assyrian Text Corpus Project.

Paterson, J. 1978. "*Transalpinae gentes*: Cicero, *De Re Publica* 3.16." *CQ* 28: 452-58.

Peacock, D.P.S. and D.F. Williams. 1986. *Amphorae and the Roman Economy: An Introductory Guide*. London: Longman.

Pearce, L. 1995. "The Scribes and Scholars of Ancient Mesopotamia." In Sasson, 1995, 2265–78.

Pedersén, O. 1998. *Archives and Libraries in the Ancient Near East 1500–300 BC*. Bethesda: CDL Press.

Pedersén, O. 2005. "Foreign Professionals in Babylon: Evidence from the Archives in the Palace of Nebuchadnezzar II." In van Soldt, 2005, 67-272.

Pfeiffer, S. 2010. "Naukratis, Heracleion-Thonis and Alexandria— Remarks on the Presence and Trade Activities of Greeks in the North-West Delta from the Seventh Century BC to the End of the Fourth Century BC." In Robinson and Wilson, 2010, 15-24.

Polanyi, K. 1944. *The Great Transformation*. New York: Holt, Rinehart, and Winston.

Polanyi, K. 1957. "Marketless Trading in Hammurabi's Time." In Polanyi et al., 1957, 12–26.

Polanyi, K. et al, eds. 1957. *Trade and Market in the Early Empires*. Glencoe, IL: Free Press.

Pomeranz, K. and S. Topik, eds. 2006. *The World that Trade Created: Society, Culture, and the World Economy, 1400 to Present*. 2nd ed. Armonk, NY: M.E. Sharpe.

Popham, M. and I.S. Lemos. 1995. "A Euboean Warrior Trader." *OJA* 14: 151-57.

Popham, M. et al. 1982a. "The Hero of Lefkandi." *Antiquity* 56: 169-74.

Popham, M. et al. 1982b. "Further Excavations of the Toumba Cemetery at Lefkandi, 1981." *ABSA* 77: 213-48.

Popham, M.R. et al., eds. 1993. *Lefkandi II : The Protogeometric Building at Toumba. Part 2, the Excavation, Architectire and Finds.* Athens: British School at Athens.

Posner, R.A. 1980. "A Theory of Primitive Society, with Special Reference to Law." *Journal of Law and Economics* 23.1: 1-53.

Postgate, J.N. 1973. *The Governor's Palace Archive.* London: British School of Archaeology in Iraq.

———. 1979. "The Economic Structure of the Assyrian Empire." In Larsen, 1979, 193-221.

———. 1988. *The Archive of Urad-Šerūa and His Family. A Middle Assyrian Household in Government Service.* Rome: Roberto Denicola Editore.

———. 1989. "Ancient Assyria: A Multi-Racial State." *ARAM* 1: 1-10.

Potts, D.T. 1990. *The Arabian Gulf in Antiquity.* Vol. 2. *From Alexander the Great to the Coming of Islam.* Oxford: Oxford University Press.

Préaux, C. 1939. *L'économie royale des Lagides.* Brussels: Édition de la Fondation égyptologique reine Élisabeth.

Pulak, C. 2000. "The Balance Weights from the Late Bronze Age Shipwreck at Uluburun." In Pare, 2000, 247-66.

———. 2008. "The Uluburun Shipwreck and Late Bronze Age Trade." In Aruz et al., 2008, 289-305.

Purcell, N. 1990. "Mobility and the Polis." In Murray and Price, 1990, 29-58.

———. 1997. Review of *The Archaeology of Greek Colonisation: Essays Dedicated to Sir John Boardman,* ed. F. De Angelis and G. Tsetskhladze (Oxford: Oxbow, 1994). *Antiquity* 71: 500.

———. 2004. "The Boundless Sea of Unlikeness? On Defining the Mediterranean." *MHR* 18: 9-29.

———. 2005a. "The Ancient Mediterranean: The View from the Customs House." In Harris, 2005, 200-32.

———. 2005b. "Colonization and Mediterranean History." In Hurst and Owen, 2005, 115-39.

Raaflaub, K., ed. 1993. *Anfänge politischen Denkens in der Antike.* Munich: Oldenbourg Wissenschaftsverlag.

Radner, K. 1999a. "Money in the Neo-Assyrian Empire." In Dercksen, 1999, 127- 57

———. 1999b. "Traders in the Neo-Assyrian Period." In Dercksen, 1999, 101–26.

———. 2004. "Assyrische Handelspolitik: Die Symbiose mit unabhängigen Handelszentren und ihre Kontrolle durch Assyrien." In Rollinger and Ulf, 2004, 152–69.

———. "Hired Labour in the Neo-Assyrian Empire." *State Archives of Assyria Bulletin* 16: 185-226.

———. 2011. "Mass Deportation: The Assyrian Resettlement Policy." Assyrian Empire Builders. Retrieved June 25, 2012, from http://www.ucl.ac.uk/sargon/essentials/governors/massdeportatio n.

Raepsaet, G. 2008. "Land Transport, Pt. 2: Riding, Harnesses, and Vehicles." In Oleson, 2008, 581-605.

Raschke, M.G. (1978). "New Studies in Roman Commerce with the East." *ANRW* 2.9.2: 604–1378.

Rathbone, D. 1983. "The Grain Trade and Grain Shortages in the Hellenistic East." In Garnsey and Whittaker, 1983, 45-53.

Rathbone, D. and P. Temin. 2008. "Financial Intermediation in First-Century AD Rome and Eighteenth-Century England." In Verboven et al., 2008, 371-419.

Rauh, N.K. 1989. "Auctioneers and the Roman Economy." *Historia* 38.4: 451-71.

———. 1993. *The Sacred Bonds of Commerce: Religion, Economy, and Trade Society at Hellenistic Roman Delos, 166 - 87 B.C.* Amersterdam: J. C. Gieben.

———. 1999. "Rhodes, Rome, and the Eastern Mediterranean Wine Trade, 166-88 BC." In Gabrielsen et al., 1999, 162-86.

———. 2003. *Merchants, Sailors and Pirates in the Roman World.* Stroud: Tempus.

———. 2013. "Anchors, Amphoras, and ashlar masonry: New evidence for the Cilician pirates." In Hoff and Townsend, 2013, 59-86.

Rauh, N.K. et al. 2008. "*Ochlos nautikos:* Leisure Culture and Underclass Discontent in the Roman Maritime World." In Hohlfelder, 2008, 197-242.

Rauh, N. et al. 2009. "Life in the Truck Lane: Urban Development in Western Rough Cilicia." *JOAI* 78: 253-312.

Ray, H. 2003. *The Archaeology of Seafaring in Ancient South Asia*. Cambridge: Cambridge University Press.

Redfield, J.M. 1986. "The Development of the Market in Archaic Greece." In Anderson and Latham, 1986, 29-58. London: Croon Helm.

Reed, C.M. 2003. *Maritime traders in the ancient Greek world*. Cambridge: Cambridge University Press.

Reger, G. 1994. *Regionalism and Change in the Economy of Independent Delos*. Berkeley: University of California Press.

———. 2003. "Aspects of the Role of Merchants in the Political Life of the Hellenistic World." In Zaccagnini, 2003, 165-97.

———. 2005. "The Manufacture and Distribution of Perfume." In Archibald et al., 2005, 253-97.

———. 2007. "Traders and Travelers in the Black and Aegean Seas." In Gabrielsen and Lund, 2007, 273-85.

———. 2011a. "Inter-regional Economies in the Aegean Basin." In Archibald et al., 2011, 368-89.

———. 2011b. "Formation of Taste and Fashion. Perfumes and Imitations in the Hellenistic and Early Imperial World." *Marburger Beiträge zur antiken Handels-, Wirtschafts- und Sozialgeschichte* 28: 21-44.

Reineke, W. 1979. "Waren die *šwtjw* wirklich Kaufleute?" *AF* 6: 5-14.

Rhodes, P.J. and R. Osborne, eds. 2003. *Greek Historical Inscriptions 404-323 BC*. Oxford: Oxford University Press.

Rickman, G. 1971. *Roman Granaries and Store Buildings*. Cambridge: Cambridge University Press.

Ridgway, D. 1997. "Nestor's Cup and the Etruscans." *OJA* 16: 325-344.

———. 2012. *OCD*[4] s.v. "Colonization, Greek."

Riggsby, A.M. 2010. *Roman Law and the Legal World of the Romans*. Cambridge: Cambridge University Press.

Robinson, D. and A. Wilson, eds. 2010. *Alexandria and the North-Western Delta*. Oxford: Oxford Centre for Maritime Archaeology

Roller, D.W. 2006. *Through the Pillars of Herakles: Greco-Roman Exploration of the Atlantic*. London: Routledge.

Rollinger, R. et al., eds. 2001. *Herodot und das Persische Weltreich/Herodotus and the Persian Empire*. Wiesbaden: Harrassowitz.

Rollinger, R. and C. Ulf, eds. 2004. *Commerce and Monetary Systems in the Ancient World: Means of Transmission and Cultural Interaction*. Wiesbaden: Franz Steiner.

Rose, C.B. 2008. "Separating Fact from Fiction in the Aiolian Migration." *Hesperia* 77: 399-430.

Rosenstein, N.S. 2008. "Aristocrats and Agriculture in the Middle and Late Republic." *JRS* 98: 1-26.

Rostovtzeff, M. 1941. *The Social and Economic History of the Hellenistic World*. Oxford: Oxford University Press.

Roth, J. 1999. *The Logistics of the Roman Army at War (264 B.C. - A.D. 235)*. Leiden: Brill.

Roth, M. T. 1997. *Law Collections from Mesopotamia and Asia Minor*. 2nd ed. *Writings from the Ancient World 6*. Atlanta: Scholars Press.

Rougé, J. 1966. *Recherches sur l'organisation du commerce maritime en Méditerranée sous l'Empire romain*. Paris: S.E.V.P.E.N.

———. 1980. "Prêt et societé maritimes dans le monde romain." *MAAR* 36: 291-304.

Rougemont, G. 2005. "Nouvelles inscriptions grecques de l'asie central." In Bopearachchi and Boussac, 2005, 127-36.

Ryholt, K. 2005. *The Petese Stories* II (P. Petese II). *The Carlsberg Papyri 6. CNI Publications 29*. Copenhagen: Museum Tusculanum Press.

Sage, E. T. 1916. "Advertising among the Romans." *CW* 9: 202-208.

Saggs, H. W. F. 1955. "The Nimrud Letters: 1952, Part II." *Iraq* 17: 126-60.

Sagona, C., ed. 2008. *Beyond the Homeland: Markers in Phoenician Chronology*. Leuven: Peeters.

Saller, R. 2005. "Framing the Debate over Growth in the Ancient Economy." In Manning and Morris, 2005, 223-38.

Salmon, J. and G. Shipley, eds. 1996. *Human Landscapes in Classical Antiquity: Environment and Culture*. London: Routledge.

Salviat, F. 1986. "Le vin de Thasos." In Empereur and Garlan, 1986, 145-96.

de Salvo, L. 1992. *Economia privata e pubblici servizi nell'impero romano: i corpora naviculariorum, Kleiò*. Messina: Samperi.

Samons, L.J. ed. 2007. *The Cambridge Companion to the Age of Pericles*. Cambridge: Cambridge University Press.

Sancisi-Weerdenburg, H. and A. Kuhrt, eds. 1987. *Achaemenid History II: The Greek Sources*. Leiden: Nederlands Instituut voor het Nabije Oosten.

Sanders, S., ed. 2006. *Margins of Writing, Origins of Cultures*. Chicago: Oriental Institute of the University of Chicago.

Saporetti, C. 1977. "La Figura del *tamkāru* nell' Assiria del XIII secolo." *SMEA* 18: 93-101.

Sasson, J., ed. 1995. *Civilizations of the Ancient Near East*. New York: Scribner's.

Scheidel, W. 1997. "Quantifying the Sources of Slaves in the Early Roman Empire." *JRS* 87: 156-169.

———. 2004. "Creating a Metropolis: A Comparative Demographic Perspective." In Harris and Ruffini, 2004, 1-31.

———. 2009. *Rome and China: Comparative Perspectives on Ancient World Empires*. Oxford: Oxford University Press.

———. 2011. "A Comparative Perspective on the Determinants of Scale and Productivity of Roman Maritime Trade in the Mediterranean." In Harris and Iara, 2011, 21-37.

———. 2012. *The Cambridge Companion to the Roman Economy*. Cambridge: Cambridge University Press.

Scheidel, W. et al., eds. 2007. *The Cambridge Economic History of the Greco-Roman World*. Cambridge: Cambridge University Press.

Scheidel, W. and S. von Reden, eds. 2002. *The Ancient Economy*. London: Routledge.

Schloen, J.D. 2001. *The House of the Father as Fact and Symbol: Patrimonialism in Ugarit and the Ancient Near East. Studies in the Archaeology and History of the Levant 2*. Winona Lake, IN: Eisenbrauns.

Schörle, K. 2010. "From Harbor to Desert: An Integrated Interface on the Red Sea and its Impact on the Eastern Egyptian Desert." *Bolletino di archeologia online*: 44-53.

Scott-Kilvert, I. 1973. *Plutarch. The Age of Alexander*. London: Penguin.

Shaw, J. 2006. *Kommos: A Minoan Harbor Town and Greek Sanctuary in Southern Crete*. Princeton: American School of Classical Studies at Athens.

Shaw, J.W. and M.E. Shaw, eds. 2000. *Kommos IV*. Princeton: Princeton University Press.

Sherratt, E.S. 1990. "'Reading the Texts': Archaeology and the Homeric Question." *Antiquity* 64: 807–24.

———. 1999. "A Political History of Ugarit." In Watson and Wyatt, 1999, 603–733.

Sherratt, A.G and E.S. Sherratt. 1991. "From Luxuries to Commodities: the Nature of Mediterranean Bronze Age Trading Systems." In Gale, 1991, 351–86.

———. 1993. "The Growth of the Mediterranean Economy in the Early First Millennium BC." *World Archaeology* 24.3: 361–78.

Shipley, G. 1993. "Distance, Development, Decline? World-Systems Analysis and the 'Hellenistic' World." In Bilde et al., 1993, 271–84.

Sidebotham, S.E. 2011. *Berenike and the Ancient Maritime Spice Route.* Berkeley: University of California Press.

Sijpesteijn, P.J. 1987. *Customs Duties in Graeco-Roman Egypt.* Zutphen: Terra.

Singer, I. 1983. "Takuhlinu and Haya: Two Governors in the Ugarit Letter from Tel Aphek." *Tel Aviv* 10: 3–25.

Smith, R.L. 2009. *Premodern Trade in World History.* London: Routledge.

Snell, D.C. 1995. "Methods of Exchange and Coinage in Ancient Western Asia." In Sasson, 1995, 1487–97.

———. 1997. *Life in the Ancient Near East, 3100–332 BCE.* New Haven: Yale University Press.

———. 2005. *Blackwell Companion to the Ancient Near East.* Malden, MA: Wiley-Blackwell

Snodgrass, A.M. 1971. *The Dark Age of Greece.* Edinburgh: University of Edinburgh Press.

———. 1980. *Archaic: The Age of Experiment.* Berkeley: University of California Press.

———. 2000. *The Dark Age of Greece.* 2nd ed. Edinburgh: University of Edinburgh Press.

de Souza, P. 1999. *Piracy in the Greco-Roman World.* Cambridge: Cambridge University Press.

———. 2012a. "Pirates and Politics in the Roman World." In Grieb et al., 2012, 47-73.

———. 2012b. s.v. "Piracy." In *EAH.*

Stampolidis, N.C. and V. Karageorghis, eds. 2002. *Ploes/Sea Routes. Interconnections in the Mediterranean 16th-6th c. B.C.* Athens: Leventis Foundation.

Stampolidis, N.C., and A. Kotsonas. 2006. "Phoenicians in Crete." In Deger-Jalkotzy and Lemos, 2006, 337-60.

Ste. Croix, G.E.M. de. 1972. *The Origins of the Peloponnesian War.* London: Duckworth.

———. 1974. "Ancient Greek and Roman Maritime Loans." In Edey and Yamey, 1974, 41-59.

Stein, G. 1999. *Rethinking World-Systems: Diasporas, Colonies and Interaction in Uruk Mesopotamia.* Tucson: University of Arizona Press.

Stolba, V.F. 2007. "Local Patterns of Trade in Wine and the Chronological Implications of Amphora Stamps." In Gabrielsen and Lund, 2007, 149-59.

Stolper, M.W. 1985. *Entrepreneurs and Empire: The Murašû Archive, the Murašû Firm, and Persian Rule in Babylonia.* Leiden: Nederlands Instituut voor het Nabije Oosten.

Stolper, M.W. and C.E. Jones. 2008. "How Many Persepolis Fortification Tablets Are There? " *Persika* 12: 37-44.

Sullivan, B.M. 2011. "Paying Archaic Greek Mercenaries: Views from Egypt and the Near East." *CJ* 107: 31-61.

J. Swaddling et. al., eds. 1995. *Italy in Europe: Economic Relations 700 BC - AD 500.* London: British Museum.

Tadmor, H. 1958. "The Campaigns of Sargon II of Assur: A Chronological-Historical Study." *JCS* 12: 22-40, 77-100.

Tadmor, H. 1975. "Assyria and the West: The Ninth Century and its Aftermath." In Goedicke and Roberts, 36-47.

———. 1984. "The Aramaization of Assyria: Aspects of Western Impact." In H. Kühne et al., 1984, 449-70.

———. 1991. "On the Role of Aramaic in the Assyrian Empire." In Mikasa no Miya et al., 1991, 419-26.

Tandy, D.W. 1997. *Warriors into Traders.* Berkeley and Los Angeles: University of California Press.

———. 2004. "Trade and Commerce in Archilochos, Sappho, and Alkaios." In. Rollinger and Ulf, 2004, 183-94.

Tchernia, A. 1983. "Italian Wine in Gaul at the Wnd of the Republic." In Garnsey et al., 1983, 87-104.

Temin, P. 2001. "A Market Economy in the Early Roman Empire." *JRS*

91: 169-81.

Terpstra, T.T. 2011. "Trade in the Roman Empire: A Study of the Institutional Framework." Dissertation, Columbia University, New York.

———. 2013. *Trading Communities in the Roman World: A Micro-Economic and Institutional Perspective. Columbia Studies in the Classical Tradition, 37.* Leiden: Brill.

Thompson, D.J. 1983. "Nile Grain Transport under the Ptolemies." In Garnsey et al., 1983, 64-75.

———. 2000. "Philadelphus' Procession: Dynastic Power in Mediterranean Context." In Mooren, 2000, 365-88.

Thür, G. (Forthcoming). "Transaction Costs in Athenian Law." In *Law and Transaction Costs in the Ancient World*, ed. D, Kehoe, et al. Ann Arbor: University of Michigan Press.

Torelli, M. 1971. "Il santuario di Hera a Gravisca." *PdP* 26: 44-67.

———. 1977. "Il santuario greco a Gravisca." *PdP* 32: 398-468.

Trivellato, F. 2009. *The Familiarity of Strangers. The Sephardic Diaspora, Livorno, and Cross-Cultural Trade in the Early Modern Period.* New Haven: Yale University Press.

Tsetskhladze, G.R. 2008. "'Grain for Athens.' The View from the Black Sea." In Alston and van Nijf, 2008, 47-62.

Tsetskhladze, G.R., ed. 2006/08. *Greek Colonisation: An Account of Greek Colonies and Other Settlements Overseas*, 2 vols. Leiden: Brill.

Tsetskhladze, G.R. and A.M. Snodgrass, eds. 2002. *Greek Settlements in the Eastern Mediterranean and the Black Sea.* Oxford: British Archaeological Reports.

Turner, V. 1969. *The Ritual Process: Structure and Anti-structure.* Chicago: University of Chicago Press.

Uchendu, V.C. 1967. "Some Principles of Haggling in Peasant Markets." *Economic Development and Cultural Change* 16.1: 37-50.

Vallet, G. et al., eds. 1999. *La colonisation grecque en Méditerranée occidentale, La colonisation Grecque en Méditerranée occidentale: Actes de la rencontre scientifique en hommage a Georges Vallet (Rome-Naples, 15–18 novembre 1995).* Paris: de Boccard.

van de Mieroop, M. 1997. *The Mesopotamian City.* Oxford: Oxford University Press.

————. 2004. "Economic Theories and the Ancient Near East." In Rollinger and Ulf, 2004, 54-64.

————. 2007. *The Eastern Mediterranean in the Age of Ramesses II.* Malden, MA: Wiley-Blackwell.

van der Spek, R.J. 2006. "The Size and Significance of the Babylonian Temples under the Successors." In Briant and Joannès, 2006, 261-307.

van Dommelen, P. 2012. "Colonialism and Migration in the Ancient Mediterranean." *ARA* 41: 393-409.

van Driel, G. 1989. "The Murašûs in Context." *JESHO* 32: 203-29.

————. 1998. "The 'Eanna Archive'." *BiOr* 55: 60-79.

————. 1999. "Agricultural Entrepreneurs in Mesopotamia." In Klengel and Renger, 1999, 213-23.

————. 2000. "Institutional and Non-institutional Economy in Ancient Mesopotamia." In Bongenaar, 2000, 5-23.

————. 2002. *Elusive Silver: In Search of a Role for a Market in an Agrarian Environment. Aspects of Mesopotamia's Society.* Leiden: Nederlands Instituut voor het Nabije Oosten.

van Driel-Murray, C. 2008. "Tanning and Leather." In Oleson, 2008, 483-495.

Vanschoonwinkel, J. 2006. "Greek Migrations to Aegean Anatolia in the early Dark Age." In Tsetskhladze, 2006, 115-41.

van Soldt, H.W. 1989 "Labels from Ugarit." *Ugarit Forschungen* 21: 375–88.

————. 1995. "Babylonian Lexical, Religious and Literary Texts and Scribal Education at Ugarit and Its Implications for the Alphabetic Literary Texts." In Dietrich and Loretz, 1995, 171-212.

————. 2005. *Ethnicity in Ancient Mesopotamia: Papers read at the 48th RAI, Leiden, 1-4 July 2002.* Leiden: Nederlands Instituut voor het Nabije Oosten.

————. 2010. *Society and Administration in Ancient Ugarit* (PIHANS 114). Leiden: Netherlands Institute for the Near East (NINO).

van Tilburg, C. 2012. s.v. "Toll." In *EAH*.

Vargyas, P. 1985. "Marchands hittites à Ugarit." *OLP* 16: 71-79.

————. 1986. "Trade and Prices in Ugarit." *Oikumene* 5: 103-16.

Veenhof, K.R., ed. 1996. *House and Households in Ancient Mesopotamia.* Istanbul: Nederlands Historisch-Archaeologisch Instituut te Istanbul.

Veldhuis, N. 1997. *Elementary Education at Nippur: the Lists of Trees and Wooden Objects*. Ph.D. diss., University of Groningen.

Verboven, K. 2002. *The Economy of Friends. Economic Aspects of Amicitia and Patronage in the Late Republic*. Brussels: Éditions Latomus.

———. 2008. "*Faeneratores, negotiatores* and Financial Intermediation in the Roman World (Late Republic and Early Empire)." In Verboven et al., 2008, 211-29.

Verboven, K., et al., eds. 2008. *Pistoi dia tèn technèn: Bankers, Loans and Archives in the Ancient World. Studies in Honour of Raymond Bogaert*. Leuven: Peeters.

Villeneuve, F. 2004. "Une inscription latine sur l'archipel Farasân, Arabie Séoudite, sud de la Mer Rouge." *CRAI* 2004: 419-29.

Vita, J.-P. 1999. "The Society of Ugarit." In Watson and Wyatt, 1999, 455-98.

Vita, J.-P. and J. Galán. 1997. "Šipṭi-Baʿalu, un 'égyptien' à Ougarit." *Ugarit Forschungen* 29: 709-13.

Vokotopoulou, I. and A.-P. Christidis (1995). "A Cypriot Graffito on an SOS Amphora from Mende, Chalcidice." *Kadmos* 34: 5-12.

Von Reden, S. 2010. *Money in Classical Antiquity*. Cambridge: Cambridge University Press.

Wachsmann, S., ed. 1998. *Seagoing Ships and Seamanship in the Bronze Age Levant*. College Station, TX: Texas A&M University Press.

Waerzeggers, C. 2003/4. "The Babylonian Revolts against Xerxes and the 'End of Archives'." *AOF* 50: 150-73.

———. 2010. "Babylonians in Susa: The Travels of Babylonian Businessmen to Susa Reconsidered." In Jacobs and Rollinger, 2010, 777-813.

———. 2010. *The Ezida Temple of Borsippa: Priesthood, Cult, Archives*. Leiden: Nederlands Insituut voor het Nabije Oosten.

Waetzoldt, H. and H. Hauptman, eds. 1997. *Assyrien im Wandel der Zeiten: XXXIX. Rencontre assyriologique internationale, Heidelberg, 6.-10. Juli 1992*. Heidelberg: Heidelberger Orientverlag.

Wallerstein, I. 1974. *The Modern World-System*. New York: Academic Press.

Warburton, D. 2009. "Economics, Anthropological Models and the Ancient Near East." *Anthropology of the Middle East* 4: 65-90.

Waters, M.W. 2002. "A Letter from Ashurbanipal to the Elders of Elam (BM 132980)." *JCS* 54: 79-86.

Watson, W.G.E. and N. Wyatt, eds. 1999. *Handbook of Ugaritic Studies. Handbuch der Orientalistik 1, Der nahe und mittlere Osten 39.* Leiden: Brill.

Weber, M. 1947. *The Theory of Social and Economic Organization.* Transl. of unfinished *Wirtschaft und Gesellschaft* I by A.R. Henderson. London: Hodge & Co.

————. 1976 [1896, 1909]. *The Agrarian Sociology of Ancient Civilizations.* Transl. by R.I. Frank. London: New Left Books.

————. 1996 [1904-05]. *The Protestant Ethic and the Spirit of Capitalism.* Transl. by T. Prescott of posthumous 1920-1 publication of a revision in *Gesammelte Aufsätze zur Religionssoziolgie.* London: Routledge.

Westerdahl, C. 2005. "Seal on Land, Elk at Sea: Notes on and Applications of the Ritual Landscape at the Seaboard." *IJNA* 34.1: 2–23.

Whitby, M. 1998. "The Grain Trade in Athens in the Fourth Century BC." In Parkins and Smith, 1998, 99-143.

Whittaker, C. R. 1986. "Cliometrics and the Historian." *Opus* 5: 127-32.

Wiemer, H.-U. 2002. *Krieg, Handel und Piraterie: Untersuchungen zur Geschichte des hellenistischen Rhodos. Klio. Beiträge zur Alten Geschichte, Beihefte, Neue Folge Band 6.* Berlin: Akademie Verlag.

Wild, J. P. 2008. "Textile Production." In Oleson, 2008, 465-82.

Wilcken, U. 1967. *Alexander the Great.* Trans. G.C. Richards. New York: Norton.

Wilkinson, T. et al., 2011. *Interweaving Worlds: Systemic Interaction in Eurasia 7th to 1st millennia BC.* Oxford: Oxbow Books.

Wilson, A. 2009. "Approaches to Quantifying Roman Trade." In Bowman and Wilson, 2009, 213-49.

————. 2011a. "Developments in Mediterranean Shipping and Maritime Trade from the Hellenistic Period to AD 1000." In Robinson and Wilson, 2011, 33-59.

————. 2011b. "The economic influence of developments in maritime technology in antiquity." In Harris and Iara, 2011, 211-33.

Wilson, J.-P. 1997-98. "The 'Illiterate Trader'?" *BICS* 42: 29-52.

Winter, I. 1995. "Homer's Phoenicians: History, Ethnography, or Literary Trope (A Perspective on Early Orientalism)." In Carter and Morris, 1995, 247-71.

Winter, N. 2002. "Commerce in Exile: Terracotta Roofing in Etruria, Corfu and Sicily, a Bacchiad Family Enterprise." *EtrStud* 9: 227-36.

Wiseman, D.J. 1968. "The Tell Al Rimah Tablets, 1966." *Iraq* 30: 175-205, pls. LVII-LXVI.

Wood, N. 1983. "The Economic Dimension of Cicero's Political Thought: Property and State." *Canadian Journal of Political Science* 16: 739-56.

Wunsch, C. 2003. "The Egibi Family." In Leick, 2003, 236-47.

———. 2010. "Neo-Babylonian Entrepreneurs." In Baumol and Mokyr, 2010, 40-61.

Yamada, S. 2005. "Karus on the Frontiers of the Neo-Assyrian Empire." *Orient: Report of the Society of Near Eastern Studies in Japan* 40: 56-90.

Yiftach-Firanko, U., ed. 2013. *The Letter: Law, State, Society and the Epistolary Format in the Ancient World*. Wiesbaden: Harrassowitz.

Yon, M. 2006. *The City of Ugarit at Tell Ras Shamra*. Winona Lake, IN: Eisenbrauns.

Young, G. K. 2001. *Rome's Eastern Trade: International Commerce and Imperial Policy, 31 BC - AD 305*. London: Routledge.

Zanda, E. 2011. *Fighting Hydra-Like Luxury: Sumptuary Regulation in the Roman Republic*. London: Bristol Classical Press.

Zaccagnini, C. 1983 "On Gift Exchange in the Old Babylonian Period." In Carruba et al., 1983, 189-253.

———. 2003. *Mercanti e politica nel mondo antico*. Rome: L'Erma di Bretschneider.

Zawadzki, S. 2006. *Garments of the Gods: Studies on the Textile Industry and the Pantheon of Sippar according to the Texts from the Ebabbar Archive*. Fribourg; Göttingen: Academic Press: Vandenhoeck & Ruprecht.

Zenner, W.P. 1991. *Minorities in the Middle: a Cross-cultural Analysis*. Albany: State University of New York.

INDEX

A

Abydos (Abydus): 15, 35

Achaeans: 42, 53

Achaemenids: 87-88, 90, 92, 95, 100, 102, 104, 112, 118

See also Persian Empire, Darius, Xerxes

Achziv (Phoenician coastal town): 51, 55

Adriatic Sea: 55-56

Aegean Sea: 9, 23, 35, 51-52, 55, 66, 70, 113

Aegina, Aeginetans: 56, 60, 62-63, 65, 66

Aeolian, Aeolic, Aeolis: 49, 62

Afghanistan: 122, 138

Africa: 104, 113, 119, 153-154

Agriculture: 2, 45, 61, 63, 65, 66, 74, 76, 83, 90-91, 94, 99, 133, 142, 146, 160, 164-165, 171

See also Grains.

Ahhiyawa: See Mycenaean

Akhenaten: 21

Akkadian: 7, 8-9, 16, 18-19, 21, 23, 25

Alashiya: 7

Alba: 153-154

Black Sea: 55-56, 66, 103, 104, 112-113, 118, 131, 134

Blood Money: 14

Borsippa: 87-88

    See also Babylonia

Bottomry: 18, 67, 70

    See also Credit

Bronze (as a commodity): 12, 24, 27, 34, 44, 49-50, 148

Brundisium: 148, 154

Byblos: 15, 18, 32, 34, 40

      C

Caesarea Maritima: 148

Camels: 86, 155-156

Campania: 145, 155

Canaan, Canaanite: 13, 24, 35, 44-45

Canopic (mouth of the Nile) see Nile River

Capua: 150, 156

Caravan: 1, 13-15, 19, 21, 38, 43, 80, 112

Carchemish: 79, 83

Caria: 107, 117

Carthage: 112, 116

Çatal Hüyük: 49

www.ingramcontent.com/pod-product-compliance
Lightning Source LLC
Chambersburg PA
CBHW050648270326
41927CB00012B/2922